Through
Peasant Eyes

The threads of connection between Primitive Christianity and the world are to be sought not in the high regions of culture and power but in the lower levels of the common life of the people.

Adolf Deissmann, 1922

Through Peasant Eyes

More Lucan Parables,
Their Culture
and Style

by
Kenneth E. Bailey

William B. Eerdmans Publishing Company
Grand Rapids, Michigan

To Ethel Jean

Copyright © 1980 by Wm. B. Eerdmans Publishing Company
255 Jefferson Ave. S.E., Grand Rapids, Mich. 49503

Library of Congress Cataloging in Publication Data

Bailey, Kenneth E.
  Through peasant eyes.

  Bibliography: p. 173.
  1. Jesus Christ—Parables. 2. Bible. N.T.
Luke—Criticism, interpretation, etc. I. Title.
BT375.2.B24   226'.806   80-14297
ISBN 0-8028-3528-7

CONTENTS

vi CONTENTS

PREFACE

The song writer composes a song and it is finished. The sculptor chisels at his marble and one day the statue is completed. But the exegete's task is never finished. He can only pause to record, somewhat fearfully, his findings at a certain point in time, with the prayer that they will be of some use to others and that he has been faithful with what thus far has been given to him. This is very much our feeling as we bring this study to a close. Wiser and more learned scholars have trod this same ground before us, and others will follow after. The parables of Jesus do not unlock all of their secrets to anyone. We can only invite the reader to join us along the path we have been privileged to walk for twenty-five years with the hope that the reader will find the direction of the journey meaningful.

   The footnote system used in this study has attempted to make sources easily identifiable for the reader and, at the same time, to save the printing costs. All books cited in the text are listed by author in the Bibliography. Where more than one source is quoted from a single author a key word from the title is given in the text. In the case of the Mishna we have listed the tractate with reference as well as the appropriate page in the Danby edition. For the Talmud we have done the same for the Soncino edition, edited by Epstein. The essays quoted from *The Jewish People in the First Century* (cited as *JPFC*) are listed together in the Bibliography. The same has been done for the *Theological Dictionary of the New Testament* (cited as *TDNT*). The great commentary of Ibn al-Ṭayyib was published in Arabic in Cairo in 1908. However, the edition was theologically edited, as the introduction affirms. Thus we have used both the printed text and the Paris Arabic Manuscript 86 as sources for this important work. The translations from the Arabic versions and studies are all the responsibility of the author. Because of their extent it has seemed redundant to add "(my translation)" to each quotation. Responsibility for the accuracy of the translations is solely my own.

The list of those to whom we are indebted is too long to record in full. Only a few from among the many can be mentioned. Special gratitude is sincerely offered to my Arab Christian friends of two decades, who stretch from the Sudan to Iraq, who have taught me far more than I have communicated to them. Mention must be made of the great scholars of the Arab Christian past, such as Ibn al-'Assāl, Ibn al-Ṣalībī, and Ibn al-Ṭayyib. These and other Arab Christian scholars of the medieval period remain virtually unknown and our debt to them through their Bible translations and commentaries is boundless. We are grateful also to the British Museum, the National Library of Paris, and the Vatican Library for microfilms of their works.

A special word of thanks must be extended to the good people of St. Stephen's Presbyterian Church of Oklahoma City, who have graciously made funds available for the acquiring of the bulk of the resources for the research of this study. In addition, they provided challenging stimuli and warm encouragement on the occasion of the presentation to them, in lecture form, of most of this material. My colleagues and students at the Near East School of Theology here in Beirut have been a constant creative forum for parabolic study. No word of gratitude is adequate to express my debt to my dear wife, Ethel, who, in addition to her love, criticism, and encouragement, has corrected my abominable spelling and typing and has produced a clean and flawlessly typed manuscript. To her this book is affectionately dedicated.

Beirut, Lebanon
Fall, 1979

INTRODUCTION

In a recent review article Walter Brueggemann comments on what he calls the "crisis of categories" in biblical studies. Brueggemann thoughtfully observes,

> Anyone who tries to teach Scripture in a classroom today is aware of the impatience of students with scholarly methods that appear pedantic and seem concerned with peripheral questions and do not cut through to the decisive pay-offs of the material (Brueggemann, 432).

He expresses a concern for "the vitality and dynamic of the text" (*ibid.*). This study is an attempt to use scholarly methods but yet to reach "the pay-offs of the material." It is written from within the "hermeneutical circle," that is, from within the family of faith to the community of believers, with the earnest hope of recovering something of the "vitality and dynamic of the text" that is available when it is seen from a Middle Eastern cultural perspective. When this Middle Eastern world is taken seriously in terms of both form and content a great deal of new insight is available. The rediscovery of these insights is the purpose of this study. The community of faith within which I write is that of Middle Eastern Arab Christianity. I have lived, worked, and worshiped within this community for nearly thirty years. Although critical questions will not be avoided, it is not our intent to review and debate all recent Western scholarly opinions. Thus much of the documentation that is expected in a technical publication the reader will find missing. A more technical approach to the parables is already available (Bailey, *Poet*). My own debt to the works of others cannot be adequately expressed in words, yet our purpose here is to introduce into the discussion *new data* rather than review interpretive insights already known.

Most current scholarship on the parables concentrates on the redactional question of how a particular evangelist uses, shapes, or creates material in the service of his own theological interests to meet particular needs in the church of his day. In this study we will attempt to examine ten of the parables of Jesus as Palestinian stories set in the ministry of Jesus. It could be argued that the material is created or shaped significantly by the Palestinian community in their obedience to the resurrected Lord who continues to teach them through the Spirit. As Bultmann has affirmed, material emerging from the historical Jesus is culturally indistinguishable from any creation of the Palestinian community (Bultmann, *Jesus*, 12–14). Yet after years of life in a Middle Eastern, oral-tradition peasant community, we find no convincing reason to question the basic authenticity of the parables as parables of Jesus of Nazareth. The material *is* Palestinian. No doubt the material has been reused by the evangelists for their own theological purposes. But it is our view that this reuse does not significantly obscure the original intent of the material that can be determined when the underlying culture and the literary form are carefully examined. The redactional quest for the theology of the evangelists is a valid pursuit worthy of much effort, but it is not our concern here. Rather, the original Palestinian setting, along with the timeless theological content, is the goal of our inquiry. This study is written out of a deep conviction that the literary form and the underlying culture of the parables need more careful attention than they have had thus far in contemporary studies. It is hoped that what is presented will be understandable to the nonspecialist as well as being of some interest to the specialist.

Before proceeding to the task, a few definitions are required, along with some attention to methodology. Initially we must ask the knotty question, ''Just what is a parable?''

WHAT IS A PARABLE?

A lengthy debate surrounds this question. One scholar will admit to over seventy parables in the synoptic Gospels, and the next limits them to thirty. Classifications such as parable, example-story, simile, etc., are well-known distinctions that have been used by interpreters to sort out types of parables. At the same time, Jeremias, the twentieth century's most influential interpreter of the parables, observed,

> This word (parable) may mean in the common speech of post-biblical Judaism, without resorting to a formal classification, figurative forms of speech of every kind: parable, similitude, allegory, fable, proverb, apocalyptic revelation, riddle, symbol, pseudonym, fictitious person, example, theme, argument, apology, refutation, jest (Jeremias, *Parables*, 20).

With this in mind we prefer to look at the way a parable *functions* in the text of the New Testament rather than concentrate on its *type*. When we do this it quickly becomes clear that parables are not illustrations. Manson has stated this most profoundly where he observes that "minds trained in Western modes of thought" are accustomed to theological arguments set forth in abstractions. Then to help "popularize these conclusions" they may be illustrated from ordinary life. But, says Manson,

> The true parable . . . is not an illustration to help one through a theological discussion; it is rather a mode of religious experience (Manson, *Teaching*, 73).

A part of what we understand Manson to be saying can perhaps best be seen by creating a comparison. In Luke 9:57–58 the text reads, "As they were going along the road a man said to him, 'I will follow you wherever you go.'" If Jesus had been a Westerner he might have responded something like this:

> Bold statements are easy to make but you have to consider seriously what it will cost you to follow me. It seems evident that so far you have yet to do so. I must say to you plainly that I can offer you no salary or security. If my point is not yet clear, perhaps an illustration will help. For example, I do not even have a bed of my own to sleep on.

But Jesus replies,

> Foxes have holes,
> and the birds of the air have nests;
> but the Son of man has nowhere to lay his head (Luke 9:58).

Rather than the abstract statement followed by a clarifying illustration we have a dramatic confrontation, briefly stated in unforgettable terms. A lofty affirmation about the person of Jesus permeates the parabolic answer. An impact is made on the listener/reader that calls for a response. Theological implications oblige the mind to move out from this compact center in a number of directions. The response of the original disciple is missing. The reader must now respond. All of this takes place at once in an intense dramatic confrontation. A parable has been spoken! To assume that we can capture all that happens in a parable in an abstract definition is to misunderstand its nature. Yet we must try.

The parables of Jesus are a concrete/dramatic form of theological language that presses the listener to respond. They reveal the nature of the kingdom of God and/or indicate how a child of the kingdom should act. With this definition in mind, we must ask next where parables are found.

PARABLES ARE WHERE YOU FIND THEM

There are at least six different types of formats in which the parables of Jesus function. It is crucial for their interpretation to see how they function in these different settings. These six are:

1. The parable in a theological dialogue.

2. The parable in a narrative event.

3. The parable in a miracle story.

4. The parable in a topical collection.

5. The parable in a poem.

6. The parable standing alone.

Each of these requires brief examination. The first is the parable in a theological dialogue. An example of this is the theological discussion between Jesus and the rich ruler in Luke 18:18-30. The climax of the discussion occurs, as we will observe, in the telling of the parable of the Camel and the Needle. The parable has a crucial function in forming the climax of the entire discussion and cannot be isolated from it.

The banquet at the house of Simon the Pharisee in Luke 7:36-50 is an example of a parable in a narrative event. The parable of the Creditor and the Two Debtors functions as a part of the narrative event. There is dialogue but the dramatic actions of the silent woman are the focus of the entire scene.

The miracle story of the healing of the woman with a spirit of infirmity in Luke 13:10-17 becomes a theological debate between the head of the synagogue and Jesus, and thus also overlaps with type one above. Yet it is in a miracle story and again the parable of the Ox and Ass functions as a crucial part of the whole.

In Luke 11:1-13 we have a topical collection on the subject of prayer. The parable of the Friend at Midnight (Luke 11:5-8) is a part of that collection. A careful distinction must be made in such a collection among the different units of tradition that are included in a collection. That is, because a number of sayings on one topic are grouped together, it is easy to fail to perceive where the paragraph breaks should come and thus misinterpret the material (cf. Bailey, *Poet*, 110f., 134f.).

Occasionally, as in Luke 11:9-13, we have a very carefully composed poem on prayer. Jesus gives three striking parables in the central stanza of the poem (*ibid.*, 134-141). Their function in that climax is the key to the understanding of the entire poem.

Finally, a parable at times stands alone. In Luke 17:1-10 we have three topics in rapid succession, each of which has some parabolic speech. There is the parable of the Millstone and the topic of judgment on the tempter. This is followed by the parable of the Grain of Mustard Seed and the apostles' request for faith. Then comes the dramatic parable of the Obedient Servant in vv. 7-10. These three stand relatively alone with no clear connection to what surrounds them and no specific context.

Thus in all but the last type the parable functions as a crucial part of a larger literary unit. It is the larger unit in each case that must be examined to determine what the parable is all about. With a working definition of what parables are in the New Testament and where they occur, we must then ask how they are to be interpreted.

THE INTERPRETATION OF PARABLES

The literature on this topic is extensive enough to lead the interpreter to despair. In this section we will not try to review that literature; rather we will set forth our own particular Middle Eastern cultural perspective and indicate our own methodology. A number of aspects of parabolic interpretation need some explanation. The first is the idea of looking at a parable as a play within a play.

(1)   The Play within the Play

In his famous drama *Hamlet,* Shakespeare uses the relatively rare phenomenon of a play within a play. In act 3, scene 2 Hamlet is desperate to "catch the conscience of the king." He (Hamlet) brings in a troop of players to reenact a story similar to the murder of his father that the present king has perpetrated. The spectator to this particular scene observes action on two levels. There is the little drama being enacted by the troop of players. Then there is the conflict between Hamlet and his uncle the king. Hamlet uses the actors and their drama to communicate with his uncle. As the troop of actors proceeds with its "play within a play," we, the audience, shift our attention from watching them to watching Hamlet and his uncle.

In the parables of Jesus we have a similar situation. The *play* is taking place between Jesus and his audience. Many times his theological enemies are his audience and thus sharp conflict is involved. The *parable* often occurs as "the play within the play." That is, in Hunter's apt phrase, the parables are "weapons of war in a great campaign against the powers of darkness which took Jesus to the cross" (Hunter, *Then,* 9). In some cases, like the scene in the house of Simon the Pharisee, we have the entire play (a long dramatic scene) and within that play the parable is told. In other cases the "play" is quite short, as in Luke 18:9 where it is reduced to a part of a verse. Sometimes it is missing entirely, as in Luke 17:7–10. Wherever possible we must try to ascertain the audience and try to understand the attitude of the original audience to the topic discussed by the parable. Some scholars see these settings for the parables as later additions that must be stripped away to discover the original message of the parable. Granted, these settings have certainly been shaped into their present form by the evangelist or his source. Yet is it not our responsibility to try to take these settings seriously and see if they are appropriate to an understanding of the original message of the parable? That is, they may well have been composed by Christians in the post-Easter Church. They are most certainly interpretations. But is it not possible that they are *correct* interpretations? Is it not possible also that some of these settings were transmitted in the tradition with the parables to which they are attached? This study is made with the assumption that these options are viable alternatives. Thus two levels of interest must be kept in focus: the theological debate between Jesus and his audience, and the use Jesus makes of parables in communicating to that audience in that debate. This brings us to consider another aspect of the relationship between Jesus and his audience, namely that of a storyteller and his listeners.

(2)   The Storyteller and His Listener

If you hear an Englishman tell a story about the days of King Arthur and his court, the teller and the listener throw an invisible mental switch. Everyone knows how the characters are expected to act in the world of the knights of the round table. In any story Sir Lancelot is expected to respect the ladies, obey the king, rescue the oppressed, and protect his own honor. The storyteller has an invisible "grand piano" on which he plays. The known pattern of life from the days of King Arthur is the "piano" on which the storyteller plays. The main points, climaxes, bits of humor, and irony are all heightened by "variations on a theme," that is, by changing, reinforcing, rejecting, intensifying, etc., the known pattern of attitude and behavior. Imagine then an Englishman telling the same story about Sir Lancelot to Alaskan Eskimos. Obviously the music of the "grand piano" will not be heard because the piano is in the minds of the English listeners who share a common culture and history with the storyteller. In the case of the parables of Jesus, *we are the Eskimos*. The people who were attuned to hear the depths of what was being said in a parable were the first-century peasants of Palestine. We in the West are separated from them by both time and distance. Two thousand years have passed, and we are culturally Westerners and not Middle Easterners. What then is to be done?

(3)   Recapturing the Middle Eastern Culture that Informs the Parables

To try to hear more precisely the music of the unseen "grand piano" is the major task of this study. The present writer has spent twenty-five years at this task already, and is fully aware of its dangers and complications. Briefly, the method we have evolved is to make use of four tools. The first is to discuss the cultural aspects of the parable with a wide circle of Middle Eastern friends whose roots are in isolated conservative village communities and try to find how the changeless Middle Eastern peasant sees things. The second is to examine carefully twenty-four translations of the New Testament in Syriac and Arabic to see how Christians in this part of the world have understood the text from the second to the twentieth centuries. The point here is that translation is *always* interpretation. The translator must decide what the text means before he can translate it. A parable passes through the translator's mind on its way to the new language. Through a careful reading of a series of such translations one is able to learn a great deal about how Middle Easterners themselves have understood a given text. The third is to look for parallels in literature as close to the New Testament as possible. Finally, the literary structure of the parable or parable passage must be examined with care.

Three of these tools are nonproblematic. Clearly one should understand the literary structure of a passage, examine literary parallels in other writings, and note translations made in the languages of the area. But the principle of "discussions with contemporary peasants" always raises the question, "How do you know that the peasants of the Middle East have not changed their culture over the centuries?" Obviously, if we can confirm in ancient literature a cultural pattern that we find surviving in the contemporary conservative Middle Eastern village, there is no problem. For example, we observe that the Middle Eastern gentleman in the village always walks down the street at a slow, pompous pace in order to preserve his honor. The father of the prodigal in Luke 15:20 *runs* down the street. For the village patriarch today to run down a village street would be humiliating and degrading. Was it the same for the village father in the time of Jesus, or has the pattern of life changed? In this case we are fortunate. Ben Sirach, a gentleman scholar in Jerusalem early in the second century B.C., tells us plainly that a "gentleman is known by his walk" (Sir. 18:20). Thus pre-New Testament literature confirms what we discover in isolated villages today in northern Syria and Iraq, in the highlands of Galilee, and in the south of Egypt. But if we do not find anything in the literature that surrounds the New Testament, what then? What if the above Sirach text had not been written? Could we then trust our contemporary insight? It is a basic presupposition of this study that there is no escape from the problem. We choose not to suspend interpretation in the fond hope that a new Dead Sea scroll will miraculously turn up answering our questions. To interpret the parable *at all* is to choose a path through a forest of alternatives, all of which are culturally conditioned. That is, if we had not found the Sirach text confirming the significance of the slow walk for a gentleman in the village, what then? We could then say, "Thus we cannot assume the father's run down the road to be significant!" But to do so is to *make* a cultural judgment. In this case the judgment is to decide that his run is not significant. We then fall back on our own subconsciously assumed Western culture as a base for interpretation. For the American, the people in a parable start acting like Americans, and for the French, they look like French, and for the German, they become Germans. When there is no alternative it seems better to start with the Middle Eastern cultural pattern with the full awareness that *if* we find more evidence our present assumptions may be confirmed, revised, or rejected. In the meantime, let us do our best. The question is not, Shall we make cultural judgments as we interpret or not? Rather, there is no escape from asking, Whose culture is to inform our interpretations? Ours or someone else's?

This situation can perhaps be clarified by one further illustration. The Westerner reads Luke 2:7, "She laid him in a manger," and assumes that Jesus was born in a stable because, of course, mangers are in stables. This judgment is a culturally conditioned decision whether the Westerner knows it or not (we put animals in stables). However, the Middle Eastern Palestinian farmer reads the same text and assumes that Jesus was born in a private home. In the Middle East the villager's home is one room with a lower level at one end where the family donkey and cow are brought at night. The family lives on the upper level. This raised terrace has mangers built into the floor at the end nearest the animals. So the Middle Eastern peasant reads the same text and decides that Jesus was born in a private home. I have seen homes here in the Middle East with mangers in the floor that were built in the eleventh century. This is my earliest evidence. We are then faced with three alternatives:

1. We can continue assuming our own Western culture and proceed with our traditional view that Jesus was born in a stable.

2. We can say, "We don't have any first-century evidence about where animals were kept and so where Jesus was born is lost to us. Without such early evidence we should not even venture a guess. Luke 2:7 must remain obscure."

3. We can tentatively agree, "We *know* that the peasant has not changed his ways from the eleventh century until now, and it is reasonable to assume that the centuries before were also culturally unchanging. The assumption of birth in a private home suits the text and everything we know about the gregarious nature of close-knit Middle Eastern society, thus there is no reason not to use the evidence we have, and affirm birth in a private home."

The question about where Jesus was born, in a stable or a private home, is not crucial (cf. Bailey, *Manger*). In the case of Luke 2:7, if we decide on the second alternative and suspend interpretation, not much is lost. But in the case of the parables a great deal is lost because the very heart of the teaching of Jesus appears in the parables. To suspend interpretation for lack of evidence is unthinkable. It is also totally unacceptable to continue reading our own culture subconsciously into the parables once we become aware of what we are doing. The third alternative then presents itself and becomes the methodological assumption that is applied in this study when, and only when, there is no other evidence available. In short, the parables are stories about people who lived in a particular time and place. We cannot interpret these stories without making culturally influenced decisions as we proceed. We will use *all* the *best* evidence at our disposal irrespective of its incompleteness. Finally, what kind of cultural questions are we intending to ask?

In our concern for understanding the culture that informs the parables we are interested in asking the *internal* question. We are not primarily interested in geography, dress, formal customs, weather, and the agricultural year. Rather we are interested in the way people feel, react, and respond. Specifically we are interested in asking five questions at crucial points in each parable in order to recapture the music of the storyteller's piano. These are the questions of *response, value judgment, relationship, expectation,* and *attitude.* How is a father expected to *respond* when his younger son asks for his inheritance while the father is still alive? What is the *relationship* between a master and his servant? What *value judgment* does the listening audience make when guests fail to attend a banquet? What is the *attitude* of Middle Easterners toward imperialistic rulers? What kind of hero does the audience *expect* in the parable of the Good Samaritan?

At times we ask these questions of the people themselves in the story. At other times we ask them of the listening audience. Both sets of questions are crucial.

Some may object that such questions are an attempt to psychoanalyze the characters in the parables and that such a process is illegitimate. Yet every listening audience in any culture has an entire complex of attitudes, value judgments, known responses, etc. (the "grand piano" mentioned above). This same fabric of parabolic communication also existed between Jesus and his first listeners. Indeed, it is in this communication network that meaning is to be found. It is precisely there that the theology of the parable is encased, and a failure to ask these questions is to subconsciously substitute non-Middle Eastern responses and, in the process, fail to understand the dynamic of the parable. It is analogous to looking at the placid surface of the water on a rocky shore and failing to put on a rubber mask to view the fascinating world of color and motion beneath the surface. Speculative mind-reading of the characters in the parables is not the point. Rather we seek out the basic Middle Eastern responses to the human situations reflected in the parables.

(4) Literary Structure

The investigation of literary structure in biblical literature has been called rhetorical criticism. It is a large and developing field that has been described and need not detain us (Bailey, *Poet*, 44-75). However, a few introductory remarks to this important discipline are essential.

We are attempting to discover the patterned repetitions of words and phrases and their significance for interpretation. The basic forms of these patterned repetitions are established in the Old Testament, to which we must turn for a few illustrations and definitions.

The poetical books of the Old Testament, along with most of the prophetic writings and many sections of other books, make extensive use of Hebrew parallelism. This literary device is built on the use of two lines that relate to one another in some special way. The second line may be synonymous with the first, in which case it is called "synonymous parallelism." When the second line is the opposite of the first the couplet is labeled "antithetical parallelism." The second line may also be the climax of the first, or an illustration of it, or complete it in some way that is more felt than understood. This parallelism is sometimes called "synthetic."

With this two-line parallelism as a tool the poets of the Old Testament developed three basic literary styles of relating these separate parts of the parallelism. We have called these *standard* parallelism, *inverted* parallelism, and *step* parallelism. All three of these literary devices occur in Isaiah 55:6–10. In this case the parallelism can be seen clearly even in an English translation such as the RSV. The author begins (in vv. 6 and 7) with three couplets of *standard* parallelism. In each case the theme stated in the first line is repeated in the second. They are as follows:

A   Seek the Lord while he may be found,
A   call upon him while he is near;
B   let the wicked forsake his way,
B   and the unrighteous man his thoughts;
C   let him return to the Lord, that he may have mercy on him,
C   and to our God, for he will abundantly pardon.

In verses 8 and 9 the author uses *inverted* parallelism, which can best be seen when printed as follows:

A   For *my thoughts* are not *your thoughts,*
  B neither are *your ways my ways,* says the Lord.
    C For as the heavens are higher than the earth,
  B so are *my ways* higher than *your ways*
A   and *my thoughts* than *your thoughts.*

We are still dealing with pairs of lines but the author has arranged them in a different order (as can be easily seen by observing the italicizing). The theme of ''my thoughts/your thoughts'' occurs at the beginning and is repeated at the end. The theme of ''my ways/your ways'' occurs in the second and fourth lines. The illustration/parable of the heavens and the earth occurs in the center. Parallelism is still used, but in this case it is *inverted* parallelism.

In verses 10 and 11 Isaiah turns to *step* parallelism, which can best be seen when printed as follows:

A   For as the *rain* and the *snow come down from heaven,*
  B and *return not* thither but water the earth,
    C *making it bring forth* and *sprout,*
      D *giving seed* to the sower and bread to the eater,

A   so shall my *word* be that *goes forth from my mouth*;
  B it shall *not return* to me empty
    C but *it shall accomplish that which I purpose,*
      D and *prosper in the thing for which I sent it.*

The four lines of the second verse match the four lines of the first verse in an ABCD–ABCD pattern, making a step design, and thus this poetic device can be called *step* parallelism. The first line of each stanza speaks of something ''going out.'' The second talks of it ''not returning.'' The last two present the results.

These three stylistic devices can be used in various combinations, but the basic literary building blocks are the three types of parallelism outlined above. A great variety of patterns is often found in *inverted* parallelism (sometimes called chiasm). Thus this device needs special attention.

Isaiah 55:8–9, examined above, is a clear case of inverted parallelism. In this case we are dealing with couplets of poetry and the pairs of lines relate to one another in an inverted fashion. In biblical literature the inversion of themes at times goes far beyond simple parallelisms. Sets of couplets, paragraphs, chapters, and even an entire book can be understood as having been composed on the basis of a series of themes that are stated and then repeated in an inverted fashion (cf. Bertram, 165–68). Thus we are obliged to go beyond inverted parallelism and talk of the *inversion principle*. Already in the illustration of the three couplets of *standard* parallelism given above (Isa. 55:6–7) Isaiah has used the inversion principle. He begins in the first couplet with a call to seek the Lord. The second couplet tells the wicked what must be abandoned. In the third couplet we return to the theme of the first couplet. Often (although not in this case) the writer places his climax in the center before he begins to repeat. Then again, often the center is related to the beginning and the end in some specific fashion. Just past the center there may be a *point of turning* that makes the second half significantly different from the first half. Thus there were a number of ways the author could heighten his message by the use of inversion. When these rhetorical devices occur they are important for any passage of Scripture; but the question arises, What significance do they have for parables?

In three of the passages selected for this study the parable is embedded in a theological dialogue. In two of these (Luke 7:36–50; 18:18–30) the parable proper occurs in the exact center of the dialogue and the dialogue is structured with the use of the inversion principle. More often the parables fall into a series of short scenes or stanzas. Elsewhere we have described this as the *parabolic ballad* form (Bailey, *Poet,* 72f.). Whether or not this literary form was intentional we cannot conclusively demonstrate. The movement of the parable, however, is clearly structured around these scenes. Thus they must be observed and studied for a fuller understanding of the parable. Often these scenes relate to one another in a discernible pattern, as in the parable of the Good Samaritan. These internal patterns will also be seen to be significant for interpretation.

One final note of caution must be sounded. If one is willing to accept sufficiently subtle theological relationships one can find parallelisms almost anywhere. Theological themes in the New Testament are all interrelated somehow if you stretch them enough. Around the turn of this century a British fundamentalist, E. W. Bullinger, wrote *The Companion Bible,* in which he worked at literary structure in such an irresponsible fashion that he virtually discredited the discipline for a full generation. A cautious start was again made by T. W. Manson. We are following leads from his work in this study. In working with students in the area of literary structure now for a number of years I have discovered the natural tendency to jump to conclusions and to superimpose onto the text all kinds of relationships that are not there. In this study doubtless some of our analysis needs further refinement. We can only hope that some useful progress has been made.

A few principles that help instill caution are perhaps in place.

a. The ideas that repeat in matching lines are the most important ideas in the line and demonstrate themselves to be so in the overall poem. If only minor words match then the structure suggested is imaginary.

b. Structural forms fall into types. A series of similar types needs to be found in different places in the Old and New Testaments before the researcher can be confident that he has identified anything of significance (cf. Bailey, *Poet*, 44–76).

c. The Old Testament Hebrew poetic line and the syntax of Hebrew and Aramaic must always be in the background to help determine where the poetic line begins and ends. For example, "he gave him" is usually one word in Semitic languages and cannot be broken into two lines.

d. Often an older piece of literature has a few extra comments attached to it for a new reader. These extra comments stand out because they break the literary pattern. The presence of such additional phrases in some of the literary structures of the New Testament introduces a game that any number can play. Mark off enough phrases as extra comments and you can make almost any literary pattern out of any New Testament paragraph. The greatest caution must be exercised in identifying any word or phrase as a later editor's comment. The break in that pattern made by the extra comment needs to be unmistakable. There must be a clear and discernible reason that has led someone at some stage in the transmission of the material to add a brief comment.

e. No translation can be trusted. Earlier, more formal translations, like the RSV, can be used with profit by the nonspecialist. Many recent English translations have taken great liberties in rearranging the words and phrases into an appropriate order for the English language. A good start can be made with an RSV translation, but a knowledge of the original languages is essential for a precise study of the literary structure of a passage.

f. When there is a structure in the text the relationships between lines are bold and unmistakable. Subtlety is a deadly enemy.

g. If the matching blocks of material are relatively long there needs to be a *series* of matching elements. For example, if one finds in any Pauline letter a reference to the cross, he unwarily may continue reading until he comes to a second reference and then affirm a connection between the two. He may have skipped over a dozen themes in order to find one that he calls a parallel. Bullinger's work is flawed by this error on nearly every page. Take any four paragraphs in the New Testament and you can find *something* that matches and affirms an ABBA or an ABAB structure for the four paragraphs.

h. Inversions have been found unconsciously expressed in a variety of places such as letters, office memos, and casual conversations (Schegloff, 78–89). In this study we are looking for a deliberate repetition that has its roots in the Hebrew parallelism of the Old Testament. The interpreter needs to look for special features such as a central climax that relates to the beginning and the end; a point of turning just past the center; hints of double inversion (cf. Bailey, *Recovering*, 269, 290f.); redundancy introduced to complete the parallelism; and bold repetitions that seem to be clearly deliberate. When such features occur the interpreter can be fairly confident that he is dealing with a conscious literary construction that is significant for exegesis.

It has been said of the saxophone, "It is an instrument that is easy to play poorly." In this same vein, rhetorical criticism is a tool for New Testament studies that is easy to use poorly.

(5)   The Problem of the One and the Many

Through the long centuries of the life of the Church the dominant method of interpretation was the allegorical method, in which every little part of the parable was given some mystical meaning. Parabolic interpretation became so confused that it is no wonder the Latin proverb emerged stating *Theologia parabolica non est theologia argumentative,* and thus affirming that no doctrine could be based on any parable. With the allegorical method anyone could read almost anything into almost any parable. The break away from allegory started with the Reformation and was finalized by a German scholar, A. Jülicher, at the beginning of this century. Because of the irresponsible extravagances of the past a number of scholars moved to the other extreme and rejected *all* allegory, insisting that there is only *one* teaching in each parable. It is our view that parables have in them more than a single theme and that these themes can be understood without either destroying the unity of the parables or falling back into the allegorizations of the past. It is instructive to remember David and Nathan. Nathan tells a story to David about a rich man, a poor man, and a lamb (II Sam. 12:1–6). David had stolen another man's wife and had had her husband killed. Nathan's story to David has three symbols:

> The rich man symbolizes David.
>
> The poor man symbolizes Uriah.
>
> The lamb symbolizes Bathsheba.

Two separate aspects of this parable must be observed with care. The first is this set of symbols that David (the original listening audience) understood instinctively. These (mentioned above) are *symbols,* not allegorizations. A symbol *represents* something else, an allegory *is* something else and has no other existence. These three symbols function in the story and without them the parable is pointless. But having identified the three symbols that *the original audience* (David) instinctively identified, we are *not* free thereby to start making other symbolical identifications. That is, we could take the city, the flocks and herds, the cup, the traveler, and the morsel, and assign them meanings of one kind or another, and in the end make the parable mean whatever we might want. Yet there *are* symbols in the parable. Moule perceptively compares a parable to a modern political cartoon that the reader has to "understand" (Moule, 96f.). The modern political cartoon *has* symbols. The cartoonist makes symbolic identifications that he knows the majority of his readers will interpret correctly. Thus, like the modern cartoon, the Gospel parable also has symbols. *The symbols to look for are the ones the original teller puts in the story for the purpose of communicating with the original audience.* The storyteller, in the telling of the parable, skillfully uses these symbols to press the original listener to make a single decision/response. In the case of the above, David is pressed to understand "I am the man." It is in that single response that the unity of the parable is to be found.

This brings us to the second question of "What does it mean for me?" We are now some 3000 years away from David and his world. If the parable is told specifically to call to repentance an Oriental king who has committed a particular evil, what can such a story mean to us living in a very different world? The answer to this question is to be found in the theological cluster that is at the heart of every parable. The parable has a cluster of theological motifs that together press the original listener to make his single response/decision. Nathan is trying to get David to make *one* move, but a number of theological themes combine in the telling of the story to press David to make that move. What are some of them? We can suggest the following:

1. The king is under the law, not above it. It is God's law, not the king's. God is offended.

2. The law specifies special rights for the "stranger within the gates." Uriah is a Hittite. David has denied Uriah these rights.

3. Unlike Egypt and Babylon, the women of the kingdom are not for the king's choosing like grapes on a vine.

4. David has many wives, Uriah only one. Simple justice has been violated.

All of these together press David to make the *single* move that he does make. Thus, even though I am not an Oriental monarch who has stolen my neighbor's wife, there is theological content in the parable that leaps the centuries and profoundly applies to me and to all of us. Once we identify the original listener and perceive the single response expected of him, we can discover the cluster of themes that evoked that response. It is in that cluster of theological themes that we find the message for all people in any place at any time. The lesson of Nathan's parable for today is *far* more than "Do not steal your neighbor's wife." Primarily it answers the ageless question, "Is the leader of a nation above the law?" In this study we will try to identify the original listener and attempt to discover what Jesus was trying to get him to understand and do. Then, through an analysis of that initial response/decision, we will be able to see what the text says to us. We will attempt to discern the multiplicity of theological themes in a parable (where they exist) without destroying its unity and without allegorizing its details.

In summary, in order to understand the parables of Jesus and to discern their message for today, the interpreter needs to go through eight basic steps, which can be carried out to some degree by the nonspecialist, and be pursued in much greater detail by the specialist. These steps can be briefly stated as follows:

1. Determine the audience. Is Jesus talking to the scribes and Pharisees, to the crowds, or to his disciples?

2. Examine carefully the setting/interpretation provided by the evangelist or his source.

3. Identify the "play within a play" and look at the parable on these two levels.

4. Try to discern the cultural presuppositions of the story, keeping in mind that the people in them are Palestinian peasants.

5. See if the parable will break down into a series of scenes, and see if themes within the different scenes repeat in any discernible pattern.

6. Try to discern what symbols the original audience would have instinctively identified in the parable.

7. Determine what single decision/response the original audience is pressed to make in the original telling of the parable.

8. Discern the cluster of theological motifs that the parable affirms and/or presupposes, and determine what the parable is saying about these motifs.

In the following chapters we intend to apply the above method to ten of the parables in Luke with the earnest hope that what is written here will help the reader, if ever so slightly, to recover something of the impact of the parables in their original Palestinian setting, and that in so doing ''the decisive pay-offs of the material,'' the ''vitality and dynamic of the text,'' will speak afresh to us in our day.

Chapter 1

THE PARABLE OF THE TWO DEBTORS
(Luke 7:36-50)

This deceptively simple, yet artistically and theologically complex, parable/dialogue has much to offer to the careful interpreter. Like the parable of the Camel and the Needle's Eye (Luke 18:18-30), this text has a short parable set in the middle of a tightly constructed theological dialogue. Culture and drama overlap to heighten and inform the theology. Thus the parable must be examined in the light of both of these factors. The overall structure of the seven scenes will be examined, and then the separate sections studied in detail. First, then, the structure:

The overall flow of the theological mosaic is as follows:

>   Introduction (the Pharisee, Jesus, the woman)
>   The Outpouring of the Woman's Love (in action)
>   A Dialogue (Simon judges wrongly)
>   A Parable
>   A Dialogue (Simon judges rightly)
>   The Outpouring of the Woman's Love (in retrospect)
>   Conclusion (the Pharisees, Jesus, the woman)

The full text of the seven stanzas is as follows:

1 One of the Pharisees asked him to eat with him,   INTRODUCTION:
and he went into the Pharisee's house and reclined.
And behold, there was a woman who was a sinner in the city.

2   And when she learned, "He is dining in the Pharisee's house!"
    bringing an alabaster flask of *perfume,*
        and *standing* behind him *at his feet,*   IN THE HOUSE
        weeping she began to *wet* his *feet* with her *tears.* OF THE PHARISEE:
        And she *wiped* them with the *hair of her head,* A WOMAN ACTS!
    and *kissed* his *feet,*
    and *anointed* them with the *perfume.*

3   Now when the Pharisee who had invited him saw it, he said to himself,
        "If this were a prophet, he would have known   A DIALOGUE:
        who and what sort of woman this is who is touching him,
        for she is a sinner."   SIMON JUDGES
        And Jesus answered and said to him,   WRONGLY
        "Simon, I have something to say to you."
        And he answered, "Teacher! Speak up!"

4   And Jesus said,*
            "Two debtors there were   A PARABLE
                to a certain money lender.
                The one owed fifty denarii
                    and the other five hundred.
            They not being able to pay,
                he freely forgave them both.

5   Which of them will love him the more?"   A DIALOGUE:
        Simon answered,   SIMON JUDGES
        "The one, I suppose, to whom he freely forgave the more." RIGHTLY
        And he said to him,
        "You have judged rightly."

6   Then turning to the woman he said to Simon,   IN THE HOUSE
    "Do you see this woman? I entered your house!   OF THE PHARISEE:

    You gave me no water for my feet,   A WOMAN ACTS!
    but she has wet my feet with her tears, and wiped them with her hair.

    You gave me no kiss,
    but from the time I came in she has not ceased to kiss my feet.

    You did not anoint my head with oil,
    but she has anointed my feet with perfume.
                In consequence I say to you,
    her sins, which are many, have been forgiven,
    therefore she loved much.
    But he who is forgiven little, loves little."
    And he said to her, "Your sins have been forgiven." CONCLUSION:

7   Then those who were reclining with him began to say to themselves,
    "Who is this who also forgives sins?"   JESUS
    And he said to the woman, "Your faith has saved you, go in peace."

_____

(*These three words are found in the Old Syriac and many of the Arabic translations.)

The structural flow of the drama in seven scenes is clear, with the major themes repeating in the second half of the structure (with a significant difference from the first half in each case). The inversion principle is used in the repetition. The parable occurs in the climactic center. Each of these sections will need to be examined in turn.

INTRODUCTION (Scene 1)

One of the Pharisees asked him to eat with him,
and he went into the Pharisee's house and reclined.
And behold, there was a woman who was a sinner in the city.

In these first lines all three major characters are introduced. We are presented with the Pharisee (soon to be known by the name Simon); Jesus, who accepts the invitation; and a woman, "who was a sinner in the city." In Luke 15:1-2 a parallel introduction of the same basic three (Pharisees, Jesus, and sinners) appears. In Luke 15:11 the parable of the Prodigal Son begins simply, "A certain man had two sons." Again, all three characters are introduced at the beginning.

We are not told the specific occasion for this particular invitation. Jeremias is most helpful:

We may at all events infer that before the episode which the story related took place, Jesus has preached a sermon which had impressed them all, the host, the guests, and an uninvited guest, a woman (Jeremias, *Parables*, 126).

This suggestion fits all the details of the story and is the best working assumption on which to proceed. Jesus preaches. An invitation is offered to him and accepted. The scene is set at a banquet, which adds a special coloration to the drama. The Pharisee, unlike the covenanter at Qumran, did not eat his meals isolated with his community (as evidenced by this very meal). At the same time, as Neusner has pointed out, "All meals required ritual purity" (Neusner, 340). The point of special importance is that the Pharisee was in touch with non-Pharisees at mealtime, and

This fact makes the actual purity-rules and food-restrictions all the more important, for they alone set the Pharisee apart from the people among whom he constantly lived (*ibid.*).

Thus, isolation from impure food and people was especially crucial for the Pharisee when he sat down to eat. Jesus enters into this kind of a world when he accepts the invitation.

Furthermore, as Safrai observes in his description of religion in first-century Palestine, groups of interested people formed religious societies, *haberim*, and held common meals for religious study.

They featured in particular the study of the Torah, and sometimes continued late into the night when they warmed to their discussions, or when there was a lecture from their teacher or a visiting sage (Safrai, *JPFC*, II, 803f.).

This banquet may well have been such an occasion. Jesus, a "visiting sage," is invited to a meal with the local intellectuals. Spirited discussion on a theological theme of mutual interest is expected. Yet surely no one could have anticipated the dramatic surprises in store for them.

We are told cryptically that "He went in" and "reclined." When the synoptics speak of "reclining" for a meal indoors they mean a banquet (Jeremias, *Eucharistic*, 48f.). Other guests are specifically mentioned at the end of the scene, and we can assume a relatively formal occasion where the traditional roles of guest and host are expected to be acted out with precision by all concerned.

Some of the Middle Eastern cultural details assumed by the text are fully described by Tristram, an astute nineteenth-century traveler.

> . . . entertainment is a public affair. The gateway of the court, and the door . . . stand open. . . . A long, low table, or more often merely the great wooden dishes, are placed along the center of the room, and low couches on either side, on which the guests, placed in order of their rank, recline, leaning on their left elbow, with their feet turned away from the table. Everyone on coming in takes off his sandals or slippers and leaves them at the door, socks or stockings being unknown. Servants stand behind the couches, and placing a wide, shallow basin on the ground, pour water over it on the feet of the guests. To omit this courtesy would be to imply that the visitor was one of very inferior rank. . . . Behind the servants the loungers of the village crowd in, nor are they thought obtrusive in so doing (Tristram, 36-38).

Tristram's observations explain how the woman achieved access to the house and how she could stand behind Jesus at his feet. The present writer can confirm much of the above from personal experience.

This same general banquet setting has been documented by Safrai in his discussion of home and family in first-century Palestine.

> Following the custom prevailing among the Greeks, diners reclined on individual couches. . . . These couches were used for festive banquets as well as for regular meals (Safrai, *JPFC*, II, 736).

Dalman makes the same observation and finds documentation in the Talmud (Dalman, *Words*, 281; P.T. *Berakhoth* 12b). Also, Ibn al-Ṭayyib, a famous Iraqi scholar of the eleventh century, writing an Arabic commentary on this text observes,

> And the phrase "at his feet" and the phrase "she was behind him" is because he was reclining with his legs stretched out and this, along with the fact that she was "standing behind him," brings her to a position at his feet (Ibn al-Ṭayyib, folio 89ᵛ).

Ibn al-Ṣalībī, another famous Middle Eastern commentator writing in Syriac in the twelfth century, notes the significance of her being at his feet.

> She stands behind him because she is ashamed to approach his face for he knows her sins, and because of the respect she shows to his person (Ibn al-Ṣalībī, 98).

Furthermore, the feet are always placed behind the one reclining because of the offensive, unclean nature of feet in Oriental society from time immemorial until the present. In the Old Testament the ultimate triumph for the victor and insult to the vanquished was to "make the enemy a footstool" (cf. Ps. 110:1). Bitterly hated Edom is told, "On Edom I cast my shoe" (Ps. 60:8; 108:9). Moses is obliged to take off his unclean shoes at the burning bush because of the holiness of the ground (Ex. 3:5). John the Baptist uses the illustration of the untying of the shoes to express his total unworthiness in the presence of Jesus (Luke 3:16). As the scene develops, this setting becomes crucial in relation to an uninvited guest, a woman.

Thus the exterior setting is clear. Jesus is known and the community has heard him. He is invited to a banquet for further discussion. At such scenes in the traditional Middle East, the doors are open and the uninvited are free to wander in. Jesus and the other guests are reclining on low couches for the meal. Yet in the dynamics of the scene something is missing.

As Tristram observed, the host failed to wash the feet of Jesus and this is freighted with meaning for the Middle Eastern world in general, and for this story in particular as it develops. But this is not all. Jesus has also received no kiss of greeting. Again Tristram is helpful. Writing in 1894 he says:

> Besides omitting the water for His feet, Simon had given Jesus no kiss. To receive a guest at the present day without kissing him on either cheek as he enters, is a marked sign of contempt, or at least a claim to a much higher social position (Tristram, 36–38).

He goes on to explain how once in the interior of Tunis he was entertained, and in the middle of the banquet his servant whispered in his ear not to trust the host because he had not kissed him on entering. Tristram observes that his servant's warning proved "most timely" (*ibid.*, 38). The formal greetings were clearly of crucial significance in first-century times. Windisch defines the verb "to greet" as "to embrace" and observes that it can mean the embrace of greeting as well as the erotic embrace of love (Windisch, *TDNT*, I, 497). Windisch also notes, "To offer rabbis the *aspasmos* (greeting) coveted by them was the impulse of all pious Jews" (*ibid.*, 498). Jesus is identified as a rabbi (teacher) in the story. Thus, from a Middle Eastern cultural perspective, the failings of the host are glaring omissions (against Marshall, 306, 311). The anointing with oil is also omitted but is most likely less of an offense to the guest, although anointing with oil was a common procedure (cf. Deut. 28:40; Ruth 3:3; Ps. 23:5; Jth. 16:8). Thus it is clear that the accepted rituals of welcoming the guest are not merely overlooked in the telling of the story but have been callously omitted by a judgmental host.

Even in less formalized Western society, there *are* traditional pleasantries observed at the entrance of guests into a home. These include generally:

1. Remarks of welcome at the opening of the door with an invitation to enter.

2. Taking the guests' coats and depositing them in a prepared place.

3. Extending an invitation to sit down.

If all of these were deliberately omitted in the case of a guest of honor at a banquet, the insult would be unmistakable. As Scherer, a longtime resident in the Middle East in the nineteenth century, observes, "(Simon) violated the common customs of hospitality" (Scherer, 105). The significance of these omissions and Jesus' response to them will become clear as we proceed.

The traditional translation of the initial phrase describing the woman is, "And behold, a woman of the city, who was a sinner. . . ." Some early Arabic translations, including Hibat Allah Ibn al-'Assāl, read, "And a woman who was a sinner in the city. . . ." This translation is grammatically legitimate. Through these Arabic translations we can see that this is the way many Middle Eastern Christian scholars understood the text in the first millennium of the Christian era. These Arabic translations present the woman as actively engaged as a "sinner" in the city. This emphasis reminds us of the two separate aspects of the phrase in question. We are given crucial information about her life-style—she was a sinner *plying her trade* in the city. This emphasis gives the story an extra cutting edge and is quite likely a part of the original intent of the text. At the same time, her community *is* identified. She is dwelling *in the city*. Simon (as we will observe) knows perfectly well who she is. She is a part of that community (although an outcast from its religious groupings). This identification of her community will also prove important for the tension of the scene as it develops.

IN THE HOUSE OF THE PHARISEE: A WOMAN ACTS!
(Scene 2)

And when she learned, "He is dining in the Pharisee's house!"
bringing an alabaster flask of *perfume,*
    and *standing* behind him *at his feet,*
        weeping she began to *wet* his *feet* with her *tears.*
        And she *wiped* them with the *hair of her head,*
    and *kissed* his *feet,*
and *anointed* them with the *perfume.*

The inverted parallelism of the three actions of the woman are clear. The woman does three things to the feet of Jesus. She washes, kisses, and anoints them. For each separate service two actions are involved. In logical sequence these can be seen as follows:

a. She brings the perfume   — then anoints his feet with it.

b. She stands at his feet   — then kisses his feet.

c. She wets his feet with her tears   — then wipes them with her hair.

The inverted arrangement of the lines in the text (a b c—c′ b′ a′) *could* be the natural flow of the story. However, a much simpler way to describe the action would be,

> She entered and, standing at his feet, she began to wet them
> with her tears, and to wipe them with her hair, and to
> kiss them and anoint them with perfume she had brought.

Rather, six specific actions are described and it would seem that the inverted parallelism is intentional. Furthermore, the order of the three actions (wash, kiss, anoint) is maintained at the end of the scene in Jesus' speech to Simon. In this latter case, the natural flow of events would be: (1) the kiss on entering the house; (2) the washing of the feet; (3) the anointing of the head with oil. Significantly, this normal order is reversed to match the order of the actions of the woman. The grammatical forms also indicate the deliberate nature of the inverted parallelism. In the first three lines the Greek text has three participles (bringing, standing, weeping). In the last three lines there are three past tenses (wiped, kissed, anointed). Ehlen has demonstrated that the parallelism of grammatical construction in the Hymn Scroll of the Dead Sea Scrolls is an important part of the parallel construction of the poetry of the hymns (Ehlen, 33–85). Finally, as we will note (cf. below on scene 6), Jesus' description of the woman's actions are also cast in poetic parallelisms. Thus it is not surprising to find parallelism used in the description of the initial set of actions here at the beginning of the scene. The point is of more than artistic interest. When a biblical author uses the inversion of parallel lines deliberately, he often places the climax in the center. This feature appears here also with the weeping and the letting down of the hair in the middle. To these details we now turn.

In an Oriental banquet, the door of the house is open and there is a great deal of coming and going, as we have observed. The RSV translates, "When she learned that he was sitting at table in the Pharisee's house. . . ," and thus indicates that the woman finds out about Jesus' location after he has entered the house. The past tense of the verb "to be" is not in the text and the "that" (Gk. *hoti*) can better be understood as introducing direct rather than indirect speech. The story itself (cf. v. 45) tells us that either she entered with Jesus or before him because her dramatic action began "from the time I came in." Thus the story seems to assume that she has heard from the community where he was to be entertained. Indeed she was told, "He is dining in the Pharisee's house!" Bearing gifts she proceeded with him or before him to that place of meeting.

Her gifts are an expression of devotion in a sacrament of thanksgiving. The anointing of his feet is clearly intentional, because she has come prepared. Her washing of his feet is not premeditated because she has nothing with which to dry them and is obliged to use her hair. When we accept the story's own affirmation that she is present at the time of his entrance, it is easy to reconstruct what has triggered her startling action. Jesus is accepted by the community around him as a rabbi. Simon addressed him (in the Greek text) as "Teacher," which is one of Luke's words for rabbi (Dalman, *Words*, 336). All guests are treated with great deference in the Middle East and always have been. We need only recall the hospitality Abraham extended to his three visitors (Gen. 18:1-8). Levison, himself a Palestinian Hebrew Christian, describes the scene and its meaning:

> The studied insolence of Simon to his Guest raises the question of why he had invited Jesus to his house. When a guest is invited to any one's house, he expects to be offered the ordinary amenities of hospitality. When the guest is a Rabbi, the duty of offering hospitality, in its very best manner, is well recognized. But Simon invited Jesus to his house, and proceeded to violate every rule of hospitality. . . . In the East when a person is invited to one's house it is usual to receive him with a kiss. In the case of a Rabbi, all the male members of the family wait at the entrance to the house and kiss his hands. In the house, the first thing that is attended to is the washing of the guest's feet. None of these civilities were offered to the Master. . . (Levison, 58f.).

This woman has heard Jesus proclaim the freely offered love of God for sinners. This good news of God's love for sinners, even those like her, has overwhelmed her and triggered in her a deep desire to offer a grateful response. Edersheim, another Hebrew Christian, fills in the details. He translates "ointment" as "perfume" and writes, "A flask with this perfume was worn by women around the neck and hung down below the breast." Such a flask was "used both to sweeten the breath and perfume the person" (Edersheim, *Life*, I, 566). It does not take much imagination to understand how important such a flask would be to a prostitute. Her intent is to pour it out on his *feet* (she does not need it any longer). For her to anoint his head would be unthinkable. Samuel the prophet can anoint Saul and David on the head (I Sam. 10:1; 16:13), but a sinful woman cannot anoint a rabbi on the head. To do so would be extremely presumptuous. With this deeply moving, profoundly meaningful gesture of gratitude in her mind, she witnesses the harsh insult that Jesus receives when he enters the house of Simon, as Simon deliberately omits the kiss of greeting and the footwashing. The insult to Jesus has to be intentional and electrifies the assembled guests. War has been declared and everyone waits to see Jesus' response. He is expected to offer a few tight-lipped remarks about not being welcome and withdraw. Rather, he absorbs the insult and the hostility behind it and does not withdraw. In a foreshadowing of things to come, "He opened not his mouth." As we observed, to omit even the footwashing is to imply "that the visitor was one of very inferior rank" (Tristram, 38). The woman is totally overcome. They have *not even extended to him the kiss of greeting*! Her devotion, gratitude, and anger mix. She forgets that she is in the presence of a circle of men hostile to her also. Yet *she* cannot greet him with a kiss; such an action would be hopelessly misunderstood. What is to be done? Ah, she can kiss his *feet*! Rushing boldly forward she then breaks down and literally washes his feet with her tears. Now what? She has no towel! Simon would not give her one if she asked for it. So she lets down her hair and with it wipes his feet. After smothering them with kisses (the verb means literally to kiss again and again), she pours out her precious perfume on the feet of the one who announced God's love for her, who is here being abused by this calloused company. She is offering her love *and* trying to compensate for the insult that Jesus has just received (against Marshall, 306). In the process she offers a tender gesture that can easily be misunderstood. *She has let down her hair,* an intimate gesture that a peasant woman is expected to enact only in the presence of her husband. The Talmud indicates that a woman can be divorced for letting down her hair in the presence of another man (cf. Tosefta *Sotah* 59; P.T. *Gittin* 9.50d; quoted in Jeremias, *Parables,* 126, n. 57). Conservative areas of the contemporary Islamic world forbid male hairdressers to work on women's hair for the same reasons.

Even more striking is the evidence from the Talmud in connection with regulations about the stoning of an immoral woman. The rabbis are worried about the woman stimulating unchaste thoughts in the minds of the officiating priests. The text reads,

> The priest seizes her garment, it does not matter if they are rent or torn open, until he uncovers her bosom and loosens her hair. R. Judah said: if her bosom was beautiful he did not expose it, and if her hair was comely, he did not loosen it (B.T. *Sanhedrin* 45a, Sonc., 294; cf. also *Sotah* 8a, Sonc., 34).

Clearly the rabbis considered uncovering the bosom and loosening the hair to be acts that fall in the same category. In a concern to protect the officiating priests from unchaste thoughts these two acts alone are mentioned. This then demonstrates the significance of an immoral peasant woman's act of letting down her hair in the presence of Middle Eastern men. Indeed, this talmudic text demonstrates clearly the sense of shock that must have electrified the room when the immoral woman in our text loosened her hair before Simon and his guests. The provocative nature of the gesture is clear, and is not lost on Simon, as we will see.

Two of the woman's actions, as we have observed, were spontaneous responses to what she saw happening before her. But she *did* come prepared to anoint his feet with perfume. Lamartine, a French traveler in 1821, passed through the Middle East with a large retinue and was greeted everywhere as a European prince. He records that in the village of Eden, in the mountains of Lebanon, he was anointed on the head with perfume on arrival (Lamartine, 371). But here the woman anoints Jesus' feet. For an explanation of this extraordinary action we turn again to the early Arabic commentators. Ibn al-Ṭayyib (himself a physician to the caliph in Baghdad in the eleventh century), comments on this verse: "For it was the custom in the past that noblemen were anointed with ointment in the houses of kings and priests" (folio 89ᵛ). If this cultural note can be entertained it is most enlightening. For her to anoint his head would be extremely presumptuous, as we have noted. No—but she can, as a servant, anoint his feet and thereby show honor to his noble person. Thus, while Simon's gesture implies Jesus to be of inferior rank, the woman's action bestows on him the honor of a nobleman in the house of a king.

The kissing of the feet is not only compensation for what Simon has refused, but also a public gesture of great humility and abject devotion. Again Jeremias is helpful where he offers a talmudic illustration of a man accused of murder who kisses the feet of the lawyer who has gotten him acquitted and thus saved his life (Jeremias, *Parables,* 126, n. 55). Thus in summary, triggered by observing the hostility that Jesus receives from his host, this outcast woman bursts forth in a series of three dramatic gestures. Others are mocking the one to whom she is anxious to show the deepest devotion. With her tears she washes his feet and, in a strikingly intimate gesture, lets down her hair to wipe them. Unworthy to kiss even his hands, she repeatedly kisses his feet. A costly perfume ordinarily used to make her attractive (perhaps to her customers) is poured on Jesus' feet. She may also be extending to him the kind of tribute ordinarily shown only to a nobleman in the house of a king. The entire dramatic action is carried out without any language, and indeed, language is useless in the presence of such costly and tender expressions of devotion and gratitude. The drama then shifts automatically and naturally to the response of Simon, the host.

For Simon, the calculated snub of the young rabbi is not proceeding according to plan. His deliberate refusal to offer the expected hospitality triggered an unprecedented act of devotion. A sensitive man could only humbly apologize to the guest and thank the woman for having compensated for his rudeness. But such is not to be. The drama moves on.

A DIALOGUE: SIMON JUDGES WRONGLY (Scene 3)

Now when the Pharisee who had invited him saw it, he said to himself,
"If this were a prophet, he would have known
who and what sort of woman this is who is touching him,
for she is a sinner."

And Jesus answered and said to him,
"Simon, I have something to say to you."

And he answered, "Teacher! Speak up!"

In scene 1, the principal characters were introduced in the order of the Pharisee, Jesus, then the woman. The drama now reviews the three principal characters in the same order. The Pharisee is mentioned first, and he surfaces not as a humble man confessing his failures as a host, but rather as a spiritual critic of the validity of the young rabbi's prophetic claim and of the woman's spiritual state. The woman's moving drama of thankfulness has passed him by. All he sees is an immoral woman who has let down her hair and who is, by her touch, defiling one of the guests, a guest not perceptive enough to know it.

Again, the dramatic touch of the scene is evident. Simon is engaging in what Shakespeare would label an "aside." Indeed it is a soliloquy, and a very revealing one at that. From it we see something of his real intent in inviting Jesus to his house—namely, to test the claim that Jesus is a prophet. His language is contemptuous; he refers to Jesus as "this" (Plummer, 211). The key word is "touching." The Greek word means both "to touch" and "to light a fire." The word "to touch" in biblical language is used on occasion for sexual intercourse (Gen. 20:6; Prov. 6:29; I Cor. 7:1). Obviously this is not intended here, but Simon's use of this word in this context has clear sexual overtones. He is affirming that in his opinion it is all very improper and Jesus (if he were a prophet) would know who she was and would (of course) refuse this attention from *such* a woman. Clearly, Simon has completely misjudged what is happening before him. Jesus *does* know who the woman is (cf. v. 47). Her actions are not the defiling caresses of an impure woman, but the outpouring of love from a repentant woman. Simon does not rejoice at this evidence of her repentance and he feels no remorse as she compensates for *his* failures. Rather he registers only more hostility to his guest. In passing it is worth noting that Simon *also* knows who she is. Jesus' knowledge of her is more evidence that the story assumes some contact between them before this incident takes place. Simon knows her only as an immoral woman. This does not imply immorality on his part. In the Oriental village immoral women are known and identified by everyone in the community. But the entire scene demonstrates Simon's total indifference to her restoration.

Again Ibn al-Ṭayyib makes an astute observation. In commenting on why Jesus accepted the invitation in the first place he says, "He goes in the hope of his (Simon's) acceptance of her repentance" (Ibn al-Ṭayyib, folio 89ᵛ). Thus Ibn al-Ṭayyib also implies that Jesus has had some previous contact with her and that she is coming to show gratitude for the gift of forgiveness. In fact, Ibn al-Ṭayyib makes the quaint suggestion that this woman has talked to the woman of Samaria, whose story is recorded in John 4. Be that as it may, his suggestion here is very much to the point. Clearly the woman is making a dramatic turn in her entire life's orientation. The story leaves us no doubt regarding the authenticity of her repentance. Yet we are also told that she is a resident of that same city and it is clear that she is known to Simon. If Simon and his other religious friends do not accept the authenticity of her repentance, no restoration to community will take place. The Lost Sheep is brought back *to the fold*. The Prodigal Son is returned *to the family*. Zacchaeus is *"also* a son of Abraham" and can no longer be rejected as an outsider according to Jesus (Luke 19:9). So here, Simon must be led to see the authenticity of her repentance so that she will be restored to fellowship *in her community*. Whether or not Ibn al-Ṭayyib's point can be made for the opening scene of the passage is beside the point. It can be made here.

At this point Simon makes an affirmation crucial for the story as it develops and crucial for our understanding of it. He rejects the validity of her repentance. She is still "a sinner" (v. 39). The grim faces around the room make it clear that she (in spite of this moving demonstration of sincerity) is still rejected as a sinner. What is to be done? The purpose of the parable and the dialogue that follows can be understood as a deliberate attempt to break the stylized attitudes toward "sinners" and "righteous" dominant in that society and make it possible for this woman to be welcomed back into a loving, caring, accepting community.

The dialogue turns again to Jesus. A typical "righteous" teacher of religion in any age could be expected to reject the woman. Jesus accepts her expressions of love with the full knowledge that they are being misunderstood by Simon and his friends. As the dialogue moves to its climax in the brief parable Jesus says, "Simon, I have something to say to you." Plummer assumes that Jesus is asking permission to speak (Plummer, 211). This exact phrase in contemporary villages, however, is used all across the Middle East to introduce a blunt speech that the listener may not want to hear. This is precisely what develops in this scene and the idiom thus understood fits perfectly into the dialogue. Simon indirectly confesses his own failures as a host by addressing Jesus with the title of Rabbi/Teacher. If he is worthy of the title that Simon grants to him, then he is worthy of the honor due the title, but this honor Simon withholds from him. Jesus' carefully chosen words are a brief parable whose structure we may now examine.

A PARABLE (Scene 4)

And Jesus said,	
"Two debtors there were	THE DEBTORS
to a certain money lender.	THE MONEY LENDER
The one owed fifty denarii	ONE DEBTOR
and the other five hundred.	THE OTHER DEBTOR
They not being able to pay,	THE DEBTORS
he freely forgave them both."	THE MONEY LENDER

As we have noted, Luke 18:18–30 is also an extended dialogue with a brief parable in the very center. In both passages the parable itself is cast in a simple literary structure. Debtors and money lender appear in the first two lines and again (but with a difference) in the last two. The center sets out the distinction between the two that is crucial to the entire scene. The structure is so simple that it may well be unintentional. Yet it contributes to the overall artistry of the entire passage. The point is clear. The verb here translated "freely forgive" is the Pauline verb "to offer grace." The two debtors are leveled in their need and neither is able to pay. The same grace is extended to each. The difference between them is set forth in the center of the parable. But in their indebtedness (at the beginning), in their inability to pay, and in their need for grace (at the end of the parable), they stand together.

Here the density of the language and its dramatic impact is heightened by the use of wordplay. Wordplay is not unique to this passage. At the center of Luke 16:9–13 there is a skillfully constructed wordplay that appears when the passage is retrotranslated into the Aramaic of the first century (cf. Bailey, *Poet,* 112–14). The historical present here in v. 40 is further evidence of a pre-Lucan tradition (cf. Jeremias, *Eucharistic,* 150f.). Black has identified a similar play on words in this passage (Black, 181–83). The woman is a *sinner*; the parable is about *debtors* and *creditors*; and the concluding discussion turns on *sin* and *love*. Black lists the Aramaic of these words as follows:

Sinner woman	=	*Ḥayyabhta*
creditor	=	*mar ḥobha*
debtor	=	*bar ḥobha* or *ḥayyabh*
sin	=	*ḥobha*
to love	=	*ḥabbebh* or *'aḥebh*

In Aramaic the word *ḥobha* means both debt and sin. This can be seen in the two versions of the Lord's prayer (Matt. 6:12; Luke 11:4), and in the parable of Pilate and the Tower (Luke 13:2, 4; cf. below, 78f.). Jesus uses this wordplay both to compare and to contrast the sinful woman (*ḥayyabhta*) with her sin (*ḥobha*) and Simon who is socially in debt (*bar ḥobha*) and has failed to love (*ḥabbebh*). This comparison (they are both sinners) and contrast (one loves, the other does not) now becomes the focus of the continuing dialogue.

A DIALOGUE: SIMON JUDGES RIGHTLY (Scene 5)

"Which of them will love him the more?"

Simon answered,
"The one, I suppose, to whom he freely forgave the more."

And Jesus said to him,
"You have judged rightly."

With a modified form of the Socratic method, Simon is led to reason out for himself the conclusion to which Jesus would bring him. Simon is pressed with a question, and seeing that he is being trapped, he can only lamely try to escape with "I suppose. . . ." Marshall notes, "Simon realizes he is caught in a trap" (Marshall, 311). Although Simon totally misunderstood the human scene in front of him, the logic of the parable is inescapable. Love, in the parable, is a response to unmerited favor, indeed, a response to pure grace. Having established this principle from the parable Jesus proceeds to an application that refers back to the actions of the woman and shocks the guests (and the reader) with its boldness.

IN THE HOUSE OF THE PHARISEE: A WOMAN ACTS!
(Scene 6)

Then turning to the woman he said to Simon,
"Do you see this woman? I entered your house!"

You gave me no water for my feet,
but she has wet my feet with her tears, and wiped them with her hair.

You gave me no kiss,
but from the time I came in she has not ceased to kiss my feet.

You did not anoint my head with oil,
but she has anointed my feet with perfume.
           In consequence I say to you,
her sins, which are many, have been forgiven,
therefore she loved much.

But he who is forgiven little,
loves little.''

And he said to her, "Your sins have been forgiven."

In the Gospel of Luke there is a series of pairs involving one man and one woman. In Luke 4:25–27 two heroes of faith are held up as illustrations of the types of people who respond in faith and receive the benefits of God's grace. One is a woman (the widow of Zarephath), the other a man (Naaman the Syrian). In Luke 13:10–17 a woman is healed on the Sabbath. Then in 14:1–6 the same happens with a man. In each case the conversation turns on the treatment of the family ox and ass. The literary structure of the Travel Narrative parallels these two stories (Bailey, *Poet*, 79–85). In Luke 11:5–8 a man under difficult circumstances has his prayers answered. In 18:1–5 a similar parable is told of a woman. These are also parallel in the outline of the material (*ibid.*). In Luke 15:3–10 two people diligently search for what they have lost. One is a man, the other a woman. In all of these cases all of the people involved are noble examples. But here a man and a woman are compared, and the *woman* is the noble character (in spite of what the men in the room think of her) while the man is the ignoble character (in spite of his high opinion of himself). In a Middle Eastern world, still dominated almost exclusively by men, such dramatic scenes were and are a profound statement about the worth of women in a man's society (cf. Bailey, *Women*, 56–73). The shock of praising a despised woman in male company is bad enough. Yet the sharp edge of the criticism can be fully understood only in the light of the cultural expectations of the scene.

The guest in any society is expected to show appreciation for the hospitality extended to him regardless of how meager it might be. In the Middle East these expectations of the guest are solidified into an unwritten law. The host is expected to downgrade the quality of his offerings as inadequate for the rank and nobility of the guest. Irrespective of what is set before him, the guest *must* say again and again that he is unworthy of the hospitality extended to him. Richard Burton, the well-known nineteenth-century traveler and Orientalist, writes the following in his record of his famous trip to Mecca:

> Shame is a passion with Eastern nations. Your host would blush to point out to you the indecorum of your conduct; and the laws of hospitality oblige him

to supply the every want of a guest, even though he be a *déténu* (Burton, I, 37).

The possibility of a *guest* pointing out the indecorum of the *host's* actions is so remote that Burton does not even mention it. Yet amazingly in this passage it happens. Quoting from early Jewish sources Edersheim documents for us the traditional expectations of a noble guest:

> A proper guest acknowledges all, and saith, "At what trouble my host has been, and all for my sake!" While an evil visitor remarks: "Bah! What trouble has he taken?" (Edersheim, *Social,* 49).

Nelson Glueck, the famous Middle Eastern archeologist, records a modern illustration of the ancient social interchange of guest and host. Glueck was entertained by an Arab family living in the ancient ruins of Pella on the east bank of the Jordan.

> We were met and entertained at lunch by Dhiab Suleiman, the *Mukhtar* ("headman") of the village. It mattered not that he was poorly clothed, his house small, his people poverty-stricken. . . . We were exchanging polite conversational amenities with a prince of Pella. We drank his coffee, which slaked our thirst. We dipped pieces of his fragrant, freshly baked bread into a dish of sour milk, and ate the eggs which he boiled and peeled for us. We exclaimed honestly over the goodness of it all. . . . We under no circumstances could have refused his hospitality or stoned him with disdain or pity for his slender provender. I have forgotten many splendid feasts, but I shall never forget the bread we broke with him. The invitation to his board was a royal summons, and we commoners had no choice but to obey (Glueck, 175f.).

Glueck's experience has been repeated by the present writer many hundreds of times all across the Middle East, from the Sudan to Syria, for over twenty years. To attack the quality of the hospitality offered, regardless of the circumstances, is unknown in fact or fiction, in personal experience or in traditional story. Yet in the biblical drama before us, such an unprecedented attack on the inferior quality of the begrudging hospitality does take place and is forthrightly expressed in uncompromising terms. After such an outburst the listening company is pressed to make a decision regarding the speaker. The terms of this decision will need to be examined at the conclusion of the final speeches in the drama, to which we now turn.

The form of the language used here has long been identified as patterned after the Hebrew parallelisms of the Old Testament (Jeremias, *Theology,* 16). Plummer writes, "The series of contrasts produces a parallelism akin to Hebrew poetry. . ." (Plummer, 212). We have noted the use of parallelism in the first description of the woman's actions (in that case, inverted parallelism). Thus it is no surprise to the reader to find parallelism used in this matching description of the woman's deeds. The parallelisms are not merely of artistic significance but, as we will note, clarify a crucial, centuries-old mistranslation of the text.

In regard to the setting of the speech, it must be noted that Jesus, "turning to the woman . . . said to Simon." That is, the speech is addressed to Simon but is delivered facing the woman. It is thus delivered as a speech in praise of her kindness and worth. Were Jesus facing Simon we would imagine a tone of harsh accusations—You, who failed in all of these duties! But delivered facing the woman, it takes on a tone of gentleness and gratitude, expressed to a daring woman in desperate need of a kind word. The entire speech concludes with a climax addressed to her, in which she is reminded that her sins have been forgiven.

The introduction to the speech provides a setting for what follows. Jesus begins with a question, "Do you see this woman?" Simon has concentrated on collecting evidence for a negative judgment on Jesus. He is now asked to give his attention to the woman and her actions. Jesus begins the confrontation with, "I entered *your house*!" The clear line of argument is, "I came in under your roof. I became your guest. You were responsible to extend to me the traditional forms of hospitality, but you refused!" The details then state clearly, "This woman whom you despise magnificently compensated for your failure." The language is very precise. The text reads, "You gave me no water for my feet." Jesus does not say, "You failed to wash my feet." It would be presumptuous to assume that Simon should have taken the role of a servant. Rather, Jesus courteously speaks only of the water. Had Simon provided water Jesus could have washed his own feet. But Simon did not even give him water. By contrast, this woman *herself* washed his feet, not with water but with her tears, and wiped them with her crown and glory as a woman, her hair. Footwashing as a courtesy extended to guests was observed in the Middle East up until the nineteenth century (cf. Jowett, 79).

Jesus continues, "You gave me no kiss." Just what Simon was expected to kiss is not mentioned in humility and deference. In the case of the other two actions the part of the body involved is specifically mentioned. (She washed the *feet*. In the following illustration the *head* and the *feet* are mentioned.) But what should Simon have kissed? Equals kiss each other on the cheek. The student/disciple kisses the rabbi's hands, the servant his master's hand, and the son his parents' hands. In the garden Judas certainly kissed Jesus on the hand (contrary to popular opinions). In the parable of the Prodigal Son, the prodigal is prevented from kissing his father's hand or foot by the father's unprecedented falling on his son's *neck* and kissing him. In this case, it is a sign of reconciliation, not equality, but it is also clearly done to prevent the son from kissing the father's hand or feet (cf. Bailey, *Poet*, 182). Simon has greeted Jesus as "Rabbi/Teacher." Thus Simon should have kissed his hand. Yet with great sensitivity Jesus does not say this, but simply states that there was no kiss of greeting at all. By contrast, the woman has *covered* his *feet* with kisses. (As we observed

above, feet and shoes are signs of degradation in Middle Eastern society; cf.
Scherer, 78). Both contrasts are made. Simon, not one kiss; the woman, many.
Simon failed to kiss even his head; the woman has carried out the supreme
gesture of devotion by kissing his *feet*. (The kissing of the feet is rare but not
unprecedented. In the Talmud Bar Hama kisses the feet of Rabbi Papi in
gratitude for the latter's successful defense of the former's legal case; B.T.
Sanhedrin 27b, Sonc., 163.)

The third action also has a double contrast. Olive oil was commonly used
for anointing the head of a guest. Such oil was and is cheap and plentiful. It was
one of the common products of the countryside in first-century Palestine and
constituted one of its main exports (Applebaum, *JPFC*, II, 674). The head,
being the crown of the person, is considered worthy of an anointing. By contrast
the woman has anointed his *feet* (which no one anoints, even with olive oil) *and*
has used an expensive *perfume*. Thus the woman's action in anointing his feet
has a double impact on the listener/reader (cf. Tristram, 39). In three clear
actions the woman has demonstrated her superiority to Simon. And Simon has
this pointed out to him publicly in poetic speech that will be remembered.

After this scathing rebuke the cutting edge of the conclusion is introduced
with the phrase, "For the sake of this I say to you." The intent is somewhat
ambiguous. Of the possible options the best meaning seems to be, "In the light
of this exposure of your many failures I say to you. . . ." Then comes the much
debated final pair of couplets, which we translate,

> her sins, which are many, have been forgiven,
> therefore she loved much.
>
> But he who is forgiven little,
> loves little.

Jesus does not actually forgive her sins on the spot (he is misquoted by the hostile
guests in the following verse). Rather he announces a forgiveness that has already taken place in the past. The Greek text uses a perfect passive, "her
sins . . . have been forgiven." The passive is to avoid the use of the divine name
(Jeremias, *Parables*, 127). The perfect tense indicates a present condition that
results from a past action. Ibn al-Salībī, the twelfth-century Syrian scholar, came to
this same conclusion : "Her actions show that her sins had been forgiven her"
(Ibn al-Salībī, 98). Jesus announces what God has done and confirms that action to
the woman.

Finally, then, comes the much discussed phrase, "therefore she loved
much." For more than a millennium this was translated in the East and in the
West, "for she loved much." This latter translation has stood in many versions
through the centuries in spite of the fact that it directly contradicts what precedes
and what follows in the text. The question is, what is first, forgiveness or an
outpouring of love? When we look to the parable and to the concluding couplet of
the series now under examination the following can be seen:

The Text	*The Relationship between Love and Forgiveness in the Text*
In the parable of the Two Debtors:	a. Forgiveness is first. b. Then a thankful response of love.
In the concluding couplet ("He who is forgiven little, loves little"):	a. Forgiveness is first. b. Then a thankful response of love.
In the traditional translation of verse 47 ("her sins . . . have been forgiven, *for* she loved much"):	a. An outpouring of love is *first*. b. Then comes forgiveness as a reward.

It is amazing that for many centuries this clashing contradiction has stood and continues to stand in unnumbered translations. If the text has any internal integrity at all, this translation must be in error. Fortunately, at last, major versions are beginning to correct the mistake. The Catholic Jerusalem Bible reads, "For this reason I tell you that her sins, her many sins, must have been forgiven her, or she would not have shown such great love." The New English Bible translates, "Her great love proves that her many sins have been forgiven." Sadly, the 1971 revision of the RSV New Testament maintains the ancient error and still has the woman earning her forgiveness by her actions (in direct contrast to the parable). The key to the corrected translations seen in the Jerusalem Bible and the New English Bible is found in the Greek particle *hoti,* which often means "for" (as in the RSV) but can have what the grammarians call a "consecutive use," which makes the *hoti* show result and can be translated "therefore." Here in verse 47 we have a clear case of such use (cf. Jeremias, *Parables,* 127; Robertson, 1001; Bauer, 593; Plummer, 213; Blass, § 456). This brings verse 47a into harmony with both the parable and the statements that follow it and restores an internal integrity to the text and its message. Indeed, Jesus is pointing out that this woman is not a defiling sinner, but a forgiven woman who knows the extent of her evil ways and something of the grace of God, freely given to her in forgiveness. This awareness has motivated her lavish outpouring of grateful love. Jesus concludes with an obvious reference to Simon that needs careful examination.

Referring to Simon, Jesus says, "He who is forgiven little, loves little." This can be read in two ways. We can assume Jesus is saying, "You, Simon, are a righteous man, and your sins are few and thus very little of God's grace is required to cover these 'debts.' Therefore you have loved little." Much more likely the intent is, "You, Simon, have many sins (some of them we have just recounted). You have little awareness of them and have not repented. Thus you have been forgiven little and, naturally, loved little." Jesus has just listed in graphic terms some of the failures (debts) of Simon, and they reflect far more than formal inadequacies as a gracious host. Rather they indicate deep levels of pride, arrogance, hard-heartedness, hostility, a judgmental spirit, slim understanding of what really defiles, a rejection of sinners, insensitivity, misunderstanding of the nature of God's forgiveness, and sexism. The most damaging criticism of all is the fact that Simon witnessed the woman's dramatic action and still labeled her as a "sinner" (v. 39). Thereby he has refused to accept her repentance and has determined to continue to reject her as a sinner. Ibn al-Ṭayyib has some very thoughtful reflections on this point.

> And the two debtors refer to two types of sinners. One is a great sinner like the woman and the other is a little sinner like the Pharisee. By the phrase "a little sinner," either he means sin in reality or he refers to his (Simon's) conceit at his own perfection. This conceit robs him of virtue and the awareness that the one who is forgiven more loves more. Indeed, he told him (Simon) this parable for the purpose of reproving the Pharisee for the feelings he has harbored against any contact with sinners and to demonstrate to him that this woman's love for him is greater than his love because of the overflowing of his grace to her (Ibn al-Ṭayyib, folio 90ʳ).

In the same passage he also writes,

> And his saying, "The one who is forgiven little, loves little," means that the one who has many sins experiences a profound repentance, followed by a sincere love for God. But the one who has few sins boasts of his uprightness and thinks he has little need of forgiveness, and he has very little love for God (Ibn al-Ṭayyib, folio 89ʳ).

Thus, with Ibn al-Ṭayyib, we understand the text to present to the reader a picture of two great sinners. One sins without the law, one within the law. The first (the woman) has accepted forgiveness for her many sins and responds with much love. The second (Simon) has no real awareness of the nature of the evil in his life. He sees himself with few spiritual debts and thus in little need of grace. Consequently, having received little grace, he shows little (if any) love. This same contrast can be seen in the parable of the Lost Sheep. Does Jesus really think that there are any "ninety-nine who need no repentance?" Or is he rather laughing at a Pharisaical mentality that makes such an assumption (cf. Bailey, *Poet*, 154f.)? The sons in the parable of the Prodigal Son (Luke 15:11–32) and the two men at prayer in the temple (Luke 18:9–14) offer similar contrasts. The rebuke to Simon is stunning. The great unrepentant sinner (whose presence defiles) is Simon, not the woman. The prophet has not only read the woman's heart, he has read Simon's heart. The judge (Simon) becomes the accused. The drama begins with Jesus under scrutiny. The tables turn and Simon is exposed. Finally, we must ask, what is affirmed about Jesus himself?

The drama's affirmations about the person of Jesus are significant. Simon has thought that Jesus might be a prophet, perhaps even "the prophet" foretold in Deuteronomy 18:15 (a famous early Greek text, the Vaticanus, gives this reading in Luke 7:39). The test in Simon's mind is the ability to know the inner nature of people. In the drama Jesus demonstrates full understanding of the inner nature of the woman *and* of Simon. But the drama goes far beyond the simple affirmation that Jesus is a prophet. Jesus surfaces as the unique agent of God through whom God announces forgiveness and to whom a grateful response of love is appropriately demonstrated. The woman is praised for showing love to *Jesus* in response to the forgiveness she has received. Simon is sharply criticized for failing to do the same. Such functional affirmations about the person of Jesus are calculated to evoke from the listener/reader a response of recognition, affirmation, and obedience, *or* accusations of blasphemy against the impostor who presumes to act as God's unique agent. The drama does not leave us in doubt regarding the assembled guests at the banquet.

CONCLUSION: THE PHARISEE, JESUS, AND THE WOMAN (Scene 7)

Then those who were reclining with him began to say to themselves,
"Who is this who also forgives sins?"
And he said to the woman, "Your faith has saved you, go in peace."

All three principal characters were introduced at the beginning of the scene. Now at the end a concluding glance returns to these same major characters. The other diners are not impressed. They did not speak "among themselves"; along with the Syriac and Arabic versions, we prefer to translate more literally "in themselves." Like Simon, they are a bit nervous about verbalizing their criticisms (having just witnessed the withering attack that Simon has endured). Yet their criticism is beside the point. He has not actually forgiven the woman's sins (although this is not beyond him; cf. Luke 5:17–26); he has only acted in God's stead in the announcing of forgiveness and in the receiving of gratitude. They are at least puzzled, and at most offended. Again with our Arabic and Syriac versions, we prefer to read "who is this who *also* forgives sins?" Along with other outrages he *also* forgives sins (Plummer, 214). Finally comes the concluding remark to the woman, "Your faith has saved you, go in peace." Her *faith* (not her works of love) has saved her.

When the biblical author uses the inversion principle he usually states his major theme in the center and then repeats this theme in some way at the end (Bailey, *Poet,* 50ff.). This feature occurs here. The theme of God's freely offered love, accepted as unearned grace, is the major point of the parable in the center of the literary unit. This theme recurs at the end in the clear affirmation that salvation is by faith. She is mercifully sent away from the presence of her despisers in the peace of reconciliation to a loving heavenly Father whose unique agent must continue to endure hostility in the proclamation of that reconciliation to sinners like herself and like Simon. The scene (like the parable of the Prodigal Son) closes unfinished. We are not told the response of Simon (even as we do not know the final response of the older son in Luke 15 or of the three disciples in 9:57–62). Will he reevaluate the nature of his own indebtedness, repent, and offer expressions of grateful love that have so far been glaringly missing? Or will his hostility and opposition harden? Then and now the reader/listener must complete the parable in his own response to God's unique agent of forgiveness and peace. The drama ends, the literary form resolves itself, and a look backward is required.

In each parable we will seek to identify the decision/response that the original listener/reader was pressed to make, and to determine the cluster of theological motifs that comprise the impact of the parable, motifs that can instruct believers in every age. As Marshall has said, "a number of different motifs are present in the story" (Marshall, 304).

First, the original listener. Simon is pressed to understand and confess,

I am a great sinner (as was this woman). This I have not realized. I have not repented, nor have I heard the offer of the grace of God as this woman has. I have been forgiven little and thus I have loved God's agent (Jesus) little. If Jesus really wants to avoid sinners He should avoid me, not this woman whom I have despised.

The theological cluster of motifs that comprise the impact of this parable include the following:

1. Forgiveness (salvation) is a freely offered, unearned gift of God. Salvation is by faith.

2. When accepted, this salvation by faith immediately triggers costly acts of love. These acts of love are expressions of thanks for grace received, not attempts to gain more.

3. Jesus is God's unique agent through whom forgiveness is announced and to whom a grateful response of love is appropriately expressed out of an awareness that through him the believer has been forgiven much. The question in scene 7 is not answered. Each reader must bring his own response.

4. The offer of forgiveness to sinners involves the agent of that forgiveness in a costly demonstration of unexpected love. Within this theme one can overhear something of the meaning of the passion.

5. There are two kinds of sin and two kinds of sinners, namely Simon and the woman. Simon sins within the law, and the woman outside the law. Sinners like the woman often know that they are sinners; sinners like Simon often do not. Thus repentance comes hardest for the "righteous."

6. In a man's world and at a banquet of men, a despised woman is set forth as a heroine of faith, repentance, and devotion. She is the champion in these regards over a man. The inherent worth of women and the fact that the ministry of Jesus is for women and men is powerfully affirmed in the drama.

7. In a confrontation with Jesus the options are faith or offense. There is no middle ground. For Simon, either Jesus is a rude young man who insults his host, fails to show gratitude for a meal prepared in his honor, and presumes to act in God's place, or he is in fact God's unique agent who mediates forgiveness and appropriately expects humble and costly devotion to his person.

8. Jesus accepts Simon's invitation without hesitation. He is known as the friend of sinners and this includes a concern for the "righteous" as well as the outcasts.

May this great dramatic scene provide the same catharsis for us that it has for countless millions throughout the history of its telling.

Chapter 2

THE FOX, THE FUNERAL, AND THE FURROW
(Luke 9:57–62)

The Text:

    And as they were going along the road

A   a man said to him,

    "I will *follow* you   FOLLOW

        wherever you *go*."   GO

                And Jesus said to him,   COST TOO HIGH?

        "Foxes have holes,   (a parable)

        and birds of the air have roosts.

        But the Son of man has nowhere to lay his head."

B   To another he said,

    "*Follow* me!"   FOLLOW

        But he said, "Lord, let me *go* first   GO

        to *bury* my father."   COST

                But he said to him,

        "Leave the dead to *bury* their own dead.   COST

      But you *go*   GO

  and *proclaim* the kingdom of God."   FOLLOW

A'   And another said,

    "I will *follow* you, Lord,   FOLLOW

        but first let me (*go* and) take leave of those at my home."   GO

                And Jesus said,

        "No one who puts his hand to the plow   COST TOO HIGH?

        and looks back   (a parable)

        is of any use in the kingdom of God."

The three brief dialogues in this passage are often overlooked in discussions of parables. Certainly they do not fit the pattern of a parable as an extended story. Yet here also Jesus communicates his views by means of concrete comparisons. Two proverbs/parables occur in the dialogues. Each deserves the title of *mashal* as defined by first-century Palestinian usage. We choose to include this trilogy under the umbrella of the parabolic speech of Jesus. In our discussion of how to interpret parables (see the Introduction), Jesus' response to the first brash volunteer was noted as a classical illustration of his use of the parabolic method of communication. These three cameos need to be considered together because the literary structure of the three forms a single unit, and because of their similarity of subject matter. To the structure set forth above we now turn.

In a recent discussion of the literary structure of this passage Louw writes, "The semantics of proverbial discourse must be based on phrase structure analysis and not on the traditional exposition of the individual's words" (Louw, 107). This is perhaps too strong—both are needed. Louw's exposition is flawed by a failure to consider the culture that informs the text, but his discussion does draw attention to the presence of a literary structure in the text and is at points helpful. The analysis given above allows a number of interlocking features worthy of note to surface.

As is often the case in biblical literature, we are working with three stanzas (cf. Bailey, *Poet*, 69). As is typical with this three-stanza form, the first and third stanzas are linked together in a number of special ways. In this case there are four clear points of comparison that establish such linkage. Initially, in the first and third stanzas (A and A'), the person involved is a volunteer. He *offers* to follow. By contrast, the person in the middle dialogue is a recruit. He is *called* by Jesus to follow. Second, in A and A', Jesus answers with parables whose imagery comes from the outdoor world. The first is from nature and the second from the farming practices of the Palestinian countryside. The dialogue (B) has no parable; in its place is a direct command. The imagery of the dialogue is from the customs of village society, not from nature. Third, in the case of A and A', there is only one statement by each party. The second dialogue has three speeches. Finally, the literary form of the first and last conversations is identical. The flow of ideas is Follow + Go + a parable. By contrast, the central stanza breaks into inverted parallelism with its themes of Follow − Go − Cost + Cost − Go − Follow/Proclaim. This identical structure of three stanzas with step parallelism tying the outside stanzas together and the central stanza breaking into inverted parallelism is found in Luke 15:4–7 (Bailey, *Poet*, 144f.).

In addition to the features that unite the first and third dialogues, a number of semantic links tie the second and third together. Each ends with a reference to the kingdom of God. Each of the people involved pleads that he is willing, "But first. . . ." Finally, some features tie all three dialogues together. Obviously, the themes of Follow + Go + Cost are the focal points in each dialogue. The first is willing to *follow* and *go* anywhere but has not considered the *cost*. The second is asked to *follow*. He wants to *go* home to his family (and is told to *go* and *proclaim* the kingdom). The *cost* of discipleship is put in the form of a command. The third wants to *follow* and, like the second, wants to *go* home first. (The Old Syriac version has the verb "go" in this text, and we suggest that it may be original. In any case, it is implied.) He, like the first, is challenged to consider the *cost*. At the same time, stanzas A and A' are not identical. There is progression. In the first, a man offers to follow unconditionally and is challenged to consider the cost. The last volunteer seems to have done so. He offers to follow but with a very specific condition. With all of these interlocking parallelisms in mind, we now turn to an examination of each dialogue in turn.

THE FIRST DIALOGUE

A   a man said to him,
    "I will *follow* you   FOLLOW
       wherever you *go*."   GO
          And Jesus said to him,   COST TOO HIGH?
       "Foxes have holes,
       and birds of the air have roosts.
       But the Son of man has nowhere to lay his head."

This parable has no cultural riddles. Yet it may have two levels of meaning. The first level is clear. This first would-be disciple represents the *centripetal* force of mission. He is drawn *in* to join the community of disciples. No one recruits him. Yet his understanding of what is involved seems shallow. Sa'īd notes, "He does not understand that 'follow' means Gethsemane, and Golgotha, and the tomb" (Sa'īd, 258). The idea of following a rejected, suffering Son of man would come as a jarring shock to any first-century Jew. In Daniel, the Son of man is to have dominion, glory, and kingdom and, "all peoples, nations, and languages shall serve him" (Dan. 7:14). The reader of Luke has already been told, "The Son of man must suffer" (Luke 9:22). Here the volunteer is not given details but only a graphic picture of total rejection. The point is not only "You, too, may have to suffer privation, and have you considered this?" but also, "Whatever your motives, keep in mind that you are offering to follow a *rejected leader*." "Roosts" is a better translation than "nests." The birds always have roosts, but build nests only at certain times of the year. The point is (partially) that even the animals and birds have *some* place to rest, but the Son of man has none.

Aside from this obvious level of meaning drawn from the nature of foxes and birds, a political symbolism may be involved. T. W. Manson points out that the "birds of the air" were an apocalyptic symbol in the intertestamental period referring to the gentile nations. The "fox" was a symbol for the Ammonites who, as Manson says, "were a people racially akin to but politically enemies of Israel" (Manson, *Sayings,* 72). In similar fashion, Herod's family (due to Herod's Idumean parentage) was racially mixed and was always seen by the Jewish population of first-century Palestine as foreign (Stern, *JPFC,* I, 261–277). Jesus calls Herod Antipas "that fox" (Luke 13:32). Manson writes,

> Then the sense of the saying may be: everybody is at home in Israel's land except the true Israel. The birds of the air—the Roman overlords, the foxes— the Edomite interlopers, have made their position secure. The true Israel is

disinherited by them: And if you cast your lot with me and mine you join the ranks of the dispossessed and you must be prepared to serve God under those conditions (Manson, *Sayings,* 72f.).

It is our view that the political overtones of the sayings of Jesus are often overlooked. Anyone who lives in the Middle East (where every religious breath has political overtones) is obliged to consider some rarely asked questions of the text. The extensive use of the parables with their somewhat veiled symbols; the cryptic phrase, "He who has ears to hear, let him hear"; the resisted pressure to make him into a king; the need to cross to the north on various occasions out of Galilee into non-Jewish provinces, and many other passages indicate that a political dimension was constantly a part of the world in which Jesus lived (cf. Manson, *Messiah*). Even so here. An oppressed people are seldom allowed to declare publicly that they are oppressed. They must talk of their oppression in symbols. The terrors of the Herodian era, with its torture and murder, were fresh in the minds of all. No one dared criticize Rome. The Romans and their Herodian supporters were the powerful of the land and their spies were everywhere. As Manson suggests, Jesus in a veiled fashion may well be saying: Look, if you want power and influence, go to the "birds" who "feather their nests" everywhere. Follow the "fox" who manages his own affairs with considerable cunning. For, in spite of your expectations, the Son of man stands powerless and alone. Are you serious in wanting to follow a *rejected* Son of man?

The Christological affirmation of the passage is clear. Jesus is the Son of man, but his ministry is a suffering rather than a triumphal fulfillment of that title.

We are not told the outcome. The volunteer does not answer. As in many of the parables of Jesus (cf. Luke 7:47; 14:24; 15:32) the parable is left suspended. We do not know whether the volunteer tightened his belt, "set his face steadfast," and stepped into line with the others, or whether, stunned at the price to be paid and at the shocking prospect of a rejected leader, he fell back from the side of the road and watched them pass. Clearly this volunteer mirrors those in every age who glibly offer to follow Jesus with no serious reflection on the price or the implications of following a suffering, rejected master. The reader is obliged to complete the conversation with his own response.

The second would-be disciple does not volunteer, but rather is recruited. Thus we have the *centrifugal* force of mission. Jesus directs three commands to the bystander. They are as follows:

THE SECOND DIALOGUE

B To another he said, "*Follow* me!"	FOLLOW
But he said, "Lord, let me *go* first	GO
to *bury* my father." But he said to him,	COST
"Leave the dead to *bury* their own dead.	
But you *go*	GO
and *proclaim* the kingdom of God."	FOLLOW

The use of inverted parallelism has been noted above. Furthermore, the Greek language is very precise in its verb structure. The type of imperative used here (aorist) indicates a command to start a new action. The person involved has not followed and is commanded to begin to do so. His response has often been misunderstood. Plummer thinks that either the father has just died or is about to expire (Plummer, 266; Marshall, 410–12). But such an interpretation is totally foreign to our Middle Eastern scene. Ibn al-Ṣalībī comments, " 'Let me go and bury' means: let me go and serve my father while he is alive and after he dies I will bury him and come" (Ibn al-Ṣalībī, I, 223). The same point is made by Saʿīd, our contemporary Arab commentator: "The second (disciple) is looking far into the future, for he postpones following Jesus to a time after the death of his father . . ." (Saʿīd, 258). In commenting on the recruit's specific request, "Let me . . . bury my father," Saʿīd writes,

> If his father had really died, why then was he not at that very moment keeping vigil over the body of his father? In reality he intends to defer the matter of following Jesus to a distant future when his father dies as an old man, who knows when. Little does he know that Jesus in a very short time will himself give up his spirit (Saʿīd, 259).

Saʿīd's point is well taken. We are told that the three conversations take place "on the road." If this recruit's father had indeed died, then what is he doing whiling away his time at the roadside? Actually Saʿīd's case is even stronger than his own cogent argument. The phrase "to bury one's father" is a traditional idiom that refers specifically to the duty of the son to remain at home and care for his parents until they are laid to rest respectfully. The present writer has heard this specific language used again and again among Middle Easterners discussing emigration. At some point in the conversation someone will ask, "Are you not going to bury your father first?" The speaker is usually addressing the would-be emigrant who is in his early thirties. The father under discussion usually is assumed to have some twenty years to live. The point is, "Are you not going to stay until you have fulfilled the traditional duty of taking care of your parents until their death, and then consider emigrating?" Other colloquialisms reflect the same cultural background. In the colloquial Syriac of isolated villages in Syria and Iraq, when a rebellious son tries to assert his independence from his father, the father's final stinging rebuke is, *kabit di qurtly* ("You want to bury me"). The point is, "You want me to hurry up and die so that my authority over you will be at an end and you will be on your own." Obviously the same cultural assumption seen above is at work here. Among the Lebanese, an older person can still offer to a younger person a compliment when, as an expression of endearment, the older person says in Arabic, *tuqburnī ja ibnī* ("You will bury me, my son"). The meaning is, "I think so much of you that I look on you as my own child and sincerely hope that you will be the one who will care for me in my old age and lay me with respect in my grave." Again, the assumption governing the idiomatic language is that the son has the duty to remain at home until the death of the parents. Then, and only then, can he consider other options. Here we are dealing with community expectations, which can be roughly translated into Western terms as peer pressures. The recruit on the side of the road is saying, "My community makes certain demands on me and the pull of these demands is very strong. Surely you do not expect me to violate the expectations of my community?" Yet this is precisely what Jesus requires. The proclaiming of the kingdom of God can only mean announcing the kingdom of God as a present reality. Jesus says the spiritually dead can take care of the traditional responsibilities of your local community, but as for *you,* go and proclaim the arrival of the kingdom (the word *you* is emphatic in the Greek text).

THE THIRD DIALOGUE

A'   And another said,
      "I will *follow* you, Lord,   FOLLOW
         but first let me (*go* and) take leave of those at my home."   GO
            And Jesus said,
            "No one who puts his hand to the plow   COST TOO HIGH?
            and looks back
            is of any use in the kingdom of God."

Like the first volunteer, this would-be disciple brashly offers to follow the master. Like the recruit in the second dialogue, he has a precondition. This condition is often translated, "Let me first say farewell to those at my home." This request seems as legitimate as that of the recruit before it. Surely he will be allowed to go home and say good-bye! Elisha, when called to follow Elijah, asked for time to "kiss my father and my mother" (I Kings 19:20). His request was granted and he even took time to butcher and roast a pair of oxen. Is it not reasonable that this volunteer's request be granted? The answer can only come from a careful examination of his precise request.

The Greek word traditionally translated as "to say good-bye to" is *apotassō.* It can mean "say good-bye to" or "take leave of." It occurs four times in the rest of the New Testament in reference to taking leave. The RSV translation typifies the New Testament understanding of this verb. These four texts are as follows:

Mark 6:46   "After he had *taken leave of* them he went into the hills. . ."

Acts 18:18   "After this Paul . . . *took leave of* the brethren. . ."

    18:21   "But on *taking leave of* them. . ."

II Cor. 2:13   "I did not find my brother Titus there, so I *took leave of* them."

Only in Luke 9:60 do we find the same Greek verb translated as "say good-bye." The distinction between the two translations is important in Middle Eastern culture. The person who is *leaving* must request permission to leave from those who are *staying*. The people who *remain* behind can "say good-bye" to those *leaving*. This gentle formality is observed to the letter all over the Middle East on formal and informal occasions. The one who leaves requests permission to go. He asks, "With your permission?" Those who remain behind then respond, "May you go in safety," or "God go with you," or "May you go in peace" (cf. Rice, 74f.). Such responses are the granting of the permission requested. The RSV translations listed above properly observe this distinction in all four cases quoted. Jesus and Paul in each case are the ones leaving someone else. Thus they properly "take leave of" those who stay behind. On more formal occasions in the English-speaking world this idiom is not entirely lost. At a banquet the guest "takes leave of" the host. In spite of the fact that "take leave of" translates *all other* cases of *apotassō* in modern English versions, in this one case the real intent of the text has long been obscured by translating "say good-bye to." The point is that the volunteer is asking for the right to go home and *get permission* from "those at home" (i.e., his parents). Everyone listening to the dialogue knows that naturally his father will refuse to let the boy wander off on some questionable enterprise. Thus the volunteer's excuse is ready-made. Shedding crocodile tears he can loudly insist that he wants to go but his father will not permit him. The Old Syriac translation reflects this as it reads, "Let me first explain my case to those in my house." The early Syriac fathers knew perfectly well that this volunteer was not going to go home to plant one last fond kiss on his father's cheek and hear his mother's parting words of encouragement. Rather he was requesting permission to submit the question of following Jesus to their authority. Later Syriac translations did not maintain this insight.

In the Arabic versions two other distinct alternatives appear, each of them a legitimate translation of the Greek text. The Greek says literally, "greet the-ones in the house of-me." The Greek definite article (here translated "the-ones") can be masculine (meaning "the people") or neuter (meaning "the things"). Also, the verb *apotassō* is the verb *tassō* with a preposition attached to the front. The verb *tassō* by itself means "fix," "order," "determine," or "arrange for." The addition of prepositions to the beginnings of Greek words often changes their meaning. But sometimes it merely adds emphasis to the original root. *Apotassō does* mean "to take leave of" or "to say good-bye to." There is the possibility that *apotassō* in this text was intended to mean "arrange for." For nearly a thousand years some Arabic versions have translated it in this fashion. They read, "First let me *make arrangements* for those at home" (cf. Vatican Coptic 9; Vatican Arabic 610; The London-Paris Polyglot; Schawayr). If we read the definite article mentioned above as a neuter rather than a masculine, the text can be translated, "First let me arrange for my possessions at home." The Vatican Arabic 610 has this translation in its original. A corrector has changed "the things" to "the people." The difficulty with this understanding of the text is the somewhat shaky assumption that the root *tassō* ("to arrange for") is the intended meaning of the word rather than the better attested "to take leave of." Yet the Arabic versions mentioned above are evidence that some Arabic fathers saw the problem. The second volunteer is not going home to "say good-bye." Recognizing this they struggled with a translation that would make sense in their cultural world. Rather than these Arabic solutions, we prefer to return to the Old Syriac for a starting place.

The Old Syriac version noted above seems to point us in the right direction. The Greek *apotassō* does carry the meaning of "take leave of" and is usually so translated in every other text in the New Testament. We need only apply this translation to the present text with the cultural awareness that he is asking for permission to go. In that cultural scene he is clearly saying, "I will follow you, Lord, but of course the authority of my father is *higher* than your authority and I *must* have his permission before I venture out." Ibn al-Ṭayyib says simply, "The one who wants to greet his family has his heart tied to his family" (Ibn al-Ṭayyib, folio 97 ᵛ). In our Middle Eastern world, traditionally the authority of the father is supreme. It is little wonder that the father became a symbol for God. An engineer in his forties will make the traditional visit from a large metropolitan area to his father in the village to ask permission for foreign travel, or a change of job, or an important business venture. Even if the trip is ceremonial and the son is in reality running his own life, yet he will make the trip as a sign of respect. Rice correctly observes that the Middle Easterner in traditional society in the past would submit all details of his life to his parents.

> On rising, each day, a man offers his prayers, and then goes to his father and mother to kiss their hands and ask their blessing. When he begins a new business, he asks the favor of God on his enterprise and ends with a desire that his parents will approve of, and bless him, in this matter (Rice, 60).

The present author will never forget a class of Middle Eastern seminary students who literally turned white when this text was expounded with its clear affirmation that Jesus is claiming an authority higher than the authority of the second volunteer's father. It is difficult to communicate the stunning shock that comes to a Middle Eastern reader/listener when the reality of the demands of this text are made clear. This shock must have been all the more disturbing when claims were made by a young man (Jesus) in his early thirties in the first century. The only alternatives were acceptance and compliance or rejection and hostility. The form Jesus uses to make this kind of a startling affirmation must now be examined.

Jesus' response to the second volunteer is like his response to the first volunteer. Each of them is told a parable that falls into three lines. This latter parable is agricultural. Jeremias has provided an accurate and most helpful summary of a part of the agricultural background of this figure.

> The very light Palestinian plough is guided with one hand. This one hand, generally the left, must at the same time keep the plough upright, regulate its depth by pressure, and lift it over the rocks and stones in its path. The ploughman uses the other hand to drive the unruly oxen with a goad about two yards long, fitted with an iron spike. At the same time he must continually look between the hindquarters of the oxen, keeping the furrow in sight.

> This primitive kind of plough needs dexterity and concentrated attention. If the ploughman looks round, the new furrow becomes crooked. Thus, whoever wishes to follow Jesus must be resolved to break every link with the past, and fix his eye only on the coming Kingdom of God (Jeremias, *Parables*, 195).

Not only was the instrument difficult to maneuver, but also the process of plowing a field was far more exacting a task than is generally observed.

> Ploughing was careful and thorough; the first breaking of the stubble after the harvest took the form of furrows opened with broad bands between them to facilitate the absorption of the rains. In the ploughing after the first rain, closer furrows divided by ridges were opened for drainage; only at the third ploughing, before sowing, were the furrows close-set without intervening bands. The final working was to cover the seed . . . the implement was larger and heavier than the modern Arab plough, which it in general resembled (Applebaum, *JPFC*, II, 651f.).

Clearly plowing was a very precise operation with strips left initially for the absorption of water. At a later stage furrows were shaped for drainage. A third plowing prepared the soil, and a fourth covered the seed after planting. Obviously anyone wanting to fulfill such a responsibility needed to give undivided attention to what he was doing.

Thus the image is strong and clear. The tension illustrated is between loyalty to Jesus as the inaugurator of the kingdom of God and its all-consuming demands, and loyalty to the authority of the family. Both loyalties have high priority for any serious-minded Christian. When they are in conflict, that conflict is excruciatingly painful. This text is another of the "hard sayings" of which the Gospels are disturbingly full.

A part of the tension of the dialogue is the underlying assumption of the necessarily close relationship between a disciple and his teacher. In the Middle East such a relationship has always been deep and binding. The Talmud states that "A father and his son or a master and his disciple . . . are regarded as one individual" (B.T. *Erubin* 73a, Sonc., 510). Becoming the student/disciple of a sage is not a simple matter of "signing up for a course" for the purpose of acquiring information. Rather it is the cementing of a lifelong relationship to a person. With this as an understood starting point Jesus is here demanding that his authority (the demands of the kingdom) take precedence over *all* other relationships.

The person who cannot resolve the tension of conflicting loyalties and keeps turning back to look over his shoulder to see what the family is ordering is judged "useless" for the kingdom of God. In summary we observe that the symbol of plowing is aptly chosen (against Bultmann, *History*, 28). The distracted plowman might catch the plow on a rock, and perhaps break its wooden point, or he might unnecessarily tire the oxen pulling futilely against a plow caught on a rock. Or the plow point will cut back into the previously plowed furrows (and thereby destroy work already done), or cut aimlessly into the unplowed ground and make the next few furrows more difficult. Or he will ruin the field's drainage system, or damage its water absorption potential, or leave the newly planted seeds exposed to the birds, etc. Thus the plowman labors in harmony with work already done, with work yet to be accomplished, and in teamwork with his plow and his oxen. It is not too much to say that the past, present, and future are kept in a delicate harmony in the immediate task at hand. Thus a plowman distracted by a divided loyalty will not be able to maintain this harmony. He will be not only unproductive, but destructive in the context of his labors. Again the dialogue is open ended. Pressed with clear-cut, yet painful alternatives the second volunteer must decide. He volunteered with the apparent confidence that his loyalty to the kingdom would be accepted as secondary to his loyalty to his family. The parable of the plow wipes out his assumption. What will he do? We are not told. Indeed, as before, each listener/reader must respond.

In conclusion and summary it is appropriate to try to focus on what specific decision/response the original listener is pressed to make and what theological motifs comprise the impact of each dialogue.

THE FIRST DIALOGUE

The original listener/participant of the dialogue is pressed to consider something like the following:

> "This 'Son of man' is not the victorious figure you expect. He walks the way of sorrows. Are you willing to walk that way with him?"

The theological cluster of motifs includes at least the following:

1. Would-be disciples of Jesus at times fail to consider seriously the cost of discipleship.
2. Jesus is the Son of man. But he does not fulfill his ministry in power and acclaim but in rejection and humiliation.
3. Would-be disciples are not accepted until they have consciously decided to pay the price of following a rejected leader.
4. There is a centripetal force in mission. Some disciples are attracted into the company of the faithful.

THE SECOND DIALOGUE

The recruit in the second dialogue is challenged with something like the following:

> "Loyalty to Jesus and the kingdom he inaugurates is more important than loyalty to the cultural norms of your society."

The theological cluster has at least the following themes:

1. Jesus accepts *no* authority higher than his own.

2. The cultural demands of the community are not acceptable excuses for failure in discipleship (irrespective of how long-standing and sacred those demands are).

3. The "follow me" of Jesus is defined by the command, "Participate in and proclaim the kingdom of God." Thus Jesus is the unique agent of God through whom obedience to the kingdom of God is expressed.

4. There is a centrifugal force in mission. This person is a recruit, not a volunteer. Jesus reaches out to call him.

THE THIRD DIALOGUE

Jesus challenged this volunteer with the intent of the following:

"My authority is absolute. The authority of even your own family (if it conflicts with my authority) is merely a distraction to be avoided if you would be of any use to me/the kingdom."

The theological cluster of the third dialogue involves the following motifs:

1. The call of the kingdom of God must take precedence over all other loyalties.

2. The disciple with divided loyalties is a disruptive force in the work of the kingdom and is thus unfit for participation in it.

3. To follow Jesus is not defined as feeling the glow of an inner light, or perceiving an intellectual insight, but is compared to the taking up of a strenuous, creative, consuming task like putting one's hand to a plow and joining a team of oxen.

4. Service in the kingdom of God is synonymous with following Jesus. Thus Jesus is the unique agent of God through whom loyalty to God is expressed. That is, to serve/follow Jesus is to serve/follow God.

Thus an examination of the literary structure and the underlying cultural assumptions helps unlock at least a part of the meaning of these carefully constructed dialogues for the original participants and listeners and for the reader/listener of today.

Chapter 3

THE GOOD SAMARITAN
"What must I do to inherit eternal life?"
(Luke 10:25-37)

Derrett describes this parable as "a highly scientific piece of instruction clothed in a deceptively popular style" (Derrett, 227). This description is verified when the parable is seen as a part of a theological discussion.

In Luke 7:36-50 we observed a parable as a part of a wider theological dialogue. In a parallel passage in Luke 18:18-30 we will study a similar case where the parable of the Camel and the Needle is the center of a much larger theological drama. Here also the parable is a part of a theological dialogue. No doubt the dialogue has been given its present balanced form by Luke or his source. It has been argued that the original thrust of the parable has been obscured by the reuse of material for a different purpose (Linnemann, 51-58). At the same time leading scholars have affirmed the basic unity and authenticity of the entire passage (cf. Jeremias, *Parables,* 202f.; Manson, *Sayings,* 259f.; Marshall, 440f.). Our study of the parable assumes this basic unity and authenticity.

The setting makes considerable difference in the interpretation of this particular parable. In Luke 7:36-50 and 18:18-30 the shortness of the parable and the length of the dialogue lead naturally to a consideration of the parable as a part of the dialogue. By contrast, the parable of the Good Samaritan is fairly long and the dialogue surrounding it relatively short. Thus there is a natural tendency for the reader to ignore the dialogue. When we do so the parable becomes only an ethical exhortation to reach out to those in need. Indeed, the average Christian across the centuries has understood the parable almost exclusively in this way. In this study we will try to discern the structure and content of the dialogue and look at the parable as a part of that dialogue.

The dialogue between Jesus and the lawyer is made up of eight speeches that fall into two precise rounds of debate. In each round there are two questions and two answers. The formal structure of each scene is identical. Shortened to the main themes the full dialogue is as follows:

> *Round one:*   A lawyer stood up to put him to the test and said,
>
> (1) Lawyer: (Question 1) "What must I *do* to inherit eternal *life?*"
>
> (2) Jesus: (Question 2) "What about the law?"
>
> (3) Lawyer: (Answer to 2) "Love God and your neighbor."
>
> (4) Jesus: (Answer to 1) "*Do* this and *live.*"
>
> *Round Two:*   He (the lawyer), desiring to *justify himself,* said,
>
> (5) Lawyer: (Question 3) "Who is my neighbor?"
>
> (6) Jesus: (Question 4) "A certain man went down from Jerusalem. . ."
>   "Which of these three became a neighbor?"
>
> (7) Lawyer: (Answer to 4) "The one who showed mercy on him."
>
> (8) Jesus: (Answer to 3) "*Go* and continue *doing* likewise."
>
>   (Bailey, *Poet,* 73f., n. 52).

A number of important features tie the two dialogues together. (1) In each case there are two questions and two answers. (2) In each the lawyer asks the first question, but rather than answer his question Jesus poses a second. (3) In each round the lawyer then answers this second question. (4) Each round closes with Jesus' answer to the initial question (cf. Crossan, 61). (5) The first dialogue focuses on the question of *doing* something to inherit eternal life. On examination, so does the second. Desiring to "justify himself" he asks for a definition of his neighbor. Clearly he is still asking what he must do to gain eternal life. (6) Each round is introduced with an analysis of the motives of the lawyer. In the first we are told that he wants to test Jesus. In the second we find that he wants to justify himself. (7) Each round ends with instructions on what to *do.* Thus a long series of interlocking themes makes clear that the two rounds of dialogue are parallel halves of the same discussion. This interrelatedness of themes will become clearer as we examine the text in detail.

ROUND ONE:

This dialogue uses the inversion principle. The first and last speeches are on the subject of *do* and *live,* the inner two on the topic of the *law.* The conversation thus ends where it started.

The full text with its inversions is as follows:

And behold, a lawyer stood up to put him to the test, saying,

(1) Lawyer: (Question 1) "Teacher, what shall I *do* to inherit eternal *life*?"

  (2) Jesus: (Question 2) He said to him, "What is written in the law?
                      How do you read?"

  (3) Lawyer: (Answer to 2) And he answered,
                      "You shall love the Lord your God
                      with all your heart, and with all your soul,
                      and with all your strength, and with all your mind;
                      and your neighbor as yourself."

(4) Jesus: (Answer to 1) And he said to him,
                     "You have answered right; *do* this, and you will *live*."

Speech 1:

> And behold, a lawyer stood up to put him to the test, saying,
> "Teacher, what shall I *do* to inherit eternal *life*?"

Ibrāhīm Saʿīd astutely observes that there is a basic contradiction in the actions of the lawyer.

> The text says, "He stood up." This is a social courtesy and a greeting of respect. Then we read, "to test him." This is an inner deception coming from a corrupt heart (Saʿīd, 276).

Saʿīd's judgment is a bit harsh but nevertheless valid. In the Middle East the student has always stood to address his teacher out of courtesy. Here the lawyer not only stands to address Jesus, but also gives him the title of "Teacher," which is Luke's word for rabbi (Dalman, *Words,* 336). The use of this title is an affirmation that Jesus is at least an equal (Linnemann, 51). After these acts of deference the lawyer tries to "test him." The subject for the test is that of inheriting eternal life.

On the surface the question is pointless. What can anyone *do* to inherit anything? Only legal heirs inherit. Yet the wording has some precedent. In the Old Testament the idea of inheritance was primarily applied to Israel's privilege of inheriting the land of promise. This inheritance is understood as a gift of God. Israel does nothing to either deserve or earn it. Foerster, describing the word *inheritance* in the Old Testament, writes, "Israel did not conquer the land by its own achievements... but ... God's free disposition gave Israel the land as its share" (Foerster, *TDNT,* III, 760). In the same discussion Foerster writes, "Israel possesses its land only by divine ordination" (*ibid.,* 774). After the Old Testament period the phrase "inherit the earth/land" is applied to the salvation which God extends to His people (cf. Dalman, *Words*, 126). "To possess the land" in Isaiah 60:21 is interpreted by the rabbis to mean participation in the salvation of the age to come (B.T. *Sanhedrin* 11; cf. Dalman, *Words,* 126). The inheritance becomes eternal life, and the way to achieve it is to keep the law.

No less than the famous Rabbi Hillel, an older contemporary of Jesus, said, "who has gained for himself words of Torah has gained for himself the life of the world to come" (Mishna *Pirke Aboth* 2:8; cf. Charles II, 696). An anonymous rabbinical saying reads, "Great is Torah, for it gives to them that practice it life in this world and in the world to come" (Mishna *Pirke Aboth* 6:7; cf. Charles, II, 712). In a book of Psalms, probably written by Pharisees about 50 B.C. and called The Psalms of Solomon, we are given even more details. Psalm 14:1-2 claims that God is faithful

> To them that walk in the righteousness of *His commandments,*
> In the law which he commanded us that *we might live.*
> The pious of the Lord shall live by it forever (Charles, II, 645; emphasis mine).

The same Psalm (14:9-10) ends,

> Therefore their [sinners'] *inheritance* is Sheol and darkness and destruction . . .
> but the pious of the Lord *shall inherit life* in gladness.

Thus sinners inherit Sheol, while the righteous, by keeping the law, inherit life eternal. Another early noncanonical book, called Slavonic Enoch, also treats the topic of eternal life as an inheritance. In chapter 9 Enoch is taken to Eden and told:

> This place (Eden), O Enoch, is prepared for the righteous, who endure all manner of offense from those that exasperate their souls, who avert their eyes from iniquity, and make righteous judgments, and give bread to the hungering, and cover the naked with clothing, and raise up the fallen, and help injured orphans, and who walk without fault before the face of the Lord, and serve him alone, and for them is prepared this place for *eternal inheritance* (emphasis mine; cf. Charles, II, 434f.).

Quite likely the audience and perhaps the lawyer expected from Jesus some kind of listing like the above as an explanation of the requirements of the law. It would then be possible to debate the fine points of what should and what should not be on the list. Jesus thus has two obvious alternatives. He can take the Old Testament approach and insist that the "inheritance of Israel" is a gift and that man can do nothing to inherit it. Such a stance would quite likely have sparked a sterile debate. Or he can go along with rabbinic opinion and concentrate on the law. Jesus chooses the latter.

Regarding the law, Ibn al-Ṭayyib suggests another possible aspect of the background of the text. He affirms that the lawyers were most likely uneasy about Jesus' attitude toward the law. Indeed, at least some leading rabbis (as we have just noted) affirmed that eternal life was achieved through keeping the law. But they were hearing disturbing noises from this young rabbi. Did he or did he not believe that the inheritance of Israel was available through a keeping of the law? Ibn al-Ṭayyib proposes that the "test" was to discover an answer to this question (Ibn al-Ṭayyib, folios 100–104). If Ibn al-Ṭayyib's suggestion is at all correct there is all the more reason for Jesus to reply by turning to the law. But rather than offer his own views, he skillfully solicits the questioner's opinion.

Speech 2:

He said to him,
"What is written in the law? How do you read?"

The phrase, "How do you read?" can mean, "May I hear your authorities with exposition?" (Derrett, 224). If this is correct the lawyer offers exposition by selection and order but without authorities. Jeremias argues that it means "How do you *recite* (in worship)?" (cf. Jeremias, *Theology,* 187). This would explain why the lawyer turns to the creed. Elements of each explanation may be involved.

Speech 3:

And he answered, "You shall love the Lord your God
with all your heart, and with all your soul,
and with all your strength, and with all your mind;
and your neighbor as yourself."

In Matthew and Mark this combination of Deuteronomy 6:5 (love God) and Leviticus 19:18 (love the neighbor) is attributed to Jesus. Derrett observes two occurrences of this combination in The Testaments of the Twelve Patriarchs and comments that there "may well be evidence that such a combination was commonplace in some quarters in Jesus' time" (Derrett, 225). If so, it is clear that Jesus *endorsed* this opinion and made it his own. Thus the lawyer may be doing the same thing that Jesus has just done. That is, Jesus knows any lawyer will affirm "keep the law" as an answer to this question on eternal life. So Jesus draws the lawyer out on the topic of the law. The lawyer in turn may know that Jesus has originated or affirmed this combination of love for God and neighbor as the essence of the law. Thus the lawyer quotes Jesus' own position in order to get it into the discussion so that the lawyer might "test" Jesus' loyalty to the law, as Ibn al-Ṭayyib has suggested.

Whatever the origin of the combination of these two texts and whatever the motive for its appearance in the dialogue, it is pure genius as a summary of duty to God and people. One of its most remarkable features is the fact that love for God (found in Deuteronomy) is listed first even though Deuteronomy is chronologically *after* Leviticus in the Old Testament (Derrett, 223). It is through a love of *God* that the believer is to approach people. This then has profound implications for the how, why, and who of the love for the neighbor.

We note also that the quotation is expanded from the Old Testament text to include "with all your mind." In Matthew 22:37 this phrase appears in the mouth of Jesus as a substitute for the phrase "with all your strength." In Mark 12:33 it comes after "with all your heart." Indeed, the "heart" for the ancient Hebrew was (among other things) the center of the intellect (he kept the law "in his heart," Ps. 119:11). Thus the phrase "with all your mind" can be seen as an expansive translation in the Greek Gospel of the meaning of the original Hebrew text (Derrett, 224, n. 5, offers another explanation).

Speech 4:

And he said to him,
"You have answered right; *do* this, and you will *live*."

A number of observations can be made here. (1) Barth observes that "Jesus praises him for his good knowledge and faithful recitation" (Barth, 417). Indeed, the man has the right theology, but the question is, Is he willing to act on it? His intellectual stance is excellent; his performance is still in question. (2) As in the case of Simon in 7:43, Jesus evokes the right answer from the lawyer himself. He does not tell him what to do, rather the lawyer tells himself. (3) The lawyer has asked about eternal life. Jesus widens the discussion to *all* of life. The Greek text has a future, "you shall live." This most certainly means the immediate future (i.e., do this and you will come alive). It could mean the future after death (do this and you will live in the next life). However, here in the Middle East, Syriac and Arabic translators have consistently agreed on the former. The Old Syriac version turns the verb into a present and reads literally, "do this and you are living." The Peshitta and Harclean Syriac (along with the Arabic versions) construct the grammar somewhat differently but also indicate a present result of a present action; do this *now* and *now* you will live. Finally, the text is a quotation from Joseph in Genesis 42:18. Joseph is talking about the near future when his younger brother is brought to him. (In the parallel discussion of the same topic in Luke 18 below we will observe this same shift from an exclusive interest in the life to come to an inclusion of the present.) (4) The verb "do" is a present imperative meaning "keep on doing." The lawyer requested definition of a specific limited requirement—"what *having done* I will inherit. . . ." The answer is given in a command for an open-ended life-style that requires unlimited and unqualified love for God and people.

Clearly the very law which the lawyer quotes sets a standard that *no one* can fully reach. In the parallel discussion on the same question in Luke 18:18–30 a standard is set that everyone listening judges impossible. They ask, "Who then can be saved?" The answer is given, "What is impossible with men is possible with God" (18:26–27). The same theological posture is seen here. By his answer, Jesus simply says, "You want to *do* something to inherit eternal life? Very well, just *continually* love God and your neighbor with the totality of all that you are." There is *no* line drawn. No list of how much is expected, such as we noted in Slavonic Enoch, is offered. Rather, the requirements are left limitless and, as Summers observes,

Jesus and Paul agree with their Jewish contemporaries that complete obedience to the law of God was the way to be right with God. They found that way ineffective in experience however, because of man's inability to give complete obedience to the law (Summers, 125).

The first round of the debate closes. But the lawyer has not yet given up the hope that he can earn his own entrance into eternal life. The law has been quoted. Now he needs some commentary, some *midrash*. The God whom he must love is known. But who is "this neighbor" whom he must love as himself? He needs some definition, perhaps a list. If the list is not too long he may be able to fulfill its demands. Thus he initiates the second round of the debate.

ROUND II

Speech 5:

> He, desiring to *justify himself*, said,
> "Who is my neighbor?"

This hope for self-justification is not a case of "excusing himself for asking Jesus, although he knows what Jesus thinks" (Jeremias, *Parables*, 202; Marshall, 447). Rather he simply hopes yet to *do* something and gain eternal life; hence the question. Karl Barth observes,

> The lawyer does not know that only by mercy can he live and inherit eternal life. He does not want to live by mercy. He does not even know what it is. He actually lives by something quite different from mercy, by his own intention and ability to present himself as a righteous man before God (Barth, 417).

This same observation was drawn by Ibn al-Ṭayyib, who understood the question to mean that the lawyer wanted "to see himself as fully righteous" (Ibn al-Ṭayyib, folio 101^r). Ibn al-Ṭayyib continues,

> The question put to the Christ, "Who is my neighbor," is asked in order that he will answer, "Your relative and your friend." The lawyer will then answer, "I have fully loved these." Then Jesus will praise him and say to him, "You have truly fulfilled the law." The lawyer will then depart, basking before the people, in the praise of his good works, and enjoying a newly won honor and confidence based on that praise (Ibn al-Ṭayyib, folio 101^v).

It is pointless to press too far into the mind of the lawyer. Yet Ibn al-Ṭayyib's suggestions have some merit. In the parallel discussion with the ruler in chapter 18 the conversation does turn in this direction. There the law is recited. The ruler claims to have fulfilled it and probably expects praise for his noble efforts. There, as here, the questioner must be surprised by the unexpected turn of the conversation.

In harmony with Ibn al-Ṭayyib's suggestion we observe that the text of

Leviticus identifies the neighbor as being one's brother and "the sons of your own people" (Lev. 19:17–18). The rabbis understood this to include all Jews. They were divided over the proselyte and were sure that it did *not* include gentiles (Jeremias, *Parables*, 202). Jeremias notes a rabbinical saying "that heretics, informers, and renegades 'should be pushed (into the ditch) and not pulled out'" (*ibid.*, 202f.). John Lightfoot quotes a *midrash* on Ruth, chapter four:

> The gentiles, amongst whom and us there is no war, and so those that are keepers of sheep amongst the Israelites, and the like, we are not to contrive their death; but if they be in any danger of death, we are not bound to deliver them; e.g., if any of them fall into the sea you shall not need to take them out: for it is said, "Thou shalt not rise up against the blood of thy neighbor"; but such a one is not thy neighbor (Lightfoot, 107).

Thus the lawyer asked his question in a world that held a variety of views on just who the neighbor really was. Indeed, as Safrai observes, "The oral law was not fully uniform" (Safrai, *JPFC*, II, 794). There was a lively debate on points of interpretation.

The literary form is that of a seven-scene parabolic ballad and is as follows:

1	A man was going down from Jerusalem to Jericho	
	and he fell among *robbers*.	COME
	And they stripped him and beat him	DO
	and departed, leaving him half dead.	GO
2	Now by coincidence a certain *priest* was going down that road,	COME
	and when he saw him,	DO
	he passed by on the other side.	GO
3	Likewise also a *Levite* came to the place,	COME
	and when he saw him,	DO
	he passed by on the other side.	GO
4	And a certain *Samaritan*, traveling, came to him,	COME
	and when he saw him,	DO
	he had compassion on him.	DO
5	He went to him,	DO
	and bound up his wounds,	
	pouring on oil and wine.	
6	Then he put him on his own riding animal	DO
	and led him (it) to the inn,	
	and took care of him.	
7	The next day he took out and gave two denarii to the manager	DO
	and said, "Take care of him, and whatever more you spend	
	I, on my return, *I* will repay you."	

Jesus' immortal reply to the lawyer's query is here seen as a part of the continuing theological dialogue with the lawyer. It is an introduction to a second question. As in the first round, Jesus wants to solicit from the questioner his own answer. The parable is told to make this possible.

Yet on a deeper level, as T. W. Manson has astutely observed, "The question is unanswerable, and ought not to be asked. For love does not begin by defining its objects: it discovers them" (Manson, *Sayings,* 261). The unanswerable question remains unanswered; rather it is transformed in the response that Jesus makes. Initially the structure must be examined. This particular form we have called the "parabolic ballad" because of the balladlike stanzas into which the story falls (cf. Bailey, *Poet,* 72). The action shifts dramatically from scene to scene. The first three are dominated by the robbers, the priest, and the Levite. In each case the action can be characterized by the verbs *come, do,* and *go.* Each of them comes, does something, and leaves. The pattern is broken by the Samaritan who, contrary to all expectation, does not leave. From then on, each line describes an action (seven in all) on the part of the Samaritan in service to the wounded man. The list is long because the lone Samaritan must make up for the actions of everyone else. He compensates for their failures in an inverse order, hence the inverted parallelism, some of which has already been noted by Crossan (Crossan, 62). The Levite (scene 3) could at least have rendered first aid. This is the Samaritan's first cluster of actions (scene 5). The priest (scene 2) was certainly riding and could have taken the man to safety. The Samaritan does this as well (scene 6). The robbers (scene 1) take his money and leave him half dead with no intention of returning. The Samaritan (scene 7) *pays* from his own pocket, and leaves him provided for with a promise to return and pay more if necessary. The climax occurs in the center with the unexpected compassion of the Samaritan. The three-line form of each scene may be artificial. What is clear is that the parable is a drama in seven scenes. Each of these scenes needs careful attention.

Scene 1: The Robbers

A man was going down from Jerusalem to Jericho and he fell among *robbers.*   COME
And they stripped him and beat him   DO
and departed, leaving him half dead.   GO

The seventeen-mile descending road through the desert from Jerusalem to Jericho has been dangerous all through history. Pompey had to wipe out "strongholds of brigands" near Jericho (Strabo, *Geogr.* xvi.2.41; noted in Plummer, 286). Ibn al-Ṭayyib observes that there were many thieves on the Jericho-Jerusalem road (Ibn al-Ṭayyib, folio 102ʳ). The crusaders built a small fort at the halfway mark to protect pilgrims; thus robbers in the area must have been a

serious threat. William Thomson has a dramatic description of a group of pilgrims traveling over the same road in 1857 with a large armed guard. One
traveler fell behind and was "attacked, robbed and stripped naked" (Thomson,
II, 445). Thus this road has always provided a perfect setting for this kind of
drama.

The story intentionally leaves the man undescribed (Marshall, 447). Yet a
Jewish audience would naturally assume that the traveler is a Jew. He is beaten,
stripped, and left "half dead." The beating probably means he struggled with his
attackers. In 1821 a British traveler, J. S. Buckingham, journeyed through Palestine. Near Capernaum he met a party that had been attacked by robbers. Two of
their group had resisted and were beaten so badly that they had to be left behind
(Buckingham, 475; cf. also Jeremias, *Parables,* 203). The rabbis identified
stages for death. The "half dead" of the text is the equivalent for a rabbinic
category of "next to death," which meant at the point of death. The next stage
was called "one just expiring" (Lightfoot, 108). Clearly the man is unconscious
and thus cannot identify himself. Nor can his identity be ascertained by any
onlooker.

The wounded traveler's condition is not a curious incidental. He is unconscious and stripped. These details are skillfully constructed to create the
tension that is at the heart of the drama. Our Middle Eastern world was and is
made up of various ethnic-religious communities. The traveler is able to identify
strangers in two ways. He can talk to the unknown man on the road and identify
him from his speech, or, even before that, he can identify him by his manner of
dress. In the first century the various ethnic-religious communities within Palestine used an amazing number of languages and dialects. In Hebrew alone there
was classical Hebrew, late Biblical Hebrew, and Mishnaic Hebrew. But in addition to Hebrew, one could find settled communities in Palestine that used
Aramaic, Greek, Southwest Ashdodian, Samaritan, Phoenician, Arabic, Naba-
tean, and Latin (cf. Rabin, *JPFC,* II, 1001–1037). The country had many settled
communities of pagans (cf. Flusser, *JPFC,* II, 1065–1100). No one traveling a
major highway in Palestine could be sure that the stranger he might meet would
be a fellow Jew. A few quick questions and his language and/or dialect would
identify him. But what if he was unconscious beside the road? In such a case one
would need to take a quick glance at the stranger's clothes. In Marissa in Palestine wall drawings of distinctive Hellenistic garb have been recently discovered.
These appear in early gallery tombs of a Sidonian community living there in
Palestine (Foerster, *JPFC,* II, 973). These tomb paintings demonstrate conclusively that Jewish and non-Jewish costumes could be distinguished by sight in
Palestine in the first century. The various ethnic communities of Dura-Europos,
with their distinctive styles of clothing, are depicted in frescoes of the second-
third century. This pattern remained unchanged, and even separate villages of
Palestine and Lebanon had their distinctive traditional dress. Lamartine, traveling through Palestine in 1832, records observing a large group of Arabs at a
distance and casually notes that they were from Nablous, "whose costume the
tribe displayed" (Lamartine, 389). In the first century, at least, Greek and Jew each

had their distinctive dress. But what if the man beside the road was stripped? He was thereby reduced to a mere human being in need. He belonged to no man's ethnic or religious community! It is such a person that the robbers leave wounded beside the road. Who will turn aside to render aid?

Scene 2: The Priest

Now by coincidence a certain *priest* was going down that road,   COME
and when he saw him,   DO
he passed by on the other side.   GO

The priest is most certainly riding. We deduce this from the fact that the priests were among the upper classes of their society. In this connection Stern observes, "Towards the close of the Second Temple period, the priesthood constituted the prestigious and élite class in Jewish society" (Stern, *JPFC*, II, 582). Elsewhere he refers to them as being in the "upper classes" (*ibid.*, 561, 582). In the Middle East no one with any status in the community takes seventeen-mile hikes through the desert. The poor walk. Everyone else in general, and the upper classes in particular, always ride. This is the natural assumption of the parable. The same kind of assumption prevails in the American scene when a farmer says, "I am going to town." If the destination is seventeen miles away you *know* he will be driving. He does not mention his car. There is no need to do so. Indeed, when the Samaritan appears, he too is riding but this fact is not mentioned. His riding animal happens to function in the story and so is mentioned but only after the Samaritan has ridden onto the scene. Furthermore, without this assumption the story loses a great deal of its thrust. If the priest had been walking, what could he have done besides offer first aid and sit, hoping that someone might come by with a riding animal who could *really* help him? The parable turns on the presupposition that what the Samaritan *did*, at least the priest *could* have done. If this is not true we would be obliged to conclude, "Of course the Samaritan should help the man; he is the only one who really can." Rather the parable assumes an equal potential for service, at least on the part of the priest and the Samaritan. Finally, the Samaritan might be a poor man, yet his animal is assumed. How much more the priest. Indeed, the upper-class status of the priest assures an image of a well-mounted aristocrat. Thus the parable in its original setting gives us a picture of a priest riding by, seeing the wounded man (presumably at some distance), and then steering his mount to the far side of the road and continuing on his way.

In trying to reconstruct the world in which this priest lives and thinks it is instructive to turn to Sirach 12:1-7:

If you do a good turn, know for whom you are doing it,
    and your good deeds will not go to waste.
Do good to a devout man, and you will receive a reward,
    if not from him, then certainly from the Most High. . . .
Give to a devout man,
    do not go to the help of a sinner,

Do good to a humble man,
  give nothing to a godless one.
Refuse him bread, do not give him any,
  it might make him stronger than you are;
then you would be repaid evil twice over
  for all the good you had done him.
For the Most High himself detests sinners,
  and will repay the wicked with a vengeance.
Give to the good man,
  and *do not go to the help of a sinner* (emphasis mine).

Thus, help offered to sinners may be labor against God Himself who detests sinners. Furthermore, sinners' hands should not be strengthened. Clearly Ben Sirach cautions against helping *any* stranger. The priest may have been influenced by such ideas current in his time. More likely, he is the prisoner of his own legal/theological system. The priest's problem, writes Derrett, is "a balancing of commandments" (Derrett, 212). The rabbis taught,

Whence do we know that if a man sees his fellow drowning, mauled by beasts, or attacked by robbers, he is bound to save him! From the verse, thou shalt not stand by the blood of thy neighbor (B.T. *Sanhedrin* 73a, Sonc., 495).

But the priest did not actually see it happen. Furthermore, how can he be sure the wounded man is a neighbor? When confronted with a mute, stripped body he is paralyzed. With speech impossible and distinctive dress missing, the observer cannot identify him. But not only is there the possibility that the wounded man is a non-Jew, but also he might be dead; if so, contact with him would defile the priest. The priest collects, distributes, and eats tithes. If he defiles himself he can do none of these things, and his family and servants will suffer the consequences with him.

A tithe of the tithe, called a "wave offering," was given by Levites to priests for consumption by the priest and his household. They could be eaten only in a state of ritual purity (Safrai, *JPFC*, II, 819). Also, while under the ban on defilement he could not officiate at any service and could not wear his phylacteries (*ibid.*, 799). Furthermore, the written law listed five sources of defilement. Contact with a corpse was at the top of the list. The oral law added four more. Contact with a non-Jew was the first of this additional list (*ibid.*, 829). Thus this poor priest was in critical danger of contracting ritual impurity in its most severe form from the point of view of both the written and the oral law.

Contracting ritual purity was a very serious matter. Safrai writes,

the rules of purity were . . . always considered an end in themselves, not just a means to an end. They were held to be the best way of avoiding sin and attaining the heights of sanctity as all texts affirm, from Philo to the tannaitic period (*ibid.*, 832).

Thus the priest is struggling with trying to be a good man. He seeks to avoid sin and attain sanctity. An additional part of his struggle is related to the fact that he is (like the wounded man) traveling *down* from Jerusalem to Jericho. Large numbers of priests served in the temple for two-week periods and lived in Jericho. Any priest leaving Jerusalem on his way to Jericho would naturally be assumed to have fulfilled his period of service and be on his way home (Safrai, *JPFC,* 870). We are told that "Ritual purification ordinarily took place in the Temple" (*ibid.,* 877). Furthermore, the twice daily sacrifice in the temple was carried out by priests, Levites, and Jewish laymen called the "delegation of Israel." During the service a gong was struck at the time of the offering up of the incense. At the sound of this gong the chief of the delegation of Israel made all the unclean stand at the Eastern gate in front of the altar. Some commentators affirm that these people were unclean priests who were obliged to stand there "to shame them for their remission in contracting uncleanness" (Danby, 587, n. 12; cf. Mishna *Tamid* 4, 6). It is easy to imagine the burning humiliation that the priest would feel if he contracted ritual impurity. Having probably just completed his two weeks as a *leader* of worship in the temple, is he now to return in humiliation and stand at the Eastern gate with the unclean? Furthermore, in addition to the humiliation involved, the process of restoring ritual purity was time consuming and costly. It required finding, buying, and reducing a red heifer to ashes, and the ritual took a full week. Thus it is easy to understand the priest's predicament as he suddenly comes upon an unconscious man beside the road.

More specifically, he cannot approach closer than four cubits to a dead man without being defiled, and he will have to overstep that boundary just to ascertain the condition of the wounded man. Then, if he *is* dead, the priest will have to rend his garments. This action "conflicted with an obligation not to destroy valuable things" (Derrett, 213). Derrett thinks that wives, servants, and colleagues would have applauded his neglect of the wounded man and that the Pharisees would have found him justified in stopping and yet "entitled to pass by" (*ibid.,* 215). Finally, the commandment not to defile was unconditional, while the commandment to love the neighbor was conditional. Therefore the priest had a legal right to pass by (*ibid.,* 213). In commenting on the Jewish background of this parable Oesterley writes,

> The whole reason of the growth and development of the Oral Law was the need of providing for the ever-increasing new cases which the experiences of life brought to the fore. The *system,* therefore, was to blame; so that the priest and the Levite are looked upon as victims of an evil, or at least an inadequate, system (emphasis his; Oesterley, 163).

The priest was the victim of a rule book ethical/theological system. Life for him was a codified system of "do's and don'ts." This mentality persists in many forms in our day and continues to claim to offer the security of having quick answers to all of life's problems and questions. The answers assure the devotee that he is in the right and seem adequate until we face an unconscious man on the side of the road. When we do, we discover that subtly *the* agenda has become, "Maintain status within the supporting community," rather than, "Reach out in freedom to the one in need beside the road." This dynamic seems to have overtaken the priest and he passes by on the other side.

Scene 3: The Levite

Likewise also a *Levite* came to the place,	COME
and when he saw him,	DO
he passed by on the other side.	GO

Both Levite and priest fall into the Come-Do-Go action pattern established by the robbers. This action pattern classifies the priest and the Levite with the robbers. The priest and the Levite contribute to the wounded man's sufferings by their neglect. The word "likewise" indicates that the Levite is also descending and thus following the priest.

The Levite almost certainly knows there is a priest ahead of him. Derrett thinks that the Samaritan also knew the others had passed the wounded man. He reasons that the Samaritan would have been bound to see the others on the road regardless of which way he was traveling, "in view of the nature of the man's injuries and the contours of the road which make a long lapse of time and prolonged absence from view unlikely" (Derrett, 217). The traces of the old Roman road are still visible and the present writer has personally walked almost its entire length. Derrett's statement about the contours of the road is true. One is able to see the road ahead for a considerable distance most of the way. Furthermore, having traveled Middle Eastern desert roads by camel, by donkey, and on foot for twenty years, I know that the traveler is *extremely* interested in who else is on the road. His life may depend upon it. A question put to a bystander at the edge of the last village just before the desert begins; a brief exchange with a traveler coming the other way; fresh tracks on the soft earth at the edge of the road where men and animals prefer to walk; a glimpse in the clear desert air of a robed figure ahead; all of these are potential sources of knowledge for the Levite traveler. As I have determined by investigation, Middle Eastern peasants assume that the Levite does know there is a priest ahead of him on the road. For them the *story* assumes it. It is perhaps truer to the story to assume the Levite's knowledge of the priest on the road ahead of him than to assume his ignorance. This detail is significant for the fabric of the drama. Our reasoning is as follows. The Levite is not bound by as many regulations as the priest. Derrett observes, "a Levite might, had he wished, have allowed himself more latitude than would a priest" (*ibid.*, 211). Jeremias writes, "the Levite was only required to observe ritual cleanliness in the course of his cultic activities" (Jeremias, *Parables*, 203). Thus he *could* render aid, and if the man were dead or died on his hands, the repercussions for him would not be as serious.

In contrast to the priest, the Levite approaches the man. This is reflected in his actions. The priest, traveling, saw and passed by. But the Levite *came to the place,* then saw and passed by. Plummer writes, ''The Levite came up to him quite close, saw and passed on'' (Plummer, 287). The Levite does ''come to the place'' (even if *genomenos* is omitted). Thus the Levite may have crossed the defilement line of four cubits and satisfied his curiosity with a closer look. He then decided against offering aid and passed by. Fear of defilement cannot be his strongest motive. Fear of the robbers may be. More likely it is the example of the higher ranking priest that deters him. Not only can he say, ''If the priest on ahead did nothing, why should I, a mere Levite, trouble myself,'' but,

> the Levite in his turn may have thought with himself, that it could not be incumbent on him to undertake a perilous office, from which the priest had just shrunk; duty it could not be, else that other would never have omitted it. For him to thrust himself upon it now would be a kind of affront to his superior, an implicit charging of him with inhumanity and hardness of heart (Trench, 314).

More than charging him with ''hardness of heart'' by stopping, the Levite would be criticizing the priest's interpretation of the law! When the professional reads the data one way, is the poor layman to call his judgment into question?

The Levite, like the priest, cannot find out whether or not the wounded man is a neighbor. This may be why he approaches him. Perhaps he can talk? Failing to find out, he then continues on. Whatever his reasons the result is the same; in spite of his religious profession, nothing in his total orientation leads him to help the wounded man.

The Levite is of a lower social class than the priest and may well be walking. In any case, he could have rendered minimal medical aid even if he had had no way to take the man to safety. If he was walking we can imagine him saying to himself, ''I cannot carry the man to safety and am I to sit here all night and risk attack from these same robbers?'' In any case, he fades from the scene following the priest.

Scene 4: The Samaritan

And a certain *Samaritan,* traveling, came to him,	COME
and when he saw him,	DO
he had compassion on him.	DO

As in 14:18-20 and 20:10-14 we are dealing with a progression of three characters. After the appearance of the priest and the Levite the audience expects a Jewish layman (Jeremias, *Parables,* 204). Not only is priest-Levite-layman a natural sequence, but, as we have observed, these same three classes of people officiated at the temple. Even as delegations of priests and Levites went up to Jerusalem and returned after their specified two weeks, so also the ''delegation of Israel'' went up to serve with them. After their terms of service one would naturally expect all three to be on the road returning home. The listener notes the first and the second and anticipates the third. The sequence is interrupted, however. Much to the shock and amazement of the audience, the third man along the road is one of the hated Samaritans. Heretics and schismatics are usually despised more than unbelievers. The centuries of animosity between the Jews and the Samaritans are reflected in the wisdom of Ben Sirach (50:25–26), *ca.* 200 B.C.

> There are two nations that my soul detests,
>   the third is not a nation at all:
> the inhabitants of Mount Seir, and the Philistines,
>   and the stupid people living at Shechem.

So the Samaritans are classed with the Philistines and Edomites. The Mishna declares, "He that eats the bread of the Samaritans is like to one that eats the flesh of swine" (Mishna *Shebiith* 8:10, Danby, 49). At the time of Jesus the bitterness between Jews and Samaritans was intensified by the Samaritans having defiled the temple during a passover just a few years earlier by scattering human bones in the temple court (cf. Josephus, *Antiquities*, 18:30). Oesterley observes,

> The Samaritans were publicly cursed in the synagogues; and a petition was daily offered up praying God that the Samaritans might not be partakers of eternal life (Oesterley, 162).

Jesus could have told a story about a noble Jew helping a hated Samaritan. Such a story could have been more easily absorbed emotionally by the audience. Rather, we have the hated Samaritan as the hero. The present writer can only confess that in twenty years he has not had the courage to tell a story to the Palestinians about a noble Israeli, nor a story about the noble Turk to the Armenians. Only one who has lived as a part of a community with a bitterly hated traditional enemy can understand fully the courage of Jesus in making the despised Samaritan appear as morally superior to the religious leadership of the audience. Thus Jesus speaks to one of the audience's deepest hatreds and painfully exposes it.

The Greek word "compassion" (*splanchnizomai*) has at its root the word "innards" (*splanchnon*). It is a very strong word in both Greek and Semitic imagery (cf. Bailey, *Cross*, 55f.). Indeed, the Samaritan has a deep "gut level reaction" to the wounded man. The Old Syriac version reflects the intensity of this word by translating, "He was compassionate to him and showed mercy," using two strong verbs. The Samaritan is not a gentile. He is bound by the same Torah that also tells him that his neighbor is his countryman and kinsman. He is traveling in *Judea* and it is less likely for him than for the priest and the Levite that the anonymous wounded man is a neighbor. In spite of this, *he* is the one who acts.

The text has a clear progression as we move through the scenes. The priest only goes *down the road*. The Levite comes *to the place*. The Samaritan comes *to the man*. As Derrett has observed, he too risks contamination, which if incurred extends to his animals and wares (Derrett, 217). With at least one animal and quite likely more (as we will note), and perhaps some goods, he is a prime target for the same robbers who just might respect a priest or a Levite as a "man of religion" but will have no hesitation in attacking a hated Samaritan.

The Samaritan has one advantage. As an outsider he will *not* be influenced as a Jewish layman might be by the actions of the priest and the Levite. We do not know which way the Samaritan is going. If he is going uphill he has just passed the priest and the Levite and is thus keenly aware of their actions. If he too is traveling downhill he, like the Levite, most likely knows who is ahead of him. Thus, somewhat like the Levite, he can say, "This unconscious man is probably a Jew and these Jews have abandoned him to die. Why should I get involved?" As we will note, if he does involve himself he will risk retaliation from the family and friends of the very Jew he is aiding. In spite of all these considerations he feels deep compassion for the wounded man and that compassion is immediately translated into concrete actions.

Scene 5: First Aid

He went to him,
and bound up his wounds,
pouring on oil and wine.

The center of the parable displays the unexpected appearance of the compassionate Samaritan. The rest of the action is the expression of that compassion. In this scene the Samaritan offers the first aid that the Levite failed to offer.

As in many of the parables, the language is deceptively simple. The Samaritan must first clean and soften the wounds with oil, then disinfect them with wine, and finally bind them up. However, this is not the order of the phrases in the text. The binding up of the wounds is mentioned first. Granted, the Greek syntax makes the actions simultaneous. But the Syriac and Arabic versions without exception give us two past tenses—he bound up and he poured. These translations make the peculiar order of the actions even more striking. Is it not possible to see the binding of the wounds deliberately mentioned first to heighten the impact of the theological overtones of the act? As Derrett has noted, the binding up of wounds is "imagery used of God as He acts to save the people" (*ibid.*, 220). God says to Jeremiah, "I will restore health to you, and your wounds I will heal" (Jer. 30:17). In the first ten verses of Hosea 6 there are no less than twelve phrases echoed here:

he has torn
he will bind us up
he will revive us
he will raise us up
that we may live before him
he will come to us
your love is like . . . the dew that goes early away
I desire steadfast love and not sacrifice
they transgressed the covenant
robbers lie in wait for a man
priests . . . commit villainy
in the house of Israel I have seen a horrible thing

God's first healing act is to bind up Ephraim's wounds. Indeed these phrases together could make a fitting prologue to the parable. Each phrase can apply to some part of the drama as it unfolds. Specifically in this text Ephraim is torn and left and finally cries out for help. We are then told that Yahweh

will bind us up
will revive us
will raise us up
will come to us.

All four phrases equally apply to the Samaritan who also first "bound up his wounds." The symbolism is clear and strong. God is the one who saves and chooses His agents as He wills. Similarly here God's sovereignty acts to save, and the agent is amazingly a Samaritan, a rejected outsider. As we will observe, the imagery can be understood to have Christological implications.

Furthermore, the oil and wine were not only standard first-aid remedies. They were also "sacrificial elements in the temple worship" (Derrett, 220). Likewise, the verb "pour" is from the language of worship. There were libations in connection with the sacrifices. Yet for centuries the call had been sounded for going beyond ritual in an effort to respond adequately to what God had done for them. Hosea (6:6) and Micah (6:7–8) called for steadfast love and not sacrifice. We have this same move, from the language of the sacrificial service to a discussion of actions of self-giving love, in Pauline writings, where he talks of his own life as a libation poured out "upon the sacrificial offering of your faith" (Phil. 2:17). Paul also calls for the Roman Christians to offer their own lives as a "living sacrifice" (Rom. 12:1). Thus for the prophets the language of the sacrificial altar evokes a concern for self-giving love. For Paul such language overlaps with such a call. The Jewish priest and Levite were the religious professionals who knew the precise rituals of the prescribed liturgy. In worship they officiated at the sacrifices and libations. They poured out the oil and the wine on the high altar before God. Here in the parable this same freighted language is applied to the Samaritan just after the priest and Levite have failed miserably in their ability to make the "living sacrifice." It is the hated Samaritan who pours out the libation on the altar of this man's wounds. As Derrett observes, "To show what is the *ḥesed* (steadfast love) which God demands one cannot be more apt than to show oil and wine employed to heal an injured man" (Derrett, 220). The Samaritan's total response to the man's needs (including this simple libation) is a profound expression of the steadfast love for which the prophets were calling. It is the *Samaritan* who pours out the true offering acceptable to God.

Yet, if and when the man regains consciousness, the Samaritan may be insulted for his kindness, because "Oil and wine are forbidden objects if they emanate from a Samaritan" (*ibid.*, 220). Not only have they come from an unclean Samaritan but the tithe has not been paid on them and by accepting them the wounded man incurs an obligation to pay tithes for them. He has recently been robbed and obviously has no way to pay even his hotel bill. As Derrett succinctly points out, the Pharisees would have been pleased if the wounded man had shouted, " 'Begone, Cuthean, I will have none of your oil or your wine!' " (Derrett, 221).

Scene 6: Transport to the Inn

Then he put him on his own riding animal
and led him (it) to the inn,
and took care of him.

As we have noted, these are acts of mercy that the mounted priest failed to carry out. The peculiar phrase here translated "his own riding animal" is not the ordinary genitive construction. The phrase most likely indicates that he had other animals, perhaps with merchandise. This animal is his own mount (cf. Jeremias, *Parables*, 204; Bishop, 172; Derrett, 217). The Old Syriac makes the riding animal into a donkey, which well may be the original behind the Greek text. We are not exactly sure about the Samaritan's next act. The Greek text can be read, "He *brought him* to the inn," or "He *led it* (the donkey) to the inn." The verb can mean either *bring* or *lead* and the pronoun can be masculine (he, the man) or neuter (it, the animal). Middle Eastern donkeys can easily carry two people, and if we assume the first, the Samaritan is riding with the wounded man. If we assume the second, he is acting out the form of a servant and leading the animal to the inn. The social distinctions between riders and leaders of riding animals is crucial in Middle Eastern society. Much to his surprise and humiliation, Haman (who expects to be the rider) finds himself leading the horse on which his enemy Mordecai is riding (Est. 6:7-11). These same social attitudes remain unchanged through the centuries. The famous Swiss traveler of the early nineteenth century, Louis Burckhardt, once shocked his Middle Eastern traveling companions by allowing his servant to ride his camel while he, Burckhardt, walked (Sim, 254). On numerous occasions I have tried to convince a young man leading the donkey on which I was riding to ride with me. The person involved always refused because to ride with me would be (from his point of view) presumptuous. So we may have here a case of a middle-class merchant with a number of animals and some goods who takes upon himself the form of a servant and *leads* the donkey to the inn.

His willingness to go to the inn and remain there overnight administering to the needs of the wounded man is a further act of self-giving love. Mosaic legislation established cities of refuge for people under the threat of death from blood vengeance retaliation. This legislation provided an escape valve for a custom it could not eradicate. The concept of retaliation, deeply reflected in the Old Testament, is still with us. Modern law in many Middle Eastern countries also makes certain allowances for blood vengeance killings. Thomson admits that originally he thought of the subject as "a curious question of ancient history." Then in villages of upper Galilee he saw it as a continuing part of life.

But as in the Jewish community in the time of Moses, so here, the custom of blood-revenge is too deeply rooted to be under the control of these feudal lords of the land; indeed, they themselves and their families are bound by it in its sternest demands. It is plain that Moses, clothed with all the influence and power of an inspired law-giver, could not eradicate this dreadful custom, and was merely commissioned to mitigate its horrors by establishing cities of refuge, under certain humane regulations, which are fully detailed in Numbers xxxv, and in Deuteronomy xix . . . the law of retaliation remains in all its vigor, and is executed with energy by the . . . tribes around (Thomson, I, 447).

Thus this phenomenon was a problem for Old Testament society and continued in full force through the nineteenth century. Thomson goes on to explain that this retaliation is made against any member of an attacker's extended family or his associates when *any* bodily injury is sustained. The actual assailant is sought if he is available; if not, anyone related to him in the remotest way may suffer. Thomson explains,

It is one of the cruel features of the *lex talionis*, that if the real murderer cannot be reached, the avengers of blood have a right to kill any other members of the family, then any relation, no matter how remote, and finally any member of this confederation. . . . Several of my intimate acquaintances have literally been cut to pieces by the infuriated avengers of blood and in some instances these poor victims had no possible implication with the clan involved (Thomson, I, 448).

What we are dealing with is an irrational response, not a reasoned action. We have no evidence of any inn in the middle of the desert. The natural assumption of the story is that the Samaritan took the man downhill to Jericho. Ibn al-Ṭayyib makes this assumption (folio 104^r; also Dalman, *Sacred*, 245; Ibn al-Ṣalībī, II, 121). In any case the inn is either in a community or in touch with one. The Samaritan, by allowing himself to be identified, runs a grave risk of having the family of the wounded man seek *him* out to take vengeance upon him. After all, who else is there? The group mind of Middle Eastern peasant society makes a totally illogical judgment at this point. The stranger who involves himself in an accident is often considered partially, if not totally, responsible for the accident. After all, why did he stop? Irrational minds seeking a focus for their retaliation do not make rational judgments, especially when the person involved is from a hated minority community. Much of what we are arguing for requires no special Middle Eastern cultural attitude but is rather a common human response. An American cultural equivalent would be a Plains Indian in 1875 walking into Dodge City with a scalped cowboy on his horse, checking into a room over the local saloon, and staying the night to take care of him. Any Indian so brave would be fortunate to get out of the city alive *even* if he had saved the cowboy's life. So with the Samaritan in the parable, his act of kindness will make *no* difference. Caution would lead him to leave the wounded man at the door of the inn and disappear. The man may still be unconscious, in which case the Samaritan would be completely protected. Or the Samaritan could remain anonymous to the wounded man. But when he stays at the inn through the night to take care of the man, and promises to return, anonymity is not possible.

The courage of the Samaritan is demonstrated first when he stops in the desert (for the thieves are still in the area). But his real bravery is seen in this final act of compassion at the inn. The point is not his courage but rather the price he is willing to pay to complete his act of compassion. This price he continues to pay in the final scene.

Scene 7: The Final Payment

The next day he took out and gave two denarii to the manager
and said, "Take care of him, and whatever more you spend,
I, on my return, *I* will repay you."

So the story has come full circle. The inversion of themes in the stanzas of this parabolic ballad makes clear the reasons for this final scene. The parable as a story could just as easily have ended when the wounded man was brought to safety. But no, having made up for the failures first of the Levite, then of the priest, finally he compensates even for the robbers. Specifically the Samaritan's reversal of the actions of the robbers can be seen as follows:

The Robbers	*The Samaritan*
Rob him	Pays for him
Leave him dying	Leaves him taken care of
Abandon him	Promises to return

This comparison reveals the magnificent construction of the parable. The more natural place to take the wounded man would have been to the house of some relative or friend, if not his own home. But the parable is constructed to make this last scene possible. Obviously the Samaritan could not pay his family or friends, and there would be no point in his returning had the drama ended in the wounded man's village.

However, the actions of this scene are not just filler. They are true to first-century life. The wounded man has no money. If he cannot pay the bill when he leaves he will be arrested for debt (Derrett, 218). Innkeepers in the first century had a *very* unsavory reputation. The Mishna warns,

Cattle may not be left in the inns of the gentiles since they are suspected of bestiality; nor may a woman remain alone with them since they are suspected of lewdness; nor may a man remain alone with them since they are suspected of shedding blood (Mishna *Abodah Zarah* 2:1, Danby, 438).

Jewish inns did not fare any better in popular opinions, for in Targum Jonathan the word "prostitute" is regularly translated "woman who keeps an inn" (cf.

Josh. 2:1; Judg. 16:1; I Kings 3:16). Thus the wounded man cannot anticipate a noble quality of life at an inn. From the parables of Jesus himself we know that people were imprisoned for bad debts (Matt. 18:23–35). Obviously the wounded man has nothing left. Thus if the Samaritan does not pledge to pay his final bill, whatever it comes to, the wounded man (on recovery) will not be able to leave. Derrett notes, "The Samaritan enabled him to 'get out of town' " (Derrett, 218). Derrett also observes that a Jew dealing with a Jew could have gotten his money back. But, "Our Samaritan had no hope of enforcing reimbursement" (*ibid.*, 219). The Samaritan is an unknown stranger. Yet, in spite of the cost in time, effort, money, and personal danger, he freely demonstrates unexpected love to the one in need. Is not this a dramatic demonstration of the kind of love God offers through His unique agent in the Gospel?

The exegesis of the early centuries consistently identified the Good Samaritan with Jesus himself. Indeed, in John 8:48, the Jews throw a taunt at him with the words, "Are we not right in saying that you are a Samaritan and have a demon?" But of far greater consequence is the costly demonstration of unexpected love that we see in the actions of the Samaritan. He appears suddenly and unexpectedly from the outside and acts to save. The traditional leaders of the community fail, yet God's agent arrives to "bind up the wounds" of the sufferer. As Barth has written,

> The good Samaritan . . . is not far from the lawyer. The primitive exegesis of the text was fundamentally right. He stands before him incarnate, although hidden under the form of one whom the lawyer believed he should hate, as the Jews hated the Samaritans (Barth, 419).

We have already observed functional Christology in 7:36–50. In this passage the overtones of Christology are in the parable itself, not in the narrative framework provided by the evangelist or his source. Is it not possible here to touch something of Jesus' own understanding of his own ministry as God's unique agent who comes as a suffering servant to save?

How then does this parable function in the dialogue between Jesus and the lawyers? The full text of this second round of the dialogue is as follows:

ROUND TWO:

He, desiring to justify himself, asked,

(5) Lawyer: (Question 3) "Who is my neighbor?"

  (6) Jesus: (after the telling of the parable asked Question 4)
"Which of these three do you think became a neighbor to the man who fell among the robbers?"

  (7) Lawyer: (Answer to 4) He answered,
"The one who showed mercy on him."

(8) Jesus: (Answer to 3) And Jesus said to him,
        "Go and you, *you do* likewise."

In the center of these four speeches we see Jesus reshaping the lawyer's question. He will not give the lawyer a list. He refuses to tell the lawyer who is and who is not his neighbor. Rather, the real question becomes, "To whom must you *become* a neighbor?" This question is then answered. The last statement is not a general admonition to good works but rather an answer to the lawyer's question about self-justification. The first round of questions and answers ended with a command to *do* something. This round ends in the same manner. The lawyer, in the opening question of this round, wants to know how many people he has to love to achieve righteousness by his own efforts. The word "you" is emphatic in the final statement. Jesus says to him, "Here is the standard that *you* must meet." Derrett understands from the parable that "unless we show love to all humanity . . . we cannot claim . . . to have obtained entrance to the Messianic age" (Derrett, 227). Hunter explains the same phrase as meaning, "This is what neighbor-love means, my friend, and if you want eternal life, this is the kind of action God requires of you" (Hunter, *Interpreting,* 73). Both authors are right. The only difficulty is—who is able to do these things? Who can meet this standard? We can almost hear the crowds say under their breath (as they do in 18:26), "Who then can be saved?" Here each half of the dialogue moves in this direction. Thus each round of dialogue ends with the same conclusion. What can I *do* to inherit eternal life? What can I *do* to justify myself? The only conclusion he can come to is, "These things are beyond me. Clearly I cannot justify myself, but all things are possible with God" (cf. Luke 18:27).

Finally then, seeing the parable in its dialogue setting, what is the lawyer to conclude and what theological motifs comprise the theological cluster of the passage? We would suggest the following:

The lawyer is pressed to understand:

> I must *become* a neighbor to anyone in need. To fulfil the law means that I must reach out in costly compassion to all people, even to my enemies. The standard remains even though I can never fully achieve it. I cannot justify myself and earn eternal life.

The following theological motifs are contained in the overall scene:

1. The parable makes clear that any attempt at self-justification is doomed to failure. The standard is too high. Eternal life cannot be earned.
2. Yet the parable holds up an ethical standard to strive after, even though it cannot be fully achieved. Like the command to "be perfect" it remains a standard even though in its fullest expression it is impossibly high.
3. A code book approach to ethics is inadequate. As Derrett writes, "When the Pharisaic system can have such defects it needs serious re-examination" (Derrett, 222).
4. The Samaritan, a hated outsider, demonstrates compassionate love. Thus the parable is a sharp attack on communal and racial prejudices.
5. For Jesus, love is something you feel *and* do.
6. The parable gives us a dynamic concept of the neighbor. The question, "Who

is my neighbor?'' is reshaped into ''To whom must I become a neighbor?''
The answer then is—everyone in need, even an enemy!

7. God's sovereignty is not bound by the official leadership of the community of
   the faithful. When that leadership fails, God is still free to choose new agents,
   as He did with Amos, for the expression of His salvation.

8. Two types of sin and two types of sinners appear in the parable. The robbers
   hurt the man by violence. The priest and Levite hurt him by neglect. The story
   implies the guilt of all three. The failed opportunity to do good becomes an
   evil.

9. The passage makes a statement about salvation. Salvation comes to the
   wounded man in the form of a costly demonstration of unexpected love. In the
   process it seems to make a statement about the Savior. We cautiously suggest
   that Jesus, the rejected outsider, has cast himself in the role of the Samaritan,
   who appears dramatically on the scene to bind up the wounds of the suffering
   as the unique agent of God's costly demonstration of unexpected love.

May the theology and the ethical demands of this time-honored passage
inform and impower us afresh today.

Chapter 4

THE RICH FOOL
(Luke 12:13-21)

The Text:

One of the multitude said to him,
  "Rabbi, bid my brother divide the inheritance with me."
But he said to him,
  "Man, who made me a judge or divider over you?"

And he said to them,   GENERAL PRINCIPLE
  "Take heed, and beware of every kind of insatiable desire.
  For life for a person does not consist in the surpluses of his possessions."

1   And he told this parable, saying,
     "There was a certain rich man   GOODS GIVEN
     whose land brought forth plenty.

2   And he discussed with himself saying,
        'What shall I do,   PROBLEM
        for I have no place to store my crops?'

3   And he said, 'I will do this:
        I will pull down my barns and build larger barns;
        and I will store all my grain and my goods.   PLAN (PRESENT)

4   And I will say to my soul, "Soul!
        You have ample goods laid up for many years.   PLAN (FUTURE)
        Relax, eat, drink, and enjoy yourself"'

5   But God said to him, 'Fool!
     This night your soul is required of you,   GOODS LEFT
     and what you have prepared, whose will these things be?'

So is he who treasures up for himself,   GENERAL PRINCIPLE
and is not gathering riches for God."

As in the case of the Good Samaritan, we intend to take the dialogue setting of this parable seriously and see where it leads us. Here also the parable is long and the dialogue short. Yet again the setting colors the thrust of the parable as it now appears in the text. The rhetorical form of the passage will be examined and then the particulars of the text will be discussed in the light of that form. The literary form (see above) must first be examined.

The overall literary form of the passage is simple and clear. It begins with a single exchange between Jesus and an anonymous petitioner that takes the form of a demand and a response. There is one wisdom saying before the parable and a second after its close. The parable falls naturally into five stanzas. The first tells of goods given and the fifth closes the parable with these same goods left behind. In the center of the parable the rich man makes three speeches. It is clear that the first and second speeches are intended to be separate, because the second is introduced by the otherwise redundant words, "And he said." Also, one senses some time lapse between the rich man's enunciation of his problem and the announcement of his intended solution. The rich man's second and third speeches are spoken together, yet there is a shift of emphasis that divides the speech into two halves. He begins with the present, in which he will build his barns and store his crops. Then in the years to come he will enjoy the "good life." Looking, then, at these three statements, in the first (stanza 2) he outlines the problem. In the second (stanza 3), he decides on a solution. In the third (stanza 4), he reflects on his future in the light of that solution. In stanza 5, God speaks. The center is a crucial turning point, for the rich man in that speech decides what he will do to solve his problem. We have this same feature in the parable of the Unjust Steward (Luke 16:1-8). In that parable there are seven stanzas, but again the center has a soliloquy in which the principal character suddenly decides on a solution to the problem set forth in the opening stanzas (cf. Bailey, *Poet*, 95f.). This very climax in the third stanza is related to the beginning and the end of the parable. In this case the inner relationship is slight and likely unconscious, yet it is there. In the first stanza goods are *given*. In the central stanza they are *stored*. In the last stanza these same goods are *left*. Furthermore, the beginning and the end talk of God's gifts. That is, in the first stanza God gives plenty. In the fifth (as we will note below), the man's soul is discovered to be on loan from God. With this literary structure in mind we will proceed to an examination of the text.

THE INITIAL DIALOGUE

One of the multitude said to him,
"Rabbi, bid my brother divide the inheritance with me."
But he said to him,
"Man, who made me a judge or divider over you?"

As we have already seen in 10:25, the Greek word "teacher" in Luke can be traced to the Hebrew "rabbi" (cf. above, 35). The rabbi was expected to be knowledgeable regarding the law and ready to give a legal ruling. Jesus' understanding of his ministry, however, does not include passing judgment on legal cases. There was precedent for this. We are told that some sages "withdrew from public affairs and even thanked the Almighty for not knowing how to administer justice" (Safrai, *JPFC*, II, 963). Ibn al-Ṣalībī offers the intriguing suggestion that the brother involved was already a disciple and was thus under Jesus' authority. The greedy petitioner then wanted Jesus to tell the brother/disciple to forsake everything by giving it (naturally) to the brother/petitioner (Ibn al-Ṣalībī, II, 132). Such details are in harmony with the story but are imaginative and unfounded.

Yet more can be substantiated. This petitioner is not asking for arbitration, but rather ordering the judge to carry out his wishes. He has already decided what he wants and he tries to *use* Jesus. To say, "Rabbi, my brother and I are quarrelling over our inheritance; will you mediate?" is one thing. To order Jesus to implement his plan is something else. It is little wonder that Jesus' response has a tinge of gruffness in it, as we will observe.

The specific background of such a request is well-known. The father dies and leaves the inheritance as a unit to his sons. Psalm 133:1 reflects on how pleasant it is when the sons manage to cooperate harmoniously in such a situation. Daube observes that "to dwell together" is a technical term in the Old Testament. It is an assumed standard. Thus when Abraham finds it necessary to break with his kinsman Lot, "it is regarded as a sad necessity which calls for justification" (Daube, 327; cf. Gen. 13:5–7). In the New Testament the same assumptions are operative. Luke 16:9 (par. Matt. 6:24) presents the dilemma of a servant in a household where the father dies and the servant suddenly has two masters.

In our text, one brother wants help in pressuring the other brother into finalizing a division between them. The rabbis stated that if one heir wanted a division of the inheritance it should be granted. (Roman law required agreement on the part of both parties; cf. Daube, 328.) Thus the petitioner seems to be saying, "Everybody knows the opinions of the rabbis. I am right, my brother is wrong. You, Rabbi Jesus, *you* tell him so!" The "inheritance" in such a context is most naturally understood to be property. Indeed, we are here dealing with the Middle East's most sensitive problem, both then and now, namely a cry for justice over the division of land.

The question of justice for those who cry out seeking it is an important concern of many biblical writers from Amos onward. Luke himself has more material from the tradition on the question of justice for the poor and downtrodden than any other evangelist. Early in Luke Mary expresses joy at the exaltation of those of low degree (Luke 1:52). A number of the parables offer hope for the poor (cf. The Great Banquet; Lazarus and the Rich Man). Luke 4:17, along with many other references, may be cited. Yet here we see the topic of justice dealt with in a unique way. Thus it is of special importance to examine carefully the "cry for justice" that is voiced here.

This particular cry can perhaps be characterized as a "naked cry for justice." A demanding voice says, "Give me my rights." We are left to assume that this petitioner is unwilling to consider his problem from any perspective other than his own. Lesslie Newbigin states the problem eloquently:

> If we acknowledge the God of the Bible, we are committed to struggle for justice in society. Justice means giving to each his due. Our problem (as seen in the light of the gospel) is that each of us overestimates what is due to him as compared with what is due to his neighbor. . . . If I do not acknowledge a justice which judges the justice for which I fight, I am an agent, not of justice, but of lawless tyranny (Newbigin, 124f.).

Newbigin describes precisely the position of the petitioner. He has decided what *his* rights are. He only wants assistance in pressuring his brother into granting those rights.

The naked cry for justice is voiced also in Shakespeare's tragedy, *Romeo and Juliet*. Tybalt kills Mercutio. Romeo then kills Tybalt, who is a relative to the Capulets (Juliet's family). With the bodies of the two dead men in full view, the crowd gathers and, with them, the prince. Lady Capulet speaks for her family and angrily demands the death of Romeo as the murderer of Tybalt. She says, "I beg justice, which thou, prince, must give!" (act 3, scene 1). Each family is "only demanding its rights." At the end of the play the same people are again gathered in the presence of the prince, only now there are two other bodies on the stage, those of Romeo and Juliet. The prince says,

> "Where be these enemies? Capulet! Montague!
> See, what a scourge is laid upon your hate,
> That heaven finds means to kill your joys with love!
> And I, for winking at your discords too,
> Have lost a brace of kinsmen:
>   All are punish'd" (act 5, scene 3).

To grant to each party their own understanding of their "rights" can lead to tragedy. A new perspective is needed. In Shakespeare's play, even the priest makes no attempt to introduce a new perspective to the two families or pronounce a word of judgment on their hates. Indeed, it takes a special brand of courage to tell antagonists that their naked cry for justice is not enough, that they must begin with a new understanding of themselves.

This rare courage is seen not only in this passage but also in Luke 13:1–3, where nationalists report an atrocity story to Jesus. As one who has been many times in precisely this same position, the present writer knows that the telling of such a story *demands* a sympathetic response from the listener. Jesus' answer requires great courage, as we will observe. We see this same kind of response here in Luke 12:13. In each text there is a strong plea for justice from a self-confident, powerless petitioner. In each case the answer is, "Look to yourself first!"

Jesus' answer to the demand of the petitioner "has the tone of disapproval" (Meyer, II, 416). This is supported by modern and medieval colloquial Arabic speech where *ja ragul* ("O man!") usually introduces a complaint against the one addressed, as is clearly the case here. This same connotation is documented by Muir, who mentions a case of its use in the caliph's court in Baghdad in A.D. 749. Ibn Hobeira, a member of the court, addressed Abu Jafar, the caliph's brother, as "O man!" This was taken as an insult and Abu Jafar immediately apologized for it "as a slip of the tongue" (Muir, 438, n. 1). Furthermore, Moses (unsolicited) sought to be a judge and was rebuffed (Ex. 2:14a). Jesus (solicited) refuses to be a judge and rebuffs the petitioner. Yet both begin with a broken relationship between two antagonists and try, in their separate ways, to achieve reconciliation. Together the two words "judge and divider" give the sense of Jesus' complaint. There is obviously a broken relationship between this man and his brother. The man wants the broken relationship finalized by total separation. But Jesus insists that he has not come as a "divider." The obvious alternative is "reconciler." He wants to reconcile people to one another, not finalize divisions between them. This brief dialogue is in full harmony with everything we know about Jesus, and it recurs in the Gospel of Thomas (logion 72). Its authenticity has been affirmed by leading Jewish and Christian scholars (Daube, 326–29; Manson, *Sayings,* 271). If this be true, then it was originally remembered in Aramaic and later translated into Greek. It is well-known that skilled translators can use the nuances of the receptor language to highlight a particular emphasis of the original. An illustration of this is Arberry's translation of the Koran, where a great deal of beauty and wordplay comes across to the English reader. Something of the same phenomena can perhaps be seen twice in this passage. The first is in this dialogue. The translator has selected a rare word, used only in this text in all of Biblical Greek, for the word "divider." In Greek it is *meristēs.* Drop the *r* and move the *i* and the word becomes *mesitēs,* which means "reconciler." Jesus has not come as a *meristēs* (divider) but rather as a *mesitēs* (reconciler). The form of this dialogue in the Gospel of Thomas is significant in this regard:

> (A man said) to him: Speak to my brothers that they divide my father's possessions with me. He said to him: O man, who made me a divider? He turned to his disciples (and) said to them: I am not a divider, am I? (Aland, 526).

In this version of the dialogue even greater emphasis is placed on the rejection of his role as a divider. The obvious answer to his question is, "No, you are rather a reconciler." But reconciliation will require the petitioner to gain a new perspective of himself. Miller writes,

> Jesus was not showing indifference to the claims of legal justice, but was insisting that there is a greater gain than getting an inheritance and a greater loss than losing it (Miller, 110).

The question is addressed in the plural, "Who made me a judge or divider over you (plural)?" Some of our Arabic versions use the dual "over the two of you." Others maintain the plural. Is Jesus addressing the crowd or only the two brothers? It is impossible to determine with precision, but the plural seems more appropriate. Jesus seems to be refusing to play a role of divider for all. After the somewhat hostile question comes the first of the two wisdom sayings that encase the parable.

FIRST WISDOM SAYING

And he said to them,
"Take heed, and beware of every kind of insatiable desire.
For life for a person does not consist in the surpluses of his possessions."

The first sentence is usually translated in reference to covetousness. The original language carries with it the overtones of insatiable desires that make the warning even stronger. The clear implication is that the petitioner will not have his problem solved if his brother *does* grant him his portion of the inheritance. Sa'īd observes, "Jesus becomes a judge *over* them, not *between* them. He judges the motives of their hearts, not their pocket books" (Sa'īd, 339). The word "life" in Greek is *zōē*, which, in contrast to *bia*, has to do with a special quality of life and not merely physical life.

The second sentence is awkward. Literally the two sentences read,

Take heed and beware of every kind of insatiable desire
    because not *out of the surpluses* to anyone
the life of him it is
    out of his possessions.

There is a repetition of the reference to possessions/surpluses. Bruce notes this and understands it to be "two ways of saying the same thing, the second a kind of afterthought" (Bruce, *Synoptic*, 557). Marshall concurs with C. F. D. Moule that two expressions may have been combined (Marshall, 522f.). However, if we are dealing with a parallel repetition of ideas in a rhetorical form, then it is not an afterthought but a necessary repetition for the completion of the form. We grant with Bruce that "The expression here is peculiar" (Bruce, *Synoptic*, 557), but the meaning is clear. People are infected with insatiable desires of many kinds. One of them is to acquire more possessions. They seek an enriching quality of life in these possessions in the fond hope that if they can only get enough material things these things will produce the abundant life. T. W. Manson writes,

It is true that a certain minimum of material goods is necessary for life; but it is not true that greater abundance of goods means greater abundance of life (*Sayings*, 271).

Jesus' cryptic answer warns the reader in two ways. First, with these presuppositions the desire for material things will prove insatiable. Second, the dreams of the abundant life will never be achieved through such an accumulation of surpluses.

The insatiable desire for a higher standard of living is widespread in the modern world. The fond hope that LIFE will be the product of more consumption is also very much with us. With the natural resources of the world dwindling and the pressure for more possessions intensifying, some wrestling with the message of this text would seem to be imperative if we are to survive. Again we note a plural, "he said to *them*." The text is meant for all readers/listeners, not just the two brothers. This wisdom saying introduces the parable itself.

STANZA ONE—GOODS GIVEN

And he told this parable, saying,
    "There was a certain rich man
    whose land brought forth plenty."

As in the case of many of the parables, this story has a literary background. Psalm 49 discusses the problem of wealth and its meaninglessness in the face of death. According to Ben Sirach,

A man grows rich by his sharpness and grabbing,
    and here is the regard he receives for it;
he says, "I have found rest,
    and now I can enjoy my goods";
but he does not know how long this will last;
    he will have to leave his goods for others and die (Sir. 11:19–20).

Thus Jesus is dealing with a theme already well-known in the literature of the audience (cf. also Eccl. 2:1–11; Job 31:24–28). What is important is what he does with it. Here Jesus expands Ben Sirach's very short story into a drama. A number of distinctive features appear in the process. (1) Rather than one speech we have four, with two speakers. (2) God himself is heard at the end of Jesus' parable. (3) The two accounts begin with different assumptions. Ben Sirach's little story is directed to the wealthy who *acquire* their possessions (by sharpness and grabbing). In contrast, Jesus' parable discusses wealth that is a *gift* from God, not wealth acquired by human effort. That is, Ben Sirach's man reflects on "What do I do with my earnings?" Jesus' man must ask, "What do I do with what I have not earned?" That he does not perceive the question in this fashion is part of what the parable is all about. (4) Jesus' version introduces the idea of "loan." The man discovers his soul to be on loan. Was his wealth also on loan? Ben Sirach's story carries none of these subtle overtones. (5) The life-style of Ben Sirach's character is exposed (he is sharp and grabbing), but nothing evolves from it. Jesus' story subtly and yet powerfully exposes both the life-style of the rich man and the resulting isolation that it creates. (6) Jesus' account is clearly focusing on surpluses. His man is already rich when the parable opens. He is then given additional wealth. Ben Sirach's man grows rich in the parable. These unique features will be further illuminated as we proceed.

Focusing on this first stanza we see a man who is already rich. We are not told how he got his riches, and the method of acquiring them is not criticized as it was in Sirach. This man has more than enough. On top of this, with no extra effort on his part, he is given the gift of a bumper crop. He did not earn it and he does not need it. His problem is what to do with unearned surpluses. With this problem in mind we turn to stanza two.

STANZA TWO—THE PROBLEM

And he discussed with himself saying,
"What shall I do,
for I have no place to store my crops?"

The text gives us a continuous past, "he was debating with himself." The subject was a matter of considerable concern and the debate lasted some time. There was no thought of "I really do not need any of this, I am already wealthy!" Nor is there any thought of "This extra wealth is a gift for which I can take no credit. God has given the increase." Rather, the bumper crops are simply referred to as "my crops" and the only question that concerns him is how to preserve them for himself. Ambrose aptly observes that the rich man *has* storage available in the mouths of the needy (cf. Trench, 337). Augustine talks about a man who stores grain on a damp floor and needs to move it upstairs lest it spoil; thus treasure to be kept must be stored in heaven, not on earth (Trench, 338). Ecclesiastes (5:10) observes,

He who loves money
  will not be satisfied with money;
nor he who loves wealth
  with gain; this also is vanity.

For us the text relates to the very important modern questions of excess profits in a capitalistic society and surplus value theories in Marxism. According to Paul, the Christian should work for two reasons. The first is so that he will not be a burden on others (II Thess. 2:7–12). The second is "so that he may be able to give to those in need" (Eph. 4:28). To explore the meaning of all of this for a Christian in a capitalistic society would go well beyond the intent and scope of this study. We would only observe in passing that this parable, with its presuppositions, speaks clearly to crucial questions of our own day.

Furthermore, the man is "dialoguing with himself." One of the striking features of the traditional Middle Easterner is his gregarious nature. Life is lived in tightly knit communities. The leading men of the village still "sit at the gate" and spend literally years talking to one another. The slightest transaction is worthy of hours of discussion. The present writer has engaged with the notables in such discussions in the gate and knows that often there seems to be a subtle pressure *not* to introduce the information that will settle the question under discussion. The reasoning seems to be—we have a wonderful discussion going, do not close it! In any case, the elder in such a community makes up his mind *in community*. He decides what he will do after hours of discussion with his friends. He does his thinking in a crowd. The text does not read, "he said to himself," as we have with the unjust steward (16:3) and the unjust judge (18:4). Rather, this man dialogues with himself. He obviously has no one else with whom to talk. He trusts no one and has no friends or cronies with whom he can exchange ideas. When he needs a dialogue he can talk only to himself. Thus we begin to get Jesus' picture of the kind of prison that wealth can build. He has the money to buy a vacuum and live in it. Life in this vacuum creates its own realities, and out of this warped perspective we hear him announce his solution.

STANZA THREE—PLAN (PRESENT)

And he said, "I will do this:
I will pull down my barns and build larger barns;
and I will store all my grain and my goods."

Plummer (324) has noted the chiasmus in this line:

I will tear down
   of me the barns
   and greater ones
I will build up.

The language of "tear down" and "build up" is classical prophetic language that refers to the call and ministry of the prophet (Jer. 1:10). It speaks of courageous acts in the name of God that call for suffering in their fulfillment. Here this noble language is sadly cheapened by this self-indulgent rich man who is determined that he alone will consume God's gifts. These gifts (for him, surplus wealth) have suddenly become "my grain and my goods." The list of *my* crops, *my* barns, *my* goods, and finally *my* soul, has often been noted. It was in the barns that the tithes and offerings were set aside. The priests and Levites came to the barns to collect them (Safrai, *JPFC*, II, 820). Our rich man has other things on his mind, as we see from his concluding speech.

STANZA FOUR—PLAN (FUTURE)

And I will say to my soul, "Soul!
You have ample goods laid up for many years.
Relax, eat, drink, and enjoy yourself."

This speech is not sad, rather it is pitiful. This wealthy, self-confident man has arrived, he has made it. All that he has longed for has now been realized. He needs an audience for his arrival speech. Who is available? Family? Friends? Servants and their families? Village elders? Fellow landowners? Who will "rejoice with me?" The father in the parable of the Prodigal Son has a community ready at any moment to join him in a festival of joy (Luke 15:22-24). The shepherd and the woman call in their friends and neighbors to rejoice over the found sheep and coin (15:6, 9). The gregarious Middle Easterner always has a community around him. But this man? He can only address himself. His only audience is his own *nefesh*.

To claim that he should be talking to his body rather than his soul is a misunderstanding of the text. The word "soul" (*psuchē*) is the Greek translation of the Hebrew *nefesh*, which means the whole person. *Nefesh* reappears in the Syriac versions of this text, and the cognate Arabic word *nafs* is used almost exclusively in the Arabic translations. Thus the point is not that he is addressing his body as opposed to his soul. The issue is his mentality. He thinks that the total needs of the total person can be met by material surpluses well preserved for the owner's exclusive use.

The word we have translated "enjoy yourself" is a colorful word. Again the translator has managed to add a wordplay to the text by a careful selection of vocabulary. The rare word used in this passage for "to bring forth plenty" is *euphoreō*. The Greeks added the letters *eu* to the beginnings of words to intensify them. Something good becomes very good by this addition. Thus *angelleō* is to bring news: *euangelleō* is to bring good news, and in the New Testament becomes the word for proclaiming the gospel. *Phoreō* means to bear fruit; so *euphoreō* (v. 16) means to bear fruit in abundance. Then here in verse 19, the word we have translated "enjoy yourself" is *euphrainō*. The noun form of this same word is *euphrōn*, which is the state of self-enjoyment. The root of these two words is *phrōn*, which comes into English in our word dia*phragm*. The *phrōn* is the diaphragm. As Bertram observes, the diaphragm was "early regarded as the seat of intellectual and spiritual activity. The diaphragm determines the nature and strength of the breath and hence also the human spirit and its emotions" (Bertram, *TDNT*, IX, 220). So anyone with *euphrōn* possessed an added measure of the good life and all that it holds. This *euphrōn* " is often used for purely secular joy, and sometimes for the joy of the festive meal" (Bultmann, *TDNT*, II, 774). But at the same time it could also cover "the facts and processes of the intellectual or spiritual life" (*ibid.*, 772). Thus this rich man has a formula, which is:

euphoreō	euphrainō
(bring forth many things)	(enjoy all aspects of the good life)

It is not by accident that the speech to the *nefesh/psuchē* (the whole person) ends with a vision of *euphrōn*. We would suggest that the above is a deliberate play on words. Into this tidy equation comes the thundering voice of God.

STANZA FIVE—GOODS LEFT

But God said to him, "Fool! (*aphrōn*)
This night your soul is required of you,
and what you have prepared, whose will these things be?"

The New Testament has four words for "fool." These are:

anoētos — mindless

asophos — without wisdom

mōros   — fool (cf. the English word moron)

aphrōn — fool/stupid

Plummer (554) identifies the last two as "much stronger" than the first two. Luke uses the first (6:11; 24:25) and certainly knew all four. In this text he has chosen *aphrōn*. The *a* prefix negates the word, as in the English "moral" and "amoral." So here, this rich man, who thinks that his *euphoreō* (many things) will produce *euphrōn* (the good life), is in reality *aphrōn* (without mind, spirit, and emotions). His formula for the good life is sheer stupidity.

The verb "is required" in Greek is a word that is commonly used for the return of a loan. His soul was on loan and now the owner (God) wants the loan returned. At the beginning of the parable we noted that his goods were a gift. Now it is clear that his life was also not his own.

The parable assumes a time lapse between stanzas four and five. The voice of God thunders at him (presumably) after he has "prepared" his maximum security storage bins. Thus, after his arrival, he is confronted with the stark reality of the world he has created with his wealth. As Manson succinctly observes,

> The sting of the words lies, however, not in the announcement that that man must die, but in the following question, which shows clearly the real poverty of his life. He is lonely and friendless in the midst of his wealth (Manson, *Sayings,* 272).

The listener/reader already knows this. Now we see that it takes the voice of God Himself to penetrate the rich man's self-created isolation and confront him with a chilling vision of himself. There is no accusing question, such as, "What have you done for others?" or "Why have you failed to help those in need?" or "Why are there no family and friends close to you who would be the natural recipients of your wealth?" He has no doubt developed impenetrable armor for just such an attack. Rather, God thunders: look at what you have done to yourself! You plan alone, build alone, indulge alone, and now you will die alone!

The story does not tell us that the rich fool does not have any family. Everyone has some family—even Howard Hughes. Rather, the rich fool does not know who will win the power struggle after he dies. He does not know who will finally gain control over all of his carefully secured wealth. Muir gives an account of the last days of the fabulous Harun al-Rashid, the most illustrious and wealthy caliph of history:

> Traveling slowly over the mountain range into Persia, Harun one day called his physician aside, and, alone under the shelter of a tree, unfolding a silken kerchief that girded his loins, disclosed the fatal disease he laboured under. "But have a care," he said, "that thou keep it secret; for my sons" (and he named them all and their guardians) "are watching the hour of my decease, as thou mayest see by the shuffling steed they will now mount me on, adding thus to mine infirmity." There is something touching in these plaintive words of the great monarch, now alone in the world, and bereft of the support even of those who were bound to rally round him in his hour of weakness (Muir, 481).

The same kind of a picture is painted by Browning in his poem "The Bishop Orders His Tomb at Saint Praxed's Church." Indeed history and literature give ample examples of the truth of what the voice of God announces to this stupid, wealthy man.

What is his response? We are not told. This parable is also open-ended. That a parable at times has aspects of a riddle becomes evident. Where does this man's mind turn? What is the content of his next dialogue with himself? Is it, I have rejected the living community of family and friends around me! Or, I am mistaken; wealth does not bring genuine security! Or, why did I not help others when I could? Or is the reader/listener expected to overhear the discussion of Psalm 49:10 (LXX 48:11):

> the fool/stupid and the mindless alike must perish
> and leave their wealth to others.

If this is the case, Psalm 49 discusses the rich man's inability to *ransom* himself with his wealth which he leaves behind. Is this the direction the listener's mind is to go? Is this parable a commentary on Luke 9:23–24? The parable does not finally give up its secrets. The rich man's silence leaves each reader/listener to answer out of his own soul. The passage concludes with a second wisdom saying, which must now be examined.

SECOND WISDOM SAYING

> So is he who treasures up for himself,
> and is not gathering riches for God.

For centuries we have had a theologically influenced translation in this wisdom saying. The text gives us two *active* participles, "treasuring up" and "gathering riches." Two centuries ago Bengel argued against our suggested translation. He rightly points out that "for himself" (*heautō*) is not precisely paralleled in the text with the construction *theō* (for God); rather the text has *eis theon* (literally "into God"). He observes,

> nothing can be added or diminished from the perfection of God (whether a man seeks His glory or not in laying out his wealth). He is rich *toward God,* who uses and enjoys his riches in the way that God would have him (Bengel, II, 109).

Bengel correctly points out the differences. The difficulty is that Bengel, like others, is obliged to turn the active participle "is enriching" into a passive "is rich," as he has done above. The two active participles are precisely parallel. Perhaps the original language does preserve some reluctance toward making "for himself" and "for God" precisely parallel because God needs nothing; indeed, the cattle on a thousand hills are His (Ps. 50:10). Yet the parallelism is there. The Arabic and Syriac versions are divided. Some translate with an active "is enriching" and others with a passive "is rich." The thirteenth-century version of Ibn al-'Assāl has "is rich" in the text and "is enriching" in the margin (folio 236ᵛ). When we ask these Oriental versions, Enriching with what? the answer is again ambiguous. We have "with God," or "in the way of God," or "in the things that are for God," or finally, "for God." The first can only mean "seeking to become rich in the reality of God Himself." The second and third are expansions of the first. The fourth is the translation we propose. As we have noted, the Greek has *eis theon* (literally "into God"). The preposition *eis* ("into") is on occasion used for the dative of advantage and translated "for" (cf. Bauer, 229). A clear case of this is in Luke 9:13 where the disciples are worried about feeding the five thousand and suggest that they must "go and buy food for (*eis*) all these people." Then *eis* is used to "denote reference to a person or thing" (*ibid.*). Luke 14:35 has this use of *eis* where the salt is referred to as "fit neither *for* (*eis*) the land nor *for* (*eis*) the dunghill." With these uses of *eis* in Luke just before and just after our text there is no syntactical reason for not understanding our text in the same fashion. Furthermore, when we translate "gathering riches *for* God" we need not be understood as trying to add to the perfection of God. All through Scripture God receives the *gifts* of the believers. So here the rich fool is characterized as one who is spending his energies trying to enrich himself rather than laboring in the service of God so as to offer *gifts* to God. Ibn al-Ṭayyib hints at this understanding of the text:

> He (Jesus) intends from this picture some one who stores up worldly treasure and does not achieve riches in divine things (Ibn al-Ṭayyib, folio 112ᵛ).

Ibn al-Ṭayyib does not indicate that the "divine things" are gifts for God, but he does have two actives for the verbs, "stores up" and "achieve riches." Thus he indicates that in each case the text is talking about an action in which the believer must engage.

Understood in this fashion we have the perfect complement to Luke 12:33 (par. Matt. 6:20), where the treasure in heaven is clearly "for yourselves." When standing alone such a text can lead to an otherworldly egocentricity, a way to take it with you. Put your money in the bank on the other side and you will be able to keep it for yourself! But if our proposal is plausible, this text is a corrective to that understanding. The "treasure in heaven" is indeed "for yourselves" (Luke 12:33). But in some profound sense it is also a gift to God, it is "for God" (Luke 12:21). Thus the general principle here stated at the end of the parable significantly complements the general principle at the beginning. The surpluses of material things (the first general principle) are to be spent in offering gifts to God (the second general principle). The gifts from God are to be returned to Him. Furthermore, the very energy directed to enriching the self with material things is misdirected. Such energy finally destroys the self that exerts it. Rather, the believer is directed to spend himself in "enriching God."

Finally, what is the response of the brother(s) and the crowd? Again there is silence. The rich man is silent in the parable, and so is the audience listening to its telling. Thus the listener/reader is pressed to finalize the tension of the text on two levels; that of the rich man, and that of the petitioner. What is he pressed to conclude? We would suggest the following:

The petitioner from the crowd is pressed to affirm,

The real problem is not the division of inheritance, but a will to serve self rather than to serve God (by serving others, including the brother).

The theological motifs that inform the parable in its setting include the following:

1. A naked cry for justice, unqualified by any self-criticism, is not heeded by Jesus.

2. In a case of a broken personal relationship Jesus refuses to answer a cry for justice when the answer contributes to a finalizing of brokenness of that relationship. He did not come as a divider.

3. Jesus' parables often reflect a profound concern for justice for the poor. For him justice includes a concern for needs and not simply earnings (cf. Matt. 20:1–16). But here a self-centered cry for justice is understood by Jesus as a symptom of a sickness. He refuses to answer the cry but rather addresses himself to the healing of the sickness that produced the cry.

4. Material possessions are gifts from God. God does grant unearned surpluses of material things. Each life is on loan. The rich man in the parable assumed to own both ("my goods" and "my soul"). The parable presents him as mistaken in both cases.

5. The person who thinks security and the good life are to be found in material things is stupid.

6. The abundant life is to be found in "treasuring up for God" rather than for self.

7. James talks of the rich man who will "fade away in the midst of his life-style (1:11). Jesus gives a parabolic picture of precisely this same phenomenon. This fool's wealth destroyed his capacity to maintain any abiding human relationships. He has no one with whom to share his soul, and worst of all, he does not even know he has a problem.

In our continuing concern to discover the pay-offs of the material, it is perhaps appropriate to reflect again on the parabolic answer to the petitioner's demand. The voice from the crowd calls out for justice in the division of the inheritance (probably held in land). Jesus' answer is to ask for a new perspective on the problem itself. He does not investigate who is right and who is wrong and then throw his weight on the side of justice (however right such an action may be in many circumstances). Rather he introduces a new perspective, indeed a theological perspective, from which to view the problem, and then leaves the problem itself unanswered. As we have indicated, the cry for justice over the division of land is the Middle East's most sensitive problem. In the following prose-poem the present writer has tried to apply the methodology used by Jesus in this passage. Today two voices cry out in the Middle East for a just division of the "inheritance." What answer can Christians give? Like this parable in Luke 12, the intent of the following is to suggest a different perspective from which an answer could perhaps emerge.

RESURRECTION

(Ode on a Burning Tank: The Holy Lands, October 1973)

I am a voice,
   the voice of spilt blood
      crying from the land.

The life is in the blood
   and for years my life flowed in the veins of a young man.
      My voice was heard through his voice,
         and my life was his life.

Then our volcano erupted
and for a series of numbing days
   all human voices were silenced
      amid the roar of the heavy guns,
      the harsh clank of tank tracks,
      the bone-jarring shudder of sonic booms,
         as gladiators with million-dollar swords
         killed each other high in the sky.

Then suddenly—suddenly
   there was the swish of a rocket launcher—
   a dirty yellow flash—
   all hell roared.
The clanking of the great tracks stopped.
   My young man staggered screaming from his inferno,
   his body twitched and flopped in the sand

And I was spilt into the earth—
   into the holy earth
      of the Holy Land.

The battle moved on.
   The wounded vehicles burned,

scorched,
            and cooled.
The ''meat wagons'' carried the bodies away as
    the chill of the desert night
    settled on ridge and dune,
And I stiffened and blackened in the sand.

And then—and then
As the timeless silence
    of the now scarred desert returned,
there—there congealed in the land,
    in the land of prophet, priest and king—
I heard a voice—
    a voice from deep in the land,
    a voice from an ageless age,
    a voice from other blood
        once shed violently in the land.

The voice told me this ancient story;
precious blood intoned this ancient tale.

''A certain man had two sons.
One was rich and the other was poor.
    The rich son had no children
    while the poor son was blessed with many sons
                        and many daughters.

In time the father fell ill.
    He was sure he would not live through the week
    so on Saturday he called his sons to his side
        and gave each of them half of the land of their inheritance.
    Then he died.

Before sundown the sons buried their father with respect
        as custom requires.

That night the rich son could not sleep.
    He said to himself,
        'What my father did was *not just*.
    I am rich, my brother is poor.
    I have bread enough and to spare,
        while my brother's children eat one day
        and trust God for the next.
I must move the landmark which our father has set in the middle of the land
so that my brother will have the greater share.
    Ah—but he must not see me.
    If he sees me he will be shamed.
    I must arise early in the morning before it is dawn and move the landmark!'
With this he fell asleep
        and his sleep was secure and peaceful.

Meanwhile, the poor brother could not sleep.
    As he lay restless on his bed he said to himself,

'What my father did was *not just*.
Here I am surrounded by the joy of many sons
                              and many daughters,
   while my brother daily faces the shame
      of having no sons to carry on his name
         and no daughters to comfort him in his old age.
   He should have the land of our fathers.
      Perhaps this will in part compensate him
      for his indescribable poverty.
   Ah—but if I give it to him he will be shamed.
   I must awake early in the morning before it is dawn
      and move the landmark which our father has set!'
With this he went to sleep
   and his sleep was secure and peaceful.

On the first day of the week—
   very early in the morning,
   a long time before it was day,
the two brothers met at the ancient landmarker.
   They fell with tears into each other's arms.
   And on that spot was built the city of Jerusalem.''

                                        —by Kenneth E. Bailey

Chapter 5

PILATE, THE TOWER, AND THE FIG TREE
(Luke 13:1-9)

In these verses we are dealing with two units of tradition (vv. 1–5, 6–9). Each unit discusses politics and repentance, and thus it is appropriate to examine them together. The second is labeled a parable. In the first, Jesus makes his point with the use of two concrete comparisons and thus the material falls under the category of parabolic speech. We do not have intellectualizing abstractions, but rather the theology is tied to two specific illustrations of people who were suddenly killed, the first by Pilate, and the second by a falling tower. Thus each unit of tradition can be seen as a type of parable.

Elsewhere we have called this material "The Call of the Kingdom to Israel" (Bailey, *Poet,* 81). This is then balanced in the Lucan Travel Narrative with a block of material that can be labeled "The Call of the Kingdom to Israel and to the Outcasts" (14:12–15:32; Bailey, *Poet,* 81).

Of the two units in this text the first is more general and addresses itself to the people. The second, as we will discover, is directed to the leadership of the nation. In each unit the literary structure will be examined and then the text studied in detail.

PILATE AND THE TOWER (Luke 13:1–5)

This passage opens with the following statement:

> And some came at that very time who told him of the Galileans whose blood Pilate had mingled with their sacrifices.

In the West we have traditionally translated the opening phrase of this verse as, "There were some *present* at that very time who. . . ." But Eastern fathers in the

74

Syriac and Arabic tradition, almost without exception, have legitimately read the verb *pareimi* as "come" rather than "be present." Thus they translate, "And some came at that time who. . . ." This understanding of the text indicates a break between passages and does not tie this unit of tradition to what precedes it. Plummer prefers this latter reading (Plummer, 337).

So atrocity storytellers suddenly appear and report to Jesus the incident of "the Galileans whose blood Pilate had mingled with their sacrifices." We are not told the intent of the storytellers. However, this intent is relatively clear to anyone who lives, or has lived, in a world of violent political conflicts. C. H. Dodd speaks of first-century Judaism's concern to maintain its identity:

> This aim, moreover, was being pursued in a situation in which resentment of pagan domination, and national sensitiveness, were mounting towards the fatal climax of A.D. 66. We have to allow for something approaching a war-mentality among large sections of the Jewish people—and we know how that can affect one's judgment. It was not clear to those who kept watch upon him that Jesus really cared for the national cause. When he was told about Pilate's slaughter of Galileans in the temple, he responded, not with indignant denunciation of Roman brutality, but with a warning to his own people to "repent" (Dodd, *More*, 96).

Josephus records a number of massacres during this period (*Antiquities* 7:45–62; 18:60–62; 20:113–17), but not this one. Plummer tries to make an historical identification (Plummer, 338). Marshall suggests that we are dealing with an historical event, "not attested from secular sources" (Marshall, 553). Marshall is more convincing than Plummer, yet neither solution is required. Civil and national violence spawns incredible rumors. One real massacre is enough to create stories about ten others. The present writer has recently completed eighteen months of agonizing with the Lebanese people in their civil war of 1975–76. The war was sparked by a massacre of twenty-eight in a bus on the outskirts of Beirut. From that time on, endless stories of massacres (some fact and some fiction) were rampant all across the land. Such stories serve a function in a community at war. The teller and the listener together are emotionally stirred to a point of rage that can then motivate them to heroism in retaliation. But woe be to the listener who dares ask, "Have you checked your sources?" Or who says, "Do not forget our hands are not clean either." All such talk is considered disloyal and the one who dares express such sentiments can expect a verbal, if not physical, attack. The brief report in the text has all the characteristics of such a violence-inspired rumor. Pilate's soldiers could have been so insensitive to Jewish religious practices as to attack worshipers in the very act of offering a sacrifice. But such an incident would hardly have escaped Josephus, who was not slow to criticize Pilate. Some minor attack on zealots in the city of Jerusalem could easily have been blown up into the report we have in the text. The expected response is, "How long, O Lord! Destroy the house of the evil Romans! Hear the cries of thy people!" A modernization of this same incident would be to go up into a Christian village in the Lebanese mountains and announce, "They came into the church with their machine guns and gunned down the faithful *in the very act of participating in the Holy Eucharist! The blood* of the worshipers *was mingled with the holy wine on the altar! NOW WHAT DO YOU THINK OF THAT*?!" The listener *must* answer with sympathy and denunciation. In the case of Jesus, if his commitment to nationalistic goals is suspect (as Dodd suggests), then the report may well be intended to measure his loyalty to the national cause. If he does not want to voice an "indignant denunciation of Roman brutality" (Dodd, *More*, 96), then it is safest for them to walk away with Amos' admonition to silence as an operating principle (Amos 5:13). The voicing of such a denunciation would also be problematic.

Ibn al-Ṣalībī thinks that the reporters are trying to spring a trap:

> This event gave some of them an opportunity to tempt our Lord. They sent (the report) to him to see what he would answer. For if he said, "This killing is a clear case of injustice and oppression," they would then defame him before the Roman governor, claiming that he was overstepping the law and that his teachings violated that same Roman Law. But the Glorified One responded to their promptings with a call to repentance and compared this fearful event with the fall of a tower in Siloam (Ibn al-Ṣalībī, II, 139).

Ibn al-Ṣalībī's thoughtful suggestion is quite likely a part of the motivation of the questioners. They have made a political statement. If Jesus responds with a supportive reply, that answer could be used against him. But Jesus' answer demonstrates the same quality of courage seen in Jeremiah's announcements of judgment in a world of political uncertainty (Jer. 26). Jesus' response is neither denunciation of Rome, nor silence. To the form and content of that response we now turn. The literary form is as follows:

And he answered them,

1   "Do you think that those Galileans
         worse sinners they were
             than *all* the other Galileans because they suffered thus?

2   I tell you, No!
                 But unless you repent
                     you will *all* likewise perish.

3   Or those eighteen upon whom the tower fell (in Siloam and killed them).
         Do you think worse debtors they were
             than *all* the others who dwelt in Jerusalem?

4   I tell you, No!
                 But unless you repent
                     you will *all* likewise perish."

There are two verses with a common refrain that together comprise four stanzas. Each verse is an illustration of violent death. The first is by the hated imperial ruler. The second is assumed by the text to be an act of God. The theme of "all" closes each stanza and ties the four together. The first line of the third stanza may have an editorial note with some extra information. If the fall of the tower on eighteen people was a noteworthy event that had caught the popular mind at the time of the telling (which seems to be the case because Jesus assumes the audience knows the incident), then the extra information about place and result would not be necessary for the original audience. As the sayings of Jesus are collected, recorded, and circulated, some extra details need to be added. The present author has identified a significant number of such footnotes with extra information that seem to have been attached to earlier compositions (Bailey, *Poet,* 67). In this case the point is insignificant theologically. Furthermore, we are not arguing that the material is any type of poetry with a specified line length; rather it is parallelistic prose with unspecified line length. Yet, if the bracketed information is an editor's note, the lines are in closer proximity to each other. We will observe below the same four-stanza structure in the parable of the Unjust Judge (Luke 18:1–8).

In regard to content, a number of points need to be made.

1. Jesus' answer *seems* to assume that the informers are trying to provoke a discussion on the relationship between sin and suffering. As we have noted above, the intent of the informers is not stated. Rather than read the account backward and supply the missing motive from the answer we would rather read the account forward from the original political statement and understand the response as a complete surprise. An atrocity story is told. Jesus is expected to respond with a denunciation of the Roman overlords. He does not. Rather, he opens the question of sin and suffering *and* concludes with a call for *them* to repent! Political enthusiasts struggling for their concept of justice do not ordinarily take kindly to such a call! The brief reference to the question of the relationship between sin and suffering is a bridge to the conclusion that focuses on repentance.

2. On the topic of sin and suffering, the text gives a double renunciation of a one-to-one relationship between them similar to the account of the man born blind in John 9:1–3. The popular attitude is there stated. The man is born blind. The disciples assume someone has sinned—either the man or his parents. Jesus denies both. In Luke 5:19 Jesus addresses the paralyzed man on the bed and announces the forgiveness of his sins. Jesus seems there also to be speaking to this same mentality. We can assume that the paralyzed man has been told that he is paralyzed because he is a sinner. Thus healing for him cannot be accomplished until he is assured of the forgiveness of his sins. In reference to our text, Edersheim makes the intriguing suggestion that the eighteen killed by the falling tower may have been working on Pilate's aqueduct. Pilate had taken money from the temple treasury for the building of the aqueduct, much to the horror of the local population. Thus if some masonry had fallen on such workmen, the entire countryside would naturally have assumed that this was a judgment from God for collaboration in such a project (Edersheim, *Life,* 222). The suggestion is all the more intriguing because it relates the two illustrations to Pilate. Some such

background may well have been the context of the falling stonework. Yet specu-
lation is pointless. The text clearly affirms that in both cases (in the opinion of
Jesus) the suffering of those involved cannot be traced to their sins.

3. The movement of the two illustrations is significant. The informants in
effect ask, "What about the suffering of these national heroes struck down by our
enemy?" Jesus answers, "What about the suffering of those whom God strikes
down in the falling of a tower?" (There is no category of fate or chance in
biblical literature. The biblical understanding of the sovereignty of God pre-
cludes it.) Thus Jesus refuses to discuss the suffering of the politically oppressed
without broadening the discussion to include other types of sufferers. Those who
suffer political oppression often quickly assume that their suffering is the only
kind that matters, and a crass indifference may then develop to the suffering of
others around them, particularly if it is of a nonpolitical nature. The incisive
thrust of Jesus' response does not allow for such a narrowing of the discussion,
irrespective of the grim nature of the political oppression presented.

4. In the first stanza we read of "sinners" and in the third of "debtors."
The same shift with the identical words can be found in the two versions of the
Lord's Prayer. Matthew gives us, "Forgive us our *debts* as we forgive..."
(Matt. 6:12), and in Luke the same prayer is recorded, "Forgive us our *sins* as
we forgive..." (Luke 11:4). Marshall observes that the presence of these two
words in parallel texts demonstrates the Semitic background of the story (Marshall, 554). Simply stated, the first (debts) are the believer's unfulfilled duties in
discipleship and obedience; the second (sins) are the overt evil acts that the
believer commits. It has long been noted that the Aramaic word *ḥōbā'*, which
occurs in both texts in the Old Syriac, carries both meanings. If we can assume
an Aramaic background to this text (as we surely can with the Lord's Prayer),
then quite likely here also the original would have had *ḥōbā'* in both texts. A
sensitive translator into Greek may have known the two-sided nature of the word,
and, finding no equivalent in Greek, he gave us half of the content of *ḥōbā'* in
the first stanza and the other half in the second. Irrespective of this suggestion,
we do have this two-sided nature of evil expressed in the words for sin that are
parallel in these verses. The evil of which the political enthusiasts are urged to
repent is described first as "sins" (v. 2) and then as "debts" (v. 4).

5. The stunning climax of the twice-repeated refrain is the call for the
listeners themselves to repent, lest they also perish. This unexpected thrust gives
us an illustration of the courage of Jesus, an understanding of a part of the reason
why he was rejected by his community, and a profound insight into a part of his
response to the oppressed struggling for justice. When Jeremiah opposed the
political climate of his day he was protected by influential friends and his life was
spared (Jer. 26:24). So far as we know, Jesus did not have powerful friends who
could or would protect him. Nicodemus' one feeble attempt illustrates the point
(John 7:50). In studying Luke 13:1–5 with Middle Eastern classes, the present
writer has often had students marvel that Jesus was not physically attacked on the
spot. This call for repentance is thrown in the face of nationalistic enthusiasts

who stand in opposition to Roman oppression. Those who fight for a just cause often assume that the struggle for the cause makes them righteous. It does not. The more intense the struggle for justice the more the oppressed tend to assume their own righteousness. This assumption of righteousness at times expresses itself as an arrogance that refuses any criticism. The subconscious rationale seems to be, "Our cause is righteous, thus we are righteous. Furthermore, after all that we have suffered, how *dare* you inflict any more wounds on us by your criticism." Attitudes of this type have on occasion surfaced on both sides of the barbed wire in the Middle East in the past thirty years. Only the strong and the brave can dare to endure the wrath of such oppressed and turn the attention away from criticism of the hated enemy to painful self-criticism with the warning, "Unless you repent, you will *all* likewise perish." In the synagogue in Nazareth there is a similar refusal on the part of Jesus to identify with the nationalism of his day. There he chooses two foreigners (one a woman) as illustrations of the kinds of people who through faith will receive the benefits of the now present kingdom of God. There the listening audience is so upset that they try to kill him. Here in Luke 13 we have no record of the audience reaction but can assume similar hostility. Anyone who would recast Jesus as a political revolutionary must not fail to take seriously the confrontation here in Luke 13.

This same call for repentance can be seen on its deepest level as a profound concern for the welfare of those whose outrage he refuses to reinforce. Jesus' speech should not be read simply as a rejection of the nationalistic struggle, nor as a concern for things "spiritual" rather than political. Rather he seems to be saying at least, "You want me to condemn evil in Pilate. I am not talking to Pilate. He is not here. I am talking to you. Evil forces are at work in your movement that will destroy you, Pilate or no Pilate. *You* must repent or *all* of you will be destroyed by those forces." Among those who struggle for justice there develops the attitude, "We are the angels and they are the devils." Blessed is the movement that is willing to listen to a courageous voice quietly insisting, "There are devils among us and angels among them. *We* must repent." He does not tell them to submit to Pilate. He is not acquiescing to Roman oppression. Rather he bravely demonstrates a deep concern for the people in front of him who will destroy themselves and all around them if they do not repent.

Finally, what is the precise response Jesus is hoping to evoke from the nationalists who bring him the atrocity story? At least this: "We ask him to look at evil in Pilate. He wants us to see evil in our own hearts. We must repent. If we do not, that evil will destroy us."

What then comprises the cluster of theological motifs found in this Dominical response to the atrocity story? We can identify at least the following:

1. Sin is defined both by evil acts and duties left unperformed.
2. There is no one-to-one relationship between sin and suffering. Easy theological judgments about the reasons for natural and political disasters must be rejected.

3. Any intense political movement must look deep within its own soul to repent of its own evil, lest it destroy itself and the very people it seeks to serve.

4. The compassion of Jesus reaches out to all who suffer, not only to those who are politically oppressed.

THE BARREN FIG TREE (Luke 13:6-9)

A clear identification of listeners is made in Luke 12:54. We have noted a slight shift of audience in 13:1, which reads, "And some came at that time who told him. . . ." Then 13:10 gives another clear break in setting with the move to a scene in the synagogue. Thus the text assumes a continuity between 13:1-5 and 13:6-9. The parable in verses 6-9 is comprised of five stanzas. The literary structure is as follows:

1	A man had a *fig tree planted* in his vineyard.	PLANT
	And he came seeking fruit on it	SEEK FRUIT
	and he found none.	NO FRUIT
2	And he said to the vinedresser,	MASTER SPEAKS
	"Behold! These three years	THREE YEARS
	I have come seeking fruit on this fig tree	SEEK FRUIT
	and I find none.	NO FRUIT
3	*Dig it out!*	DIG OUT
	Why should it exhaust the ground?"	SAVE THE GROUND
4	But he answering said to him,	VINEDRESSER SPEAKS
	"Master! Forgive it this year also	ONE YEAR
	until I dig around it	HELP FRUIT-BEARING
	and spread on manure.	HELP FRUIT-BEARING
5	And if it bears fruit in the future—	FIND FRUIT?
	And if not,	NO FRUIT
	dig it out."	DIG OUT

The overall structure of the parable is clear and only slightly modified from patterns we have observed in other parables. The "plant, seek fruit, no fruit" themes of stanza one are balanced by "find fruit, no fruit, dig out" in the last stanza. Thus the parable begins with a planting and ends with a threatened digging up of what was planted. Stanzas two and four are parallel and match each other almost line for line. Stanza two could roughly be called "the problem" and stanza four, "the hoped-for solution." As is usually the case when the inversion principle is used, the climax occurs in the center and is then mirrored thematically in some way at the end. This literary device is used here in that the motif "dig it out" occurs in the middle and again at the end. The critical point of turning occurs, as is usual in such structures, just past the center. At that point the voice of mercy pleads for additional grace. The literary structure is simple, balanced, and artistically satisfying. Each stanza will be examined in turn.

Stanza One

A man had a *fig tree planted* in his vineyard.
And he came seeking fruit on it
and he found none.

PLANT
SEEK FRUIT
NO FRUIT

In Joel 1:7 the close association of the fig and the vine is seen where the prophet says of the locust horde,

It has laid waste my vines,
and splintered my fig trees.

And again in 1:12,

The vine withers,
the fig tree languishes.

Thus, finding a fig tree in a vineyard is not unusual. In Isaiah 5:1–7 we have the classical Old Testament parable of the vineyard. There the symbols are identified. The owner of the vineyard is the Lord of hosts, and the vineyard itself is the house of Israel (Isa. 5:7). We can assume that the same symbolic identification would have immediately been made in this parable by Jesus' audience. There is then a crucial divergence of symbols. Isaiah discusses all the vines in the vineyard collectively. Jesus' parable concentrates on one plant in the vineyard that is a fig tree, not a grape vine. This selection may be in order to draw attention to the fact that he is discussing one particular tree and not the vineyard as a whole (in contrast to Isaiah). Also it may be because the fig in Palestine bears fruit ten months of the year so that at almost any time the owner can find fruit on it. In any case, the vine and the fig are closely related all through the Old Testament and together are a symbol of peace. For in time of peace each man will sit under his own vine and his own fig tree (Mic. 4:4; Zech. 3:10). Then, finally, the fig *in its first fruit* is Hosea's symbol of a pure, innocent, responsive people.

Like grapes in the wilderness,
I found Israel.
Like the first fruit on the fig tree
in its first season,
I saw your fathers (9:10).

Also, in 9:16 failure to bear fruit is used as a symbol for the idolatrous days in which Hosea lived. Thus Jesus could have had a variety of reasons for choosing a fig tree rather than a vine for this particular parable.

Whenever there is a clear literary background for a parable it becomes crucial to see what Jesus does as he reworks well-known material. In this case, the basic symbolism is unmistakable because it is already identified in the prototype in Isaiah 5:7, as we have noted. We find no reason to reject this same symbolism in the present parable. Thus the owner is again God and the vineyard (not the tree) is "the house of Israel." The New Testament parable of the vineyard (20:9–16) has some of this same background. In the New Testament the text is specifically interpreted by the evangelist as spoken against the scribes and the chief priests. Luke 20:9 reads, "The scribes and the chief priests . . . perceived that he had told this parable against *them*." Thus the evangelists understood that parable to be against the *leadership* of the nation, not the nation itself. In Isaiah's parable the *vineyard* (the nation) is deliberately torn down by the owner (Isa. 5:5–6). By contrast, in the present parable of the Barren Fig Tree, the master is concerned for the fruitfulness of the vineyard and thus asks some very serious questions about a particular tree (the fig). It is unfruitful and is thus bleeding strength from the vineyard itself by its continuing presence. The master acts to *preserve* the health of the vineyard, not to destroy it. Thus in harmony with the clear symbolism of Luke 20:9–16 and Isaiah 5:1–7 we would see the problem discussed in this parable to be the crisis of fruitless leadership within the nation, not judgment on the nation of Israel itself (against Montefiore, *Gospels*, II, 965).

The text also preserves an authentic note of traditional culture. The landowner of the past did not get his hands dirty. Even so in this story. The vineyard owner does not himself plant a fig, but rather has it planted. The point is theologically insignificant but gives a stamp of authenticity to the parable as a story that fits Middle Eastern culture.

Thus, in a simple and straightforward manner, the problem is stated in the opening stanza.

Stanza Two

And he said to the vinedresser,	MASTER SPEAKS
"Behold! These three years	THREE YEARS
I have come seeking fruit on this fig tree	SEEK FRUIT
and I find none."	NO FRUIT

The owner and the vinedresser cooperated in the planting in the first stanza. Now they cooperate in the evaluation of the problem.

The common understanding of the time sequence is that the tree would have three years in which to grow. Then for three years the fruit was considered forbidden, according to Leviticus 19:23. The fruit of the fourth year (that is, the seventh year of the tree's life) was considered clean and was offered to the Lord (Lev. 19:24). The details in this brief parable are scanty, but the probable intent is that the master is seeking this seventh-year fruit specified in Leviticus 19:23 as an offering to the Lord. Indeed, he has been seeking it for three years. The master would not "come *seeking*" the unpurified fruit of years four to six of the tree's life. Thus for three years he sought the first fruits and has been disappointed three times. Now nine years have passed since the planting of the tree. The situation seems hopeless. If our identification of the symbolism of the parable is correct this stanza is saying that quite enough time has passed for the current leadership of the nation to produce the fruits expected of it (probably the fruits of repentance; cf. Luke 3:8). The master has waited patiently, long beyond the expected time of fruit-bearing. His conclusion is set out in stanza three.

Stanza Three

> "*Dig it out!*   DIG OUT
> Why should it exhaust the ground?"   SAVE GROUND

Not only does the disappointing tree fail to produce fruit and take up space that could be used for other useful plants, but it drains strength out of the ground, thereby exhausting it. In his concern for good soil in the good vineyard the master orders the fig tree to be dug out.

Here an authentic note in the story appears. In the West, woodsmen cut down trees. In the Middle East, the tree is "*dug out.*" The tree, with its stump and some of its root cluster, falls as one block and is removed. This agricultural practice is reflected in the text of Luke 3:9, where John says, "Even now the ax is laid to the *root* of the trees" (not the trunk). So the verb in 13:7 (*katargeō*) literally means "dig out," not "cut down." Thus the Palestinian agricultural scene, accurately reflected in the text, gives a vivid picture of a radical elimination of this unfruitful tree. The unfruitful leadership of the nation is to be rooted out. At this point in the parable a dramatic shift takes place.

Stanza Four

> But he answering said to him,   VINEDRESSER SPEAKS
> "Master! Forgive it this year also   ONE YEAR
> until I dig around it   HELP FRUIT-BEARING
> and spread on manure."   HELP FRUIT-BEARING

In biblical literature, when the stanzas relate to each other in an inverted fashion, there is often a crucial shift just past the center of the literary structure (Bailey, *Poet*, 48, 50f., 53, 61f., 72–74). This important feature, as we have noted, occurs in this parable. The speech of the master outlines the problem and is carefully matched by the speech of the vinedresser, who suggests a hoped-for solution. The prototypical parable in Isaiah 5 has *no* offer of grace. There the parable moves from the disappointment of the vineyard owner when a good crop is not forthcoming to *immediate* judgment. The owner announces that he will "remove its hedge . . . break down its wall . . . make it a waste . . . and command the clouds that they rain no rain upon it" (Isa. 5:5–6). The judgment is harsh, enacted by the owner himself and carried out at once. Some such final scene was surely expected for Jesus' version of this classical parable. The point of turning in this text is twofold. The fig tree is offered a period of grace and special attention is planned for it: the vinedresser will dig around it and add manure. Thus, when compared with the Song of the Vineyard in Isaiah, this parable has a striking emphasis on mercy that is usually overlooked in the light of the motif of judgment.

Another point of literary comparison is the story of Ahikar in the Pseudepigrapha (8:35, Charles, II, 775). The part of the story in question may be a later addition (Marshall, 555), yet it is of interest. In the story, Ahikar has a wayward adopted son who promises to reform. Ahikar tells the boy that he is like a palm tree beside a river that cast its fruit into the river. The owner decided to cut it down. The tree complained, offering to produce carobs if given one more year. The owner skeptically replied, ''Thou hast not been industrious in what is thine own, and how wilt thou be industrious in what is not thine own?'' (ibid.). Here the tree itself does the pleading, and more important we are given a negative answer. The reader is left with a strong negative impression—nothing can really be done—the situation is hopeless. Not so with the parable of Jesus. In Jesus' parable the fig tree is to be given one last chance. Again the theme of mercy is prominent.

The parable has two distinctive colloquialisms. The first is grammatical and the second cultural. The parable is told in the past tense. Suddenly in verse 8 there is an historical present, rare in Luke. That is, the text suddenly shifts to the present tense and reads, ''Answering he says (sic) to him. . . .'' This shift adds a colloquial vividness to the telling of the story and suggests that Luke is using traditional material (Marshall, 555). Then in Luke 20:19 both the people and the leaders understand that the parable of the vineyard is told against the scribes and chief priests. If our assumption is correct that this parable is also told against the religious leadership and that this would have been immediately sensed by the listening audience, then we have here a somewhat humorous peasant turn of phrase. The word ''manure'' (koprion) occurs only here in the New Testament. It is not the kind of language that is ordinarily used in religious illustrations. The vinedresser could have offered to spread on fresh earth, or water the tree each day, or even prune it back. If the fig tree represents the scribes and the chief priests, and the parable talks of the need to cast on some manure, then we have a clear case of what the comedians call ''insult humor.'' What they need is a little manure spread around them. The original audience no doubt found the imagery humorous. Mild irreverence for people in positions of power is usually appreciated by a popular audience. With such details the sparkle and vitality of the parable appears along with its unmistakable cutting edge.

Christian allegorizers have had a field day with this parable all through the centuries. The ''three years'' have become everything from ''law, prophets, and gospel'' to the three years of the ministry of Jesus. In such cases the allegorization is misleading but harmless. But in this stanza the vinedresser has often been identified with Jesus, who is then seen arguing with God the Father. Such an identification could hardly have been imagined by the original audience nor intended by Jesus. The Christian allegorizer begins with his theology of the Trinity and from that makes the above identification. But when he does so, God the Father is seen as harsh and judgmental, and Jesus appears as gracious and loving. Thus a split is caused in the Trinity. For centuries Islam has characterized Christian theology as tritheistic; when such interpretations surface, unmistakable cracks appear in the concept of the unity of God to the extent that the Islamic accusation has some validity. If we return to the parabolic prototype in Isaiah 5, the owner is the farmer who both plants the vineyard and then tears it down when it produces wild grapes. Here two people debate the fate of the vineyard among themselves. It is far more appropriate to understand the debate as between mercy and judgment. Manson observes,

> The conversation between the owner of the vineyard and his workmen is reminiscent of Rabbinical passages in which the attributes of God debate, the attribute of justice with the attribute of mercy. If God dealt with Israel by strict justice, Israel would perish. But he does not. He gives another chance. And if it is madness to fly in the face of His justice, it is desperate wickedness to flout His mercy (Manson, *Sayings*, 275).

We disagree with Manson's identification of the fig tree with Israel, but agree with his understanding of the debate between justice and mercy. Judgment requires that the tree be dug out for the stated reasons. Mercy pleads for more grace and a second chance. The same tension is reflected all through the Old Testament and is intensely focused in prophets like Hosea, who can thunder harsh oracles of judgment in one verse and in the next say,

> How can I give you up, O Ephraim! . . .
> My heart recoils within me,
>   my compassion grows warm and tender (Hos. 11:8-9).

In this parable mercy and judgment are given voices. They are personified dramatically by the owner and the vinedresser who struggle *together* over the unfruitful vine. The tension itself is deep within the heart of God.

The theology of the Song of the Vineyard in Isaiah 5 is powerfully reinforced by the use of wordplay. The last part of verse 7 reads,

> and he looked for *mishpaṭ* (justice)
>   and behold, *mishpaḥ* (bloodshed)
> for *ṣedhaqah* (righteousness)
>   but behold, *ṣe'aqah* (a cry).

In Jesus' dialogue of the vineyard there is quite likely a similar use of wordplay. This wordplay surfaces in the Old Syriac version of the parable. Given that Syriac and Aramaic are dialects of the same language, this wordplay may well have been present in the original Aramaic of the parable itself. It is as follows:

> dig it out   = *fsūqīh*
> forgive it/let it alone = *shbūqīh*

So the vinedresser pleads not *fsūqīh* (dig it out) but rather *shbūqīh* (forgive it). Thus the thrust of the main point of each voice (grace and judgment) is perhaps reinforced and made unforgettable by a skillfully constructed wordplay.

Stanza Five

> "And if it bears fruit in the future—   FIND FRUIT?
> and if not,   NO FRUIT
> dig it out."   DIG OUT

The Greek phrase *eis to mellon* is often translated "next year." But the identical construction in I Timothy 6:19 is translated "for the future." The word *mellon* is commonly used for the future (Bauer, 502), which may be a better translation in this text. The voice of grace and mercy is talking. The vinedresser is pleading for grace (give it more time) and mercy (forgive it). These elements are strengthened if a specific time for the "execution" is not stated. The time of the future judgment is left unspecified.

In the second half of the verse, the "then" of the if-then construction (the apodosis) is missing. The RSV and many other translations supply the missing words "well and good," which are implied but not stated. The construction is classical (Marshall, 556) but the reason for it may be literary. In stanza four the vinedresser suggests two horticultural acts in an attempt to revive the fruitless tree. He will "dig around it" and "spread on manure." From a literary point of view, this gives the fourth stanza four lines to match the four lines of stanza two. The same concern for balanced stanzas may be at work in stanza five. The apodosis may have been omitted so that stanza five would have only three lines to match stanza one with its three semantic units. In any case, the meaning is clear; after the "acts of redemption" are completed and sufficient time for renewal is given, the fig tree must respond. If it does not, judgment will be the only option left. The health of the vineyard is too important and the master's expectation of fruit too strong to leave an unproductive tree indefinitely occupying good ground and sapping its strength.

Even so, the salvation offered has a special quality to it. It comes exclusively from the outside. The voice of mercy pleads for forgiveness yet one more time. Then redemptive *acts* that may lead to renewal (the production of fruit) are proposed. The word ordinarily translated "let it alone" (v. 8) is the New Testament word for "forgiveness," and there is no misunderstanding about what Jesus is discussing. Forgiveness can be offered yet again, but that will mean *nothing* unless some help for the tree comes from the outside. Renewal cannot come from within the resources of the tree itself. It cannot gather the strength it needs from its own roots. The *vinedresser* must act to save the tree and at the same time the tree must respond to those acts or they are of no avail. In this simple agricultural picture can we not overhear the great themes of God's own mighty redemptive acts?

Here, as in previous parables, we do not know what happens. This story is also open-ended. Does the owner grant the reprieve? Does the tree respond? We are not told. The action freezes like a TV spot and the reader/listener must respond.

In conclusion, then, what specific response is sought from the original audience by the telling of the parable? We suggest that the original audience is pressed to understand:

> The present spiritual leadership of the nation is fruitless. Judgment threatens. God in His mercy will act to redeem. If there is no response, judgment will be the only alternative. His love for the community of faith is too deep for it to be otherwise.

The cluster of theological motifs present in the parable include the following:

1. The spiritual leaders of the household of faith are planted in "God's vineyard" and are expected to produce fruit for Him.
2. When that leadership is fruitless it not only fails in its own obedience but also sterilizes the community around it. God cares for the community and will not tolerate this situation indefinitely.
3. Mercy is extended to unfruitful leadership in the form of forgiveness and renewing grace.
4. Only in the grace of God, freely offered to the fruitless leaders, is renewal possible. God acts to forgive and renew. These acts come from beyond the leaders, who cannot renew themselves.
5. God's offer of mercy must evoke a response from within or renewal will not take place and judgment will be inevitable.

Thus the two units of tradition are closely related. The first deals with the suffering of the community that results from the Roman leaders. The people are called on to repent. The second deals with the barrenness in the community that results from the failures of the national leaders, who need forgiveness and grace. Thus in the first (13:1–5) the people must repent. In the second (13:6–9) the leaders need forgiveness. In each, politics and repentance (forgiveness) are related in ways that instruct the faithful in every age.

Chapter 6

THE GREAT BANQUET
(Luke 14:15-24)

Luke 14 and 15 have in them some of the greatest passages in all of Scripture. Here the unqualified offer of grace to sinners is set forth in all of its majesty. Often the theological masterpiece of the parable of the Prodigal Son is allowed to overshadow that of the Great Banquet, which deserves equal attention. We will examine in turn the literary background, setting, structure, and culture of the parable. The interpretation will attempt to take all of these into consideration.

In Luke this parable is told at a banquet where the people recline. Our Arabic translations, following the Greek text, give us "reclined" rather than the RSV "sat at table." What is the precise setting? Jeremias has pointed out that with the exceptions of Luke 24:30 and Mark 16:14 the word "recline" in the Gospels always means either a meal out-of-doors or a banquet of some kind (Jeremias, *Eucharistic*, 48f.). Here we have a banquet. But was there a table? In the Old Testament the presence of a table for a meal seems to assume wealth or rank (cf. II Sam. 9:7; I Kings 13:20). The same can be said for the New Testament. There are many references to meals and eating but a physical table is mentioned only four times. It occurs in the story of the Canaanite woman who humbly suggests that the dogs can eat crumbs from the master's table (cf. Matt. 15:27 and parallels). The rich man in the story of Lazarus has a table (Luke 16:21). There is a table in the upper room (Luke 22:21) and in the eschatological messianic banquet hall (Luke 22:30). Granted, the meals held out-of-doors at which Jesus and the disciples "reclined" were not eaten on tables. Yet it is perhaps best to assume (as we did in Luke 7:36) that here also the guests are reclining on couches around a low table. The parable tells of a "great banquet" where property owners are the chosen guests. The setting is the house of a ruler (14:1) who is most certainly wealthy enough to be in the class of people who recline on couches around tables and not on the floor in peasant style. Thus, "reclined around tables" would perhaps best represent the scene. We must visualize relatively wealthy people reclining in Greco-Roman style at a formal banquet.

The parable itself is introduced by a pious outburst from a fellow diner (14:15) who says, "Blessed is he who shall eat bread in the kingdom of God!" With this statement we are clearly in the world of Palestinian speech and culture. "To eat bread" is a classical Middle Eastern idiom meaning "to eat a meal." It has long been identified as a Hebraism (Plummer, 360). T. W. Manson regards this introductory statement as "probably too good to be invented" (*Sayings,* 129). Thus, the guest reclining with Jesus introduces the subject of *eating* in the kingdom. Here as elsewhere the banquet is a symbol for salvation (Marshall, 587). This salvation culminates at the end of history with a final great banquet. That last great banquet is commonly referred to as the messianic banquet of the end times. So important is this latter theme as a background for an understanding of the parable that it must be examined briefly.

The idea of the sacred meal with God is deeply embedded in the Old Testament. In Psalm 23:5 we are told that God Himself spreads a banquet for the one who trusts in Him. Even more informative for our passage is Isaiah 25:6-9. This passage is most likely poetry that uses very old poetic forms (as confirmed to me by William Holladay of Andover-Newton Theological School in private correspondence). Our translation of the text is as follows:

	Text (Isaiah 25:6–9)	*Major Themes*
6	And He will make, Yahweh of Hosts,	MAKE—A BANQUET
	for *all* the peoples on this mountain	ALL PEOPLES
	a fat banquet, a wine banquet,	
	a banquet of juicy marrow, of good wine.	
7	And He will swallow on this mountain	SWALLOW—VEIL
	the face of the covering,	ALL PEOPLES/NATIONS
	the covering over *all* the peoples,	
	and the veil spread over *all* the nations.	
8	He will swallow up death forever.	
	And the Lord Yahweh will wipe away tears	SWALLOW—DEATH
	from off *all* faces.	ALL FACES
	And the reproach of His people	
	He will take away from upon *all* the earth,	TAKE AWAY—REPROACH
	for Yahweh has spoken.	ALL THE EARTH
9	It will be said on that day,	
	"Lo, this is our *God*;	GOD
	we have *waited* for Him	WAIT
	that he might *save* us.	SAVE
	This is *Yahweh*;	GOD
	we have *waited* for Him;	WAIT
	let us be glad and rejoice in His *salvation*."	SAVE

In this remarkable text a number of important themes are brought together. Salvation is described in terms of a great banquet, which shall be for *all* the peoples/nations. The gentiles will participate after God has swallowed up death and their veil. The people swallow the banquet, God swallows up death and the covering. The veil is not removed, rather it is destroyed. Ordinarily the nations who come to the Lord must come bringing gifts (cf. Isa. 18:7; 60:4-7; Ps. 96:8). Here the banquet is pure grace—the participants from the nations bring nothing. The food offered is rich fare of the kind that is the food of kings. Verse 9 is often seen as a separate piece of tradition. Yet it *is* attached here by the editor and thus the waiting for the God who comes to save is emphasized. There is also the striking occurrence of five cases of *"all"* in verses 6-8.

This banquet theme was developed in the intertestamental period and understood to be related to the coming of the Messiah (cf. Jeremias, *Eucharistic*, 233f.), but somehow the idea that the gentiles would be invited to attend was muted. The Aramaic version of the passage, the Targum, paraphrases verse 6 as follows:

> Yahweh of Hosts will make for all the peoples in this mountain a meal; and though they suppose it is an honour, it will be a shame for them, and great plagues, plagues from which they will be unable to escape, plagues whereby they will come to their end (quoted by Gray, I, 429f.).

Clearly the vision of Isaiah is here lost. In I Enoch 62:1-16 the "kings and the mighty and the exalted and those who rule the earth" (obviously the gentiles) will fall down before the Son of man, who will drive them out from his presence. He will "deliver them to the angels for punishment" (v. 11); "they shall be a spectacle for the righteous" (v. 12); and "his sword is drunk with their blood" (v. 12). After this destruction of sinners the righteous and the elect shall eat with the Son of man forever and ever (v. 14, Charles, II, 227f.). Then, in the Qumran community, the great banquet was specifically connected with the coming of the Messiah. This is described in a short work called "The Messianic Rule" (1QSa 2:11-22). In this remarkable passage we read of how, in the last days, the Messiah will gather with the whole congregation to eat bread and drink wine. The wise, the intelligent, and the perfect men will gather with Him. These will all be assembled by rank. Verse 2:11 reads,

> And then (the Mess)iah of Israel shall (come),
> and the chiefs of the (clans of Israel) shall sit before him,
> (each) in the order of his dignity
> according to (his place) in their camps and marches (Vermes, 121).

The specifics of these ranks are carefully spelled out. First are the judges and officers; then come the chiefs of thousands, fifties, and tens; finally there are the Levites. No one is allowed in who is "smitten in his flesh, or paralyzed in his feet or hands, or lame, or blind, or deaf, or dumb, or smitten in his flesh with a visible blemish" (*ibid.*, 120). All gentiles are obviously excluded and, along with them, all imperfect Jews. Thus, Isaiah's open-ended vision has been blurred if not eliminated. For him the great day was coming when the veil of the gentiles would be destroyed and they would sit down with God's people. Enoch has the gentiles excluded, and the Qumran community in addition rejects all Jewish unrighteous along with those with any physical blemish. The pious guest in Luke 14:15 certainly assumes something of this background. Regarding the opinions of Jesus, the reader of Luke's Gospel already has an indication of his views on this topic from reading Luke 13:29, which is also an important part of the background of the parable before us. This verse is set in a structure which can be seen as follows:

Luke 13:28-34

The Ingathering for the Banquet

There will be weeping and chattering of teeth
when you see Abraham and Isaac and Jacob
and all the prophets in the kingdom of God,
and you yourselves thrown out.

And they *will come* from East and West
and from North and South
and *sit at table* in the kingdom of God.

And behold, some are last who will be first,
and some are first who will be last.

The Death of Jesus

At that very hour some Pharisees came and said to him,
"Leave and go away from here,
for Herod wants *to kill you.*"

The Great Day

And he said to them, "Go tell that fox,

'Behold I cast out demons and perfect cures
   today and tomorrow,
       and the *third day* I am made perfect.

The Great Day

Nevertheless it is necessary for me
   today and tomorrow
       and the *following/coming day* to go on my way.

The Death of Jesus

For it is not acceptable that a prophet die away from Jerusalem.'
Jerusalem, Jerusalem, *killing* the prophets
and *stoning* those who are sent to you.

The Ingathering

How often would I have *gathered* your children
as a hen *gathers* her brood under her wings,
and you would not" (cf. Bailey, *Poet,* 81).

The passage opens with the messianic banquet.

Three interlocking themes are stated and then repeated in an inverse fashion. In the preceding verses (13:23–28) we are told that in the final fulfillment of all things, some who think they are accepted will plead specifically, "We ate and drank in your presence" (13:26). That is, they will claim to have participated in table fellowship with him. But no, "I do not know you," comes the answer. Abraham, Isaac, and Jacob and all the prophets will be there, but these bystanders will be rejected. Then comes the double repetition of the threefold theme of the *ingathering* for the great banquet, a reference to the *death* of Jesus, and the *third* day (see above, p. 91).

The materials are clearly edited into this present form by Luke or his source. Each of the major themes is stated and then repeated in a reverse fashion. Significantly some of the motifs in Isaiah 25 reappear. There *will be* an ingathering. The faithful will come from all four corners of the compass. A dramatic reversal of positions is anticipated, for the last will be first, and some who are first will be last. Jerusalem is presented as the place where Jesus most earnestly desired to gather the faithful for the banquet, but they have refused. Here the ingathering for the messianic banquet is discussed, along with the twice-repeated theme of the death of Jesus, and a reference to his being made perfect on "the third day." These latter two themes are not repeated in our parable and so lie outside of the scope of this study, but are of importance for an understanding of the theology of the Travel Narrative as a whole, and for a full understanding of the messianic banquet in Luke, as well as Luke's theology of the cross. For our purposes we note specifically that Jesus anticipates a great eschatological banquet. Jerusalem's children are invited and they refuse. Some who expect to be there are turned away. The guests will come in from the four points of the compass.

To summarize the literary background of our parable we can see the great banquet of God described in inclusive terms in Isaiah 25. The Targum of the same passage reverses its terms. Enoch sees the gentiles excluded. The Qumran community turns the scene into an ordered banquet where only the worthy can attend and they by rank. In Luke 13 we read of a great ingathering and banquet with the patriarchs. Some have refused an earnest invitation. Many who expect to be there will be rejected. The guests come from the four corners of the earth. Lucan composition relates the "third day" and the death of Jesus to the banquet. With this Old Testament, intertestamental, and New Testament background in mind, we can proceed to the text.

The pious banqueter invokes a blessing on those who will be accepted on that great day. The expected response is something like, "O Lord, may we be among the righteous and be counted without blemish, worthy to sit with the men of renown on that great day." Rather than a traditional pious invocation, Jesus responds with a parable, whose literary form is as follows (cf. p. 93).

The parable begins with a reference to the banquet itself and those originally invited. We have a clear case of *inclusio* in that these same themes, with the same language, recur at the end. After the introduction the dramatic action

And he said to him,
"A man once gave a great banquet,   GREAT BANQUET
and he invited many.   MANY INVITED

1   And he sent his servant at the hour of the banquet to say, 'Come!
                                                     DO THIS
         Because all is now ready!'   BECAUSE OF THIS
         But they all alike began to make excuses.   EXCUSES

2   The first said to him, 'I have bought a field,   I DID THIS
         and I must go out and see it.   I MUST DO THIS
         I pray you have me excused.'   EXCUSE ME

3   And another said, 'I have bought five yoke of oxen,   I DID THIS
         and I go to test them.   I MUST DO THIS
         I pray you have me excused.'   EXCUSE ME

4   And another said, 'I have married a bride,   I DID THIS
         and therefore—   THUS I MUST
         I cannot come.'   NOT COME

5   So the servant came and reported this to his master.
     Then the householder in anger said to his servant, 'Go out
         quickly,   MASTER—GO
         into the streets and lanes of the city.   TO STREETS
         Bring in the poor, maimed, blind, and lame.' FILL UP

6   And the servant said, 'Sir,   SERVANT
         what you commanded has been done,   I WENT
         and still there is room.'   NOT FULL

7   And the master said to the servant, 'Go out,   MASTER—GO
         into the highways and hedges,   TO HIGHWAYS
         and compel to enter, that my house may be filled.'   FILL UP

For I tell you (pl.),
none of those men who were invited   THOSE INVITED
shall taste my banquet."   MY BANQUET

divides into seven speeches. We could even call the parable "The Banquet of the
Seven Speeches." These seven fall naturally into seven stanzas (almost seven
scenes) with certain key ideas repeating in the first four and then other key ideas
repeating in the last three. The master gives three speeches. Each of them begins
with a command related to the gathering of the guests. There are two invitations
to the original guests at the beginning of the parable, and two invitations
to outsiders (although to different people) at the end. The parable needs to be
examined one stanza at a time. To this examination we now turn.

INTRODUCTION

And he said to him,
"A man once gave a great banquet,   GREAT BANQUET
and he invited many."   MANY INVITED

STANZA ONE—A BANQUET PREPARED

"And he sent his servant at the hour of the banquet to say, 'Come!

	DO THIS
Because all is now ready!'	BECAUSE OF THIS
But they all alike began to make excuses."	EXCUSE ME

A great banquet is naturally hosted by a great man. The guests would be his peers and associates. This first invitation is serious and, as we will observe below, acceptance of it is a firm commitment. In the first stanza of the parable there is introduced a sequence of three ideas that will be repeated four times in a row. This sequence we have tried to indicate with the words at the right of the text. They are: DO THIS, BECAUSE OF THIS, and EXCUSE ME. The repetition of these three ideas will prove significant as we proceed. Then also, we notice two invitations.

A rabbinic commentary on Lamentations refers to the people of Jerusalem and notes that none of them would attend a banquet unless he was invited twice (*Midrash Rabbah Lam.* 4:2, Sonc., 216). This has often been taken as a background of the double invitation of the parable under discussion. However, the editors of the above text observe that the double invitation is "to make sure that the first invitation had not been sent to him in mistake." As the next paragraph illustrates, "such an error may have a tragic sequel" (*ibid.*, n. 5). In the text of the Midrash there follows a long story of a Jerusalemite who gives a dinner and sends out an invitation to a friend. By accident the invitation is delivered to an enemy and tragedy results. The entire context is irrelevant to the parable under discussion. Rather the double invitation is in perfect harmony with traditional Middle Eastern custom, which still persists in conservative areas. A village host must provide meat for a banquet. The meat will be killed and cooked on the basis of the number of guests. A host sends out his invitations and receives acceptance. He then decides on the killing/butchering of a chicken or two (for 2–4 guests), or a duck (for 5–8), or a kid (10–15 acceptances), or a sheep (if there are 15–35 people), or a calf (35–75). That is, the decision regarding the kind of meat and the amount is made mostly on the basis of the number of accepted invitations. Once the countdown starts it cannot be stopped. The appropriate animal is killed and must be eaten that night. The guests who accept the invitation are duty-bound to appear. The host completes his preparations. Then at the "hour of the banquet" a servant is sent out with the traditional message, "Come, all is now ready," meaning the meat is cooked and we are ready for you. Ibrāhīm Saʿīd has caught this in his comment on this verse:

> This is according to the accepted custom of noble men in the East who extend an invitation sometime before the banquet and then repeat the invitation by means of a messenger at the hour of the banquet (Saʿīd, 382).

Thomson confirms Saʿīd:

> If a sheikh, bey, or emeer invites, he always sends a servant to call you at the proper time. This servant often repeats the very formula mentioned in Luke

xiv. 17: Tefŭddŭlŭ, al 'asha hâder—Come, for the supper is ready (Thomson, I, 178).

Furthermore, Thomson finds the parable, "in all its details, in close conformity to the customs of this country" (*ibid.*, 179). The Greek text supports this cultural background. The present imperative "Come!" means literally "continue coming." The guests have begun their action by accepting the invitation. They continue it by responding to the messenger. Indeed, beginning with Esther (6:14) down through the first century, this double invitation can be documented in both Jewish and Roman works (Marshall, 587f.). Thus, the two invitations are in full harmony with the customs of the times. The initial acceptance obliges the guest to respond to the summons at the "hour of the banquet."

The language already triggers in the listeners' ears the rumblings of great events. "The *hour* of the banquet" approaches and the freighted message goes out, "Come! All is ready!" The theological intent is unmistakable. The hour of the messianic banquet has arrived. All is prepared, invitations are out; let those already invited attend the feast and enjoy the fellowship and nourishment of the long anticipated repast. But no! Here the parable takes a totally unexpected turn.

The text literally says, "They all from one began to make excuses." The phrase "from one" may be identified as an Aramaism meaning "all at once" (Creed, 191). This is supported by the reading from the Old Syriac version. Or it may be a Greek phrase meaning "unanimously" (Marshall, 588). We can catch the surprise registered in the idiom. There is also insult. Surely a last minute refusal to attend a great banquet is bad taste in any culture. In the Middle East it is considered a rude affront to the host. Thomson is again helpful: "It is true now, as then, that to refuse is a high insult to the maker of the feast" (Thomson, I, 178; cf. also Marshall, 588). Everything was flowing smoothly, the invitations were accepted, the animal butchered, the meat cooked, the guests summoned—and all at once—excuses! This brings us to the second stanza.

STANZA TWO—THE REAL ESTATE EXPERT

"The first said to him, 'I have bought a field,	I DID THIS
and I must go out and see it.	THUS I MUST DO THIS
I pray you have me excused.' "	EXCUSE ME

We observe the same repetition of themes: I did this (line one), thus I must do this (line two), therefore excuse me (line three). The statement is a bold-faced lie and everyone knows it. No one buys a field in the Middle East without knowing every square foot of it like the palm of his hand. The springs, wells, stone walls, trees, paths, and anticipated rainfall are all well-known long before a discussion of the purchase is even begun. Indeed, these items must be known, for in the past they were carefully included in the contract. Regarding the buying of land Thomson writes,

> It is not enough that you purchase a well-known lot; the contract must mention everything that belongs to it, and certify that fountains or wells in it, trees upon it, etc., are sold with the field. . . . Thus Abraham bought this field *and* the cave that was therein, *and* all the trees that were in the field, *and* that were in all the borders round about, were made sure (Thomson, II, 383; emphasis his).

The purchaser will also know the human history of the field. He will be able to tell you who has owned it for generations and to recite the profits of that field for an amazing number of past years. The few plots of agricultural land are so crucial to life that in Arab Palestine these plots had proper names (Lees, 213f.). The same overall situation has been noted in first-century Palestine. Applebaum observes the poverty of the Jewish farmer in New Testament times. He comments on

> the great skill and grit of the hard-working Jewish cultivator in wresting production from a minimal plot of ground. But over-population reduced the Jewish peasant unit of cultivation and endangered the cultivator's margin of livelihood (Applebaum, *JPFC*, II, 691).

Thus, in a world of increasing population, limited land space, and the growth of a landless tenantry, the host of the banquet is to believe that a field has been suddenly bought sight unseen.

A Western equivalent to this excuse would be the case of a suburbanite who cancels a dinner engagement by saying, "I have just bought a new house over the phone and I must go and have a look at it and at the neighborhood." The excuse is obviously paper thin and *no one* will believe it.

Again Ibrāhīm Sa'īd is helpful when he says, "What is the point of looking at the field after he has finished the purchase procedures?" (Sa'īd, 382). Sa'īd, writing in Arabic for Middle Eastern readers, assumes that the reader knows that the process of buying a field is long and complicated and often stretches over a number of years.

Derrett suggests a series of legal justifications for the guests' excuses. The land may be depreciating in value and the buyer may want (after examination) to retract the sale. He may need a written conveyance to acquire the property. He may need to assert his title by physically taking possession. Or finally, there may be religious questions regarding cultivation that relate to the keeping of the law (Derrett, 137). However, banquets were held *in the late afternoon* (Jeremias, *Eucharistic*, 44f.). In Luke 17:8 the dinner is clearly after the day's labors are over! Why, we must ask, is the "real estate expert" suddenly busy with these details? What was the dear man doing all morning? Derrett himself translates the excuse, "I am obliged to go out (of town) to view it" (Derrett, 137). So, are we to believe that he is preparing for out-of-town travel shortly before dark? If these complicated legal requirements were taking up his time, why did he accept the invitation to the banquet? After the meat was cooked and the banquet spread, at the end of the working day does he suddenly discover a

long list of pressing business details? Black points out that the word *ananken*
carries the idea of "statutory custom" or "pressure" (Black, 225f., 228). Marshall interprets this to mean a "legal obligation" (Marshall, 589). This also is
possible. However, in the timeless East one day is *always* as good as another.
What is wrong with the following morning for these legal obligations, if there
were such? The field will still be there in the morning. Real estate does not walk
away. The buyer *did* accept to attend the banquet, and Marshall recognizes that
"refusal to respond to the invitation at this point is an act of great discourtesy"
(Marshall, 588). We find compelling reasons to see this refusal as a clear case of
that same "great discourtesy."

Finally, if the man *wants* the host to believe him he can say, "I have been
negotiating for a field for months and the owner has suddenly insisted that we
settle tonight." Such an excuse would save the honor of the host and preserve the
relationship between guest and host. But this is not his purpose. He is intentionally insulting the host by offering an obviously false excuse. (We noted that the
banquet scene in Luke 7:36–50 also began with an intentional insult.) In addition
to the possible legal aspects of the term, when the guest says, "I *must* go and see
it," he is affirming that this field is of greater importance to him than his
relationship to the host. In the Middle Eastern world where personal relationships
are of supreme importance this equation strikes with special force. The speaker
only partially covers this break in relationship by his courteous request for
permission to be absent. (In passing, we observe that the close identity of the
master and his servant is apparent in these first two speeches. He is talking to the
servant and addresses the master.) The third stanza maintains the established
pattern.

STANZA THREE—THE PLOWING EXPERT

"And another said, 'I have bought five yoke of oxen	I DID THIS
and I go to test them.	I MUST DO THIS
I pray you have me excused.' "	EXCUSE ME

The three main ideas (noted on the right) are repeated now a third time.
Again the excuse is ludicrous. Teams of oxen are sold in the Middle Eastern
village in two ways. In some places the team is taken to the market place. At the
edge of the market there will be a small field where prospective buyers may test
the oxen. If they cannot pull together they are of course worthless as a team. In
the smaller villages the farmer owning a pair for sale announces to his friends that
he has a team available and that he will be plowing with them on a given day.
Word spreads quickly in an oral tradition community. Prospective buyers make
their way to the seller's field to watch the animals working and, of course, to
drive them back and forth across the field to be assured of their strength and
evenness of pull. All of this obviously takes place before the buyer even begins to
negotiate a price. Again the excuse offered here is a transparent fabrication.

If we can reuse our modern surburbanite as a cultural parallel, in this case he calls his wife and says, "I cannot make it home tonight for dinner because I have just signed a check for five used cars, which I bought over the phone, and I am on my way down to the used car lot to find out their age and model, and see if they will start." On hearing this, even the most devoted wife will worry about her husband's sanity.

Jesus highlights his point by mentioning five *pairs* of oxen and specifically states that the agent is going to *test* them. As in the case of the real estate expert, the transparent nature of the excuse is unmistakable. Again Saʿīd, our Arab Christian commentator who grew up in a small Middle Eastern village, catches this point. He writes, "This excuse is not reasonable, because the testing of oxen takes place *before* they are bought, not after" (Saʿīd, 383). The point is not to "look them over" but to "*test* them" (as Saʿīd observes), and to see if they will perform as yoked oxen or not. The Greek word *dokimazō* has this clear intent. There is a subtle shift between the first excuse and the second. The first guest had not yet begun to go. He was pleading his case as he said, "I must go out and see it." This second guest says literally, "I am going to test them." He does not state an intention but announces an action in process. Fields are land, and land is holy. But oxen are animals, and animals are unclean. The second guest is saying to the host, "These animals are more important to me than my relationship to you." In spite of the rudeness of his excuse, he is still civil and requests to be excused. The same cannot be said about the third guest, whose speech must now be examined.

STANZA FOUR—THE PASSIONATE BRIDEGROOM

"And another said, 'I have married a bride,	I DID THIS
and therefore—	THUS I MUST—
I cannot come.' "	I CANNOT COME

Patterned speech sets up expectations and those expectations focus special attention on any change in the pattern. In this stanza we have the fourth repetition of the themes, I did this (line one), thus I must do this (line two), excuse me (line three). Only in this case the completion of line two is left to the imagination and line three is brief and rude. The third guest speaks with a simple past tense, "I married a bride." (The *gunē* can be a bride. Cf. Bauer, 167.) So did a lot of the rest of us. We can, however, give him the benefit of the doubt and assume that he means the recent past, "I have just married a bride." However, the wedding was not that day. Had there been a wedding in the village the host would not have scheduled his great banquet. No village can stand two grand occasions at once. All the guests would be at the wedding, and the competition would be pointless. But even if the recent past is indicated, his speech is still crude. Middle Eastern society maintains formal restraint in talking about women.

In Arabic the words *harīm* (women), *haram* (sacred), and *harām* (forbidden) are from the same root. In a formal setting the men do not discuss their women. In the nineteenth century Thomson documented the fact that a man away from home, if he had only daughters at home, would address his letter to the son he hoped yet to father, because to address a letter to a woman would be improper. He talks of the extreme reluctance in the past of Middle Eastern men "to speak of the females of their families" (Thomson, I, 175f.). In intertestamental times Ben Sirach wrote in praise of a long list of famous people—and they are all men (Sir. 44–50). But more than that, the main meal of the day was in the middle of the afternoon (Jeremias, *Eucharistic,* 44f.). Thus this guest is saying, "Yesterday I said I would come, but this afternoon I am busy with a woman, who is more important to me than your banquet." Surely such an excuse would be rude in any society, and it is intensely rude in the Middle Eastern world and totally unprecedented. Some commentators have noted that a newly married man was exempted from military duty for a year (Deut. 20:7; 24:5; cf. Plummer, 361f.), and assume that this text is behind the excuse. Such is not the case. Deuteronomy is talking about a year's military service away from home. Our passionate guest has accepted the invitation. There is no war; he is not called to leave the village. The time away from home will be at most a few hours, and he will be back in his wife's arms late that same night. Finally, he does not even ask to be excused. The entire response is guaranteed to infuriate the most patient of hosts, East or West (Thomson, I, 179). What then does all of this mean?

The listeners to the parable could easily identify the theological movement of the story. The messianic banquet has been announced. Indeed, the "hour of the banquet" has come. Those invited (the leaders of the Jewish community) are told, "All is now ready." Thus in the person of Jesus the kingdom of God in some sense is at hand. Those who seek to "eat bread in the kingdom of God" initially must seek to eat bread with him (cf. Manson, *Sayings,* 129). Yet suddenly there is a stream of excuses. They complain that he eats with and welcomes sinners and does not keep the Sabbath in a strict fashion. Deeper reasons for his rejection may be that he does not fulfill their theological and nationalistic expectations of the Messiah. The parable says that as they reject Jesus (with these unacceptable excuses) they are rejecting the great banquet of salvation promised by God in Isaiah, that is, in some sense, even now set for them through the presence of Jesus in their midst. But not only do they reject the host, they also prefer other things. Manson writes,

> God gives the Kingdom; but the accepting of God's gift means the rejection of many other things. The Kingdom of God offers the greatest gifts; but it demands exclusive loyalty and whole-hearted devotion. The great feast is a feast and not a distribution of free rations. Those who wish to enjoy it must come in. They cannot have portions sent out for them to enjoy, while they busy themselves with other things (*ibid.,* 130f.).

With these theological implications in mind, we return to the text.

STANZA FIVE—THE OUTCASTS' INVITATION

"So the servant came and reported this to his master.
Then the householder in anger said to his servant, 'Go out
  quickly,   MASTER—GO
    into the streets and lanes of the city.   TO STREETS
      Bring in the poor, maimed, blind, and lame.' "   FILL UP

The host's anger is natural—he has been publicly insulted. But his response is grace, not vengeance. He turns to invite the outcasts of the village.
These poor, maimed, blind, and lame are *from the city*. They are a part of the
community, although ostracized from community life. Clearly these categories
symbolize the outcasts of Israel that were attracted to and welcomed by Jesus (cf.
ibid., 130).

We noted above that the Qumran community anticipated a rejection from
the messianic banquet of everyone who was "smitten in his flesh . . . or lame, or
blind" (cf. above, 90). For centuries commentators have observed that the poor
are not invited to banquets, the maimed do not get married, the blind do not go
out to examine fields, and the lame do not test oxen. The word "poor" in biblical
literature often has theological overtones meaning "humble and pious" (cf. Isa.
66:2; Matt. 5:3). Whether or not such meanings are intended here we cannot
determine, but it is clear that there is a radical reversal. The original guests
(assumed to be worthy peers of the host) refuse to respond to the good news that
the banquet is ready. They are confident that the banquet cannot proceed without
them and that the entire event will thus become a humiliating defeat for the host.
But not so—unworthy guests are invited. The host is not indebted socially to the
poor, maimed, blind, and lame, and they will not be able to respond in kind. His
offer is what we have described elsewhere as an "unexpected visible demonstration of love in humiliation" (Bailey, *Poet*, 182). The dramatic, visible nature of
the demonstration is clear. It is unexpected and breaks in upon the new group of
undeserving guests as a stunning surprise. The host may anticipate suffering,
since the original guests will be infuriated that their attempt to abort the banquet
has failed, and they will taunt the host as one who is unable to put together a
banquet without "bringing in this riffraff" (cf. Luke 15:2, "This man receives
sinners and eats with them"). Again, as in the case of the parable of the Prodigal
Son, this unexpected visible demonstration of love in suffering theologically
foreshadows the cross and demonstrates in dramatic form a part of its meaning.
The offer to the "outcasts of Israel" is an offer of costly grace. This offer, the
parable assumes, is accepted. The last two stanzas round out the final scene.

STANZA SIX—STILL ROOM

"And the servant said, 'Sir,   SERVANT
    what you commanded has been done,   I WENT
      and still there is room.' "   NOT FULL

STANZA SEVEN—THE OUTSIDERS

"And the master said to the servant, 'Go out,   MASTER—GO
   into the highways and hedges,   TO HIGHWAYS
     and compel to enter, that my house may be filled.' "   FILL UP

As we noted, the unworthy guests were *from the city* and thus a part of the community. Now, however, the servant is sent out into "the highways and hedges" to bring in people from beyond the town. The "highways" indicate the well-traveled roads. But much of the inter-village traffic moves on narrow paths built along the stone walls or hedges that line such paths. Marshall understands the "hedges" to be fences "along which beggars might rest for protection" (Marshall, 590). Beggars are found in villages and cities where large concentrations of people live. Furthermore there is no hint that this last group of guests are themselves outcasts from their society. They are from beyond the host's community and that is all we know about them. There is a general agreement among contemporary scholars that this latter invitation symbolically represents an outreach to the gentiles, and that Luke understands it in this fashion (Manson, *Sayings*, 130). However, some contend that such an outreach to the gentiles was not envisioned by Jesus and that this invitation to those outside the community is an expansion of the parable by the early Church "in a situation demanding missionary activity" (Jeremias, *Parables*, 64). To this question we now briefly turn.

Hunter has written,

> We are entitled to regard this mission to "the highways and the hedges" in Luke 14:23 as a secondary feature only if we can show that Jesus never envisaged a Gentile mission (Hunter, *Interpreting*, 57).

We would rather accept the burden of proof and ask if there is any material in Luke regarding the gentile mission that can most reasonably be traced to Jesus of Nazareth. The quest for an answer can certainly start with the parable under discussion. We have noted that Isaiah 25:6–9 is a crucial text for a clear understanding of this parable. There the inclusion of the gentiles in the great banquet of God is boldly set forth. One would then expect to find a similar inclusion of the gentiles in Jesus' banquet parable. When it occurs (given the Isaiah background) it is easier and more natural to assume it to be a part of the original parable than to argue for it as a later addition. Furthermore, in the parable the servant *does not* go out after the outsiders (gentiles) along the highways and by the hedges. The command is given but not carried out. It remains an *unfulfilled future task* as the parable closes. The order to invite the outcasts *within* the community *is* carried out in the parable. This parallels Jesus' own ministry in that he *did* carry out a ministry of inviting the outcasts of Israel into his fellowship. He *did not* carry out any major outreach to the gentiles. Indeed, the twelve were sent only to the lost within Israel (Matt. 10:5). Thus the details of the parable as it now stands precisely fit Jesus' own historical ministry. But is there other evidence in Luke or elsewhere of Jesus' interest in the gentiles?

Luke's interest in the gentiles is unmistakable (cf. Martin, 375f.). Simeon declares Jesus to be a "light for revelation to the Gentiles" (2:32). The genealogy is traced to Adam (Luke 3:38) and not to Abraham (Matt. 1:2). The quotation from Isaiah 40:3-5 in Luke 3:6 includes the phrase, "And *all flesh* shall see the salvation of God"; and the commission to the disciples at the end of Luke specifically mentions the gentiles (24:47). Our question thus becomes, Is there a direction set by Jesus himself that is then reflected on, enlarged, and fulfilled by the Church, or is all concern for the gentiles traceable only to the post-Easter situation?

The ministry of Jesus is clearly focused on "the lost sheep of the house of Israel" (Matt. 15:23). Johannes Blauw has argued that the resurrection is a great turning. There the centripetal force of mission (let the gentiles *come in* if they like, but do not *go out* to them) becomes a centrifugal force and the Church goes out to the gentiles with a message for all people (Blauw, 83f.).

Jeremias affirms the same position when he writes, "Jesus expressly rejected the idea that he was also sent to the Gentiles; his mission was confined to the lost sheep of the Israelite community" (Jeremias, *Promise*, 26). Jeremias also sees the message of the Old Testament as being always "centripetal; the Gentiles will not be evangelized where they dwell; but will be summoned to the holy Mount by the divine epiphany" (*ibid.*, 60). Jesus, he argues, understands only that the gentiles will be summoned in the final hour before the last judgment. Yet Blauw admits there are hints of the centrifugal force of mission in the Old Testament. Isaiah 42:4 reads,

> He will not fail or be discouraged
>> till he has established justice in the earth;
>> and the coastlands wait for his law.

This passage is among the famous Servant Songs of Isaiah, and clearly the servant in some sense is seen as going out to "establish justice in the earth." Then in Isaiah 49:6 (in another of the Servant Songs) the centrifugal force is more boldly stated. We read,

A   And now the *Lord says,*   LORD SAYS
    who formed me from the womb *to be his servant,*   MY SERVANT

    B   to *bring Jacob back* to him,   JACOB—BROUGHT BACK
        and that *Israel* might *be gathered* to him,   ISRAEL—GATHERED

        C   for I am *honored* in the eyes of the Lord,   HONORED
            and my *God* has become *my strength.*   MADE STRONG

A'   *He says:*   LORD SAYS
    It is too light a thing that *you should be my servant*   MY SERVANT

    B'   to *raise up* the tribes of *Jacob*   JACOB—RAISED UP
        and to *restore* the survivors of *Israel*;   ISRAEL—RESTORED

        C'   I will give you as a *light to the nations,* LIGHT TO NATIONS
            that *my salvation* may reach to the *end of the earth.*"   SALV.
                                       TO ENDS OF EARTH

We have already observed the use of step parallelism in Isaiah (cf. above, xviii). Here, through the use of repeating couplets, the unique role of the servant is highlighted. In the first series the servant is formed from the womb (A) to restore Jacob/Israel (B) and is especially honored by God who has become his strength (C). This series of ideas is relatively traditional. But the second series contains a dramatic surprise. For we discover that it is too light a thing to be the servant of God (A') just for the restoration of Jacob/Israel (B'). Thus he is given as a light for the salvation of the nations (C'). The clear progression of the text clarifies the twofold role of the servant. He *is* formed/sent for the "lost sheep of the house of Israel." But this is not enough for the greatness of the servant. He is strengthened and honored (C) so that he becomes the light of salvation to the ends of the earth (C'). Clearly there is a centrifugal force of mission set forth in the text. Thus we can say (with Blauw) that in the Old Testament the centrifugal force of mission is rare, yet it is present in the Servant Songs of Isaiah, which are prominent in the New Testament.

Are there hints, or even clear indications, of this centrifugal force of mission in the pre-Easter teachings of Jesus? We believe that there are. The central passage is the famous inauguration scene in the synagogue at Nazareth where Jesus announces and begins his ministry (Luke 4:14–30). The text quoted from the Old Testament is again from Isaiah (61:1–2), but this time it is an edited, composite quote that falls into seven idea units. These are as follows:

1	The *Spirit of the Lord* is upon me		SPIRIT OF THE LORD
	2	for He has anointed me to *preach* to the poor.	PREACH
		3 He has *sent me* to proclaim to the captives—*freedom*,	SEND OUT—FREEDOM
		4 and recovering of *sight to the blind*;	SIGHT
		3' to *send out* the oppressed—in *freedom*,	SEND OUT—FREEDOM
	2'	and to *proclaim*	PROCLAIM
1'	the acceptable *year of the Lord*.		YEAR OF THE LORD

As it now stands in Luke, this text differs from Isaiah 61:1–2 at four major points. As Lund has observed (Lund, 236–38), all four of these changes were necessary to create the present literary form of seven lines with three pairs and a climax in the center. We would add to Lund's observation the fact that the editing is not only for literary, but more significantly, for theological reasons. These four changes are as follows. First, the phrase "to bind up the brokenhearted" is removed from line 3. With this removal the line is of manageable length and begins with the word "send" and ends with the word "freedom." Second, a full line is brought in from Isaiah 58:6 and stands in the present structure as line 3'. It also begins with the word "send" and ends with the word "freedom." It has obviously been selected, at least partially, because it balances line 3 at the beginning and at the end. Third, the key word "to proclaim" (*kērussō*) in line 2' has replaced Isaiah's word, which means "to say" or "to call.'' This is because the parallel line (2) has the verb ''to preach'' (*euangelizō*). In these two verbs we have the two great New Testament words for the proclamation of the gospel. After editing they stand in the text balancing one another. Finally, the last part of Isaiah 61:2, with its references to judgment on the gentiles, is omitted. Thus line 1' comes into balance with line 1. After editing, the inverted parallelism is completed. Of special interest for our purposes are the three central lines. In such inverted parallelisms the climax usually occurs in the center of the structure and thus this center deserves special attention. Here we note the following:

> 3   He has *sent me*—to proclaim to the captives—*freedom,*
>
>   4   and recovery of sight to the blind;
>
> 3'   to *send out* the oppressed—in *freedom,*

Line 3', as we have noted, was brought in from Isaiah 58:6 and placed in this text in order to balance line 3; and line 3 itself had the phrase ''to bind up the brokenhearted'' removed in order to make it of manageable length. Thus more editing has taken place on these two lines (3 and 3') than anywhere else in the composite quotation, and they occur in the center of the seven lines. The reason for this special care and placement is evident when the rest of the discussion in the synagogue is examined.

    In Luke 4:25–27 Jesus draws on two remarkable heroes of faith from the Old Testament. Both are non-Jews. The first is the woman from Zarephath of Sidon. The second is Naaman from Syria. The text clearly has two stanzas with four lines in each stanza. The two stanzas relate to each other in step parallelism such as we noted above in Isaiah 49:5–6 and in 55:10–11. This step parallelism is as follows:

> 1   *There were many widows in Israel*
>
>   2   in the *days* of *Elijah,*
>
>   (when the heavens were shut for three years and six months
>   and there came a great famine over all the land)
>
>   3   and *Elijah* was sent to *none* of them
>
>   4   *except* to *Zarephath of Sidon,* to *a woman,* a widow.
>
> 1'   *And there were many lepers in Israel*
>
>   2'   in the *time* of the prophet *Elisha,*
>
>   3'   and *none* of them was *cleansed*
>
>   4'   *except Naaman, the Syrian.*

Each of the two stanzas has the same four themes. These are (1) many in Israel, (2) the prophet, (3) none was helped, and (4) except so-and-so. This sequence of ideas is carefully followed in each stanza. For our subject it is important to observe the second line of the first stanza. That line has some extra historical information that any synagogue audience would already know. However, Theophilus (for whom Luke was writing; cf. 1:3) would most likely not know the details of the life of Elijah and would therefore need this information. Without it the illustration is worthless. Any Greek reader will wonder just what the woman's problem was. In the second stanza, no additional information is necessary. Even if the reader knows nothing about Naaman the Syrian, it is obvious that a leper is cleansed. Thus the precise literary form of the original eight lines, with their repetitive step parallelism, makes it clear that the extra information in line 2 is added after the composition of the original eight lines. Consequently we are dealing with two literary layers. Someone has written the original matching eight lines and then at a later period someone else has added new information for non-Jewish readers. The parallelism of the original eight lines is as precise as Isaiah 49:5-6 and 55:10-11 and warrants the title of poetry. We would submit that the most natural assumption for the material is that the original poem is quoted from Jesus of Nazareth and that the additional historical information is added by Luke for his gentile readers. It is of course possible that the earliest Palestinian church has written the eight lines and Luke is expanding its construction. We are not affirming proof, but only trying to ascertain probability. These two striking illustrations in this type of a poetical form could easily maintain themselves intact for centuries if need be, in a Middle Eastern peasant society (as evidenced by the oracles of Amos, the pre-Islamic Arabic poetry, and many other cases). We would submit that there is no *historical* reason to deny that Jesus of Nazareth is the author of the original eight lines.

Then, in turn, these two illustrations stand in the text as a *midrash,* an interpretation of the heart of the Isaiah quote noted above. In the center of that quote in line 3 the prophet *is sent* to someone to proclaim freedom. In the matching line 3′ the prophet *sends out* someone else in freedom. This precise shift also occurs in the two stanzas that we have just examined. Elijah is *sent* to the woman and Elisha *sends* Naaman *out* to his freedom. Putting these side by side we observe,

> He has *sent me*—to proclaim—freedom (like Elijah who was *sent* to the woman of Zarephath)
> To *send out* the oppressed—in freedom (like Elisha who *sent* Naaman *out* in freedom)

The first of these is a case of a *centrifugal* force of mission (Elijah goes *out* of Israel and helps the woman of Zarephath); the second is the more common *centripetal* force of mission (Elisha ministers to Naaman who is attracted *in* and comes to him in Israel). To whom then is this material traceable? Is it strictly a Lucan composition or can it be, in some sense, attributed to Jesus of Nazareth? The question must be asked regarding both form and content.

In regard to the composite Isaiah quotation, we observe that it was considered perfectly legitimate for a reader in the synagogue to skip from passage to passage in his reading, particularly if he was reading from the prophets. He was not supposed to skip too far, say from the end of a book to its beginning, and should not skip from book to book. But skipping *was* ruled legitimate, and the extent of the discussion in the Mishna (*Megillah* 4:4) and in the Talmud (B.T. *Megillah* 24a) makes it clear that it was a relatively frequent practice. Furthermore, Paul often gives us composite quotes and assumes their legitimacy (cf. I Cor. 2:9). They can be found in the Gospels as well (Mark 1:2-3). Thus Jesus could well have carefully thought out his theme and prepared ahead of time his composite text from Isaiah 58 and 61. At the same time, the Greek words for "to preach good news" *(euangelizō)* and "to proclaim" *(kērussō)* look as if they have been edited to match in Greek because these are the two great New Testament words for the proclamation of the gospel. Also the word "freedom" *(aphesis)*, which comes at the end of lines 3 and 3', is the same word in the Greek Old Testament in each text. But the Hebrew Old Testament has different words, although with identical meanings. That is, lines 3 and 3' match in Hebrew, but match even better in Greek. Thus it would appear that the text in its present form may have been influenced to some extent by the Septuagint (the Greek Old Testament), and thus by the early Church. In the light of this, we would affirm that the composite Isaiah text, as it now appears in Luke, represents major themes from Isaiah selected by Jesus in his discussion in the synagogue. The present literary structure of these texts may reflect early Church editing.

Then (as we have argued), the eight-line *midrash* (excluding its later historical addition) is most probably traceable to Jesus of Nazareth and reflects a centrifugal force of mission that he endorsed but did not fulfill, except in rare incidents. Jesus composes the eight-line *midrash*. Luke adds an explanatory comment. This centrifugal force of mission permeates and informs the entire passage. We have observed that the harsh criticism of the gentiles in Isaiah 61:2 is omitted. The very illustrations selected in the *midrash* set forth two gentiles as heroes of faith to be imitated. Why are two non-Jews made the heroes of faith rather than Abraham on Mount Moriah, or Moses at the Red Sea, or Jeremiah going out to buy a field? Is not the very wrath of the worshipers in the synagogue most likely partially related to this focus on the gentiles? Jeremias himself argues convincingly that verse 22 can best be understood to mean "they all bore witness against him . . . they were astonished that he spoke of the mercy of God" (Jeremias, *Promise,* 44f.). They expect him to continue reading in Isaiah 61:2b, "and the day of vengeance of our God." Rather than talking about the "foreigners" who shall "be your plowmen and vinedressers" (Isa. 61:5), two gentiles are held up as illustrations of the kind of faith that the kingdom demands. The audience is understandably furious. Thus in this crucial passage there is clear reference to the centrifugal force of mission, the going out even to the gentiles. The entire text *does* reflect Lucan and early Church theological interests, but these interests we see as traceable in the text to Jesus himself, and beyond him to Isaiah 49:5-6.

Two further passages need to be examined briefly. The first is the parable of the lamp. In Luke 11:33 the lamp is put on a stand "that *those who enter* may see the light." Here we are back to the centripetal force of mission. Only those who come *in* will see the light. The same is reflected in Matthew 5:15 where the lamp is put on a stand to "give light to all *in the house.*" Again the focus is on the centripetal force of mission. Only those "in the house" will see the light. Yet significantly, the preceding verse reads, "You are the light of the world. A city set on a hill cannot be hid." We expect to read, "You are the light of Israel," but not so. In a fashion reminiscent of Isaiah 49:6 the light on the hill is to shine out to *all the world.* Again, as in Luke 4:16–30, the centripetal and the centrifugal forces of mission are set side by side. The city on the hill sends light *out* to *all the world,* and the lamp is seen only by those who are *in the house.* Finally, in the case of the Greek/Canaanite woman of Tyre and Sidon (Matt. 15:21–30; Mark 7:24–30), we have a clear statement of the exclusive nature of the ministry of Jesus. He says to the woman that he was sent "only to the lost sheep of the house of Israel" (Matt. 15:24). The discussion then turns on to the symbols of food and the children's bread. Jeremias affirms that

> the key to the meaning of Jesus' words to the woman who sought his help lies in the fact that she understood that Jesus was speaking of the Messianic banquet. Her "great faith" (Matt. 15:28) consisted in her recognition, as shown by her words about the crumbs that the little dogs might venture to eat, that Jesus was the giver of the Bread of Life (Jeremias, *Parables,* 118, n. 14; *Eucharistic,* 234; *Promise,* 29f.).

If we accept Jeremias' argument, we have in this text a case of a gentile woman who sees in Jesus the bringer of salvation. Thus, in the very story where he specifically states that he has come *only* for Israel, we see him reach out to minister to a gentile woman who sees him as "the giver of the Bread of Life." (In Isaiah 49:5–6 we saw the same juxtaposition of restorer of Israel + light of salvation for the nations.) Unless we make a prior theological judgment that Jesus *could not* have had an interest in the gentiles, we have here a case of just such an interest. Is not this text simply saying "to the Jew first and also the Greek" (Rom. 1:16)? In the light of the texts discussed above, is it not possible to see the ministry and teachings of Jesus directed primarily to the Jewish nation, but with clear pointers in the direction of something beyond Israel which fulfills the great Servant Song in Isaiah 49:5–6? Elijah was sent *out.* The light from the city on the hill goes *out.* The Greek woman of Sidon *is* fed by the bread of life and she meets Jesus on non-Jewish land. It is in the light of these texts that the concluding verses of the parable of the Great Banquet must be examined. T. W. Manson succinctly remarks, "the whole parable [of the Great Banquet] might be regarded as a *midrash* on Isa. 49:6" (*Sayings,* 130).

When Luke 14:23–24 is considered in the light of the above, it becomes possible to see the two concluding stanzas as a part of the original parable. Not only is the suggestion of an invitation to the gentiles theologically harmonious with other things that Jesus has done and taught, but the very literary form of the parable should suggest that the last two speeches complete the series of seven. Furthermore, at the beginning of the feast there were two invitations to the original guests; thus it is not surprising that at the end of the parable there are two invitations to unexpected guests (granted, in one case they are the same people and in the other they are not). An argument against the originality of the second invitation is that it is missing in Matthew. However, if the two accounts of the parable are examined, it is clear that the Matthean version has had considerable editing. A long series of expansions colors almost every verse. If Matthew has taken the liberty to *add* this much material following his own interests, can it not be argued that he has also deleted other details for the same reason? The two invitations to the original guests in the *beginning* of the Lucan version are shortened to one invitation in Matthew. It would seem that in like fashion the two invitations to outsiders at the *end* are also reduced to one. What then does this final invitation mean?

In stanza six the servant tells the master that after the outcasts of Israel are brought in there is still room in the banquet hall. In stanza seven the invitation goes out to the gentiles. The key word here is "compel." The Spanish inquisition and other tragic subversions of the gospel have been perpetrated by the organized church using this text as support. Nothing could be further from its original intent. In the Middle East the unexpected invitation must be refused. The refusal is all the more required if the guest is of lower social rank than the host. (The unexpected guest may be half starving and in real need of the offered food, but still he senses a deep cultural pressure to refuse.) In Luke 24:28-29 we have, culturally speaking, a similar scene. This time Jesus receives the unexpected invitation. As a courteous Oriental he "made as though he would go further." The two men, again in true Middle Eastern fashion, "compel him" to stay. He is not forced against his will. Rather, they know he *must* refuse for the first fifteen minutes of discussion as a matter of honor. In order to convince him that they really *do* want him to stay, and that they really *do* have food, they gently drag him into the house. They compel him to stay. Even so in the parable, we have a classical case of an unexpected invitation from someone of a higher rank. A stranger from outside the city is suddenly invited to a great banquet. He is not a relative or even a citizen of the host's city. The offer is generous and delightful but (thinks the stranger) *he cannot possibly mean it.* After some discussion the servant will finally have to take the startled guest by the arm and gently pull him along. There is no other way to convince him that he is really invited to the great banquet, irrespective of his being a foreigner. Grace is *unbelievable!* How could it be true, asks the outsider. For me? What have I ever done for him? I cannot pay it back? The host is not serious! It is a most pleasant prospect, but considering who I am, he cannot mean it! The host knows that this kind of shock and unbelief will face the servant/messenger at every turn, so he instructs the same to overcome reserve and unbelief by the only method possible—with a smile grab them by the arm and pull them in. Demonstrate to them that the invitation is genuine! Compel them to come in (cf. *ibid.*).

Finally, the motive for this extra invitation is "that my house may be filled.'' The purpose of this final remark seems to be a concern to demonstrate that it is possible for the banquet to be *full* without the original guests. The occasion can be a grand success even in their absence. The noble host wants the new guests to feel total acceptance. They must not look around and say, ''See how many seats are vacant. What a shame! Poor man, he is rejected by the important people and has only the few of us at his banquet.'' No! His house must be full! This brings our consideration of the seven speeches to a close. The concluding remark must now be examined.

CONCLUSION

''For I tell you (plural),	
none of those men who were invited	THOSE INVITED
shall taste my banquet.''	MY BANQUET

There is some ambiguity in the text and considerable discussion among the commentators regarding this final sentence. Is it a part of the parable itself and thereby is the householder speaking (Derrett, 141; Marshall, 590f.)? Or is it a concluding remark of Jesus to his audience reclining with him at the banquet (Jeremias, *Parables,* 171–180)? With the awareness that it is possible to read the phrase either way, the text seems most probably a remark of Jesus to his audience. In Luke 15:7, at the conclusion of the parable of the Lost Sheep, we have a similar construction with a concluding Dominical comment. Luke 15:10 has the same formula (cf. also Luke 18:6 and 18:14). We have argued elsewhere that Luke 16:8 is not a similar construction. There the master of 16:8 is better understood as the master of the parable (cf. Bailey, *Poet,* 102f.). But in this text the shift to a plural ''I tell you'' is significant. The master talks in the singular to a single servant all through the parable and, indeed, does so in the concluding speech in stanza seven. Derrett argues that the host would often send portions of a banquet to his leading friends, who were ''unavoidably absent'' (Derrett, 141). But such, we have argued, is not the case. In the parable they deliberately absented themselves with flimsy excuses and the host was *angry*. How could he be angry at the unavoidably absent? Rather they are deliberately absent and obviously he is not going to send special portions out to the guests who have just offended him to the point of anger. For the host to report such a decision as the climax of the parable would be redundant. But as a statement of Jesus to the audience it becomes profoundly meaningful. He states symbolically that those who would like to ''eat bread in the kingdom of God'' (14:15) had better hurry and accept *his* invitation to table fellowship, because they *will not* be able to participate at a distance. Thus the sudden shift to a plural seems to indicate that the parable is over and that Jesus is addressing his audience.

Yet just below the surface the two possibilities fuse. The original guests who refuse the host will certainly (by their own choice) not participate in the great banquet. Furthermore the guests reclining with Jesus are in grave danger of excluding themselves from the banquet of salvation already spread by the inaugurator of the kingdom. If the understanding of the text presented above can be sustained, the banquet is openly called "my banquet." Thus Jesus identifies himself with the host. The banquet is his banquet. He extends the original invitation to the guests. He pleads with them to attend and records that their self-exclusion is final. Again T. W. Manson's reflections are worth noting:

> Jesus does not here teach either a mechanically operating predestination, which determines from all eternity who shall or shall not be brought into the Kingdom. Neither does He proclaim that man's entry into the Kingdom is purely his own affair. The two essential points in His teaching are that no man can enter the Kingdom without the invitation of God, and that no man can remain outside it but by his own deliberate choice. Man cannot save himself; but he can damn himself. . . . He (Jesus) sees the deepest tragedy of human life, not in the many wrong and foolish things that men do, or the many good and wise things that they fail to accomplish, but in their rejection of God's greatest gift (*Sayings*, 130).

This then brings us to an examination of the symbols that the original listening audience would instinctively have identified. In the light of these we will try to determine the single response that Jesus was trying to evoke from the listeners and, finally, attempt to discern the theological cluster of the parable. First, then, the symbols.

What precisely would the original audience have instinctively identified? At least the following can be affirmed with some confidence:

the banquet = the messianic banquet that ushers in the new age

the original guests = the leaders of Israel who are rightfully the first to be invited

the lame and poor of the city = the outcasts within the house of Israel

the guests from the highways and the hedges = the gentiles

To this we must add the person of Jesus himself. To try to identify God as the host in distinction to the servant, who becomes Jesus or John the Baptist or both, is to press the symbols beyond what could have originally been instinctively perceived by the original audience. Granted, many commentators through the centuries of the life of the Church have identified the person of Jesus with the host or with the servant; and in Qumran it *was* the Messiah who summoned the faithful to the messianic banquet. But the story has a close identification between the servant and his master that is typical of the Oriental world generally. The former is considered a mirror of the latter. We have already noted that the original guests address the servant as the master and ask directly to be excused. Indeed, all through the parable the servant is his master's voice. So the referent for this combined symbol is God acting through His unique agent, Jesus. Thus Jesus is able to affirm the banquet as "my banquet." At the same time, he is the unique agent of God, through whom God is acting in the inauguration of the messianic banquet of the age of salvation and in the invitations to the different types of guests. How then are these symbols used by Jesus for pressing the original audience to a concrete response?

The original audience could hardly have missed the thrust of the parable. Jesus is saying to them,

> God's Messiah is here. He is inviting you to the messianic banquet of the day of salvation. The banquet is now ready. Do not refuse! For if you do (with your ridiculous excuses) others will fill your places from among the outcasts of Israel, and (in the future) an invitation will go out to the gentiles. The banquet will proceed without you. It will not be cancelled or postponed. The eschatological age has dawned. Respond to the invitation or opt out of participation in God's salvation.

Like the parable of the Prodigal Son, this parable is told in defense of the gospel to the outcasts. In Luke 15:2 the Pharisaic complaint is specifically that Jesus *eats* with tax collectors and sinners. Table fellowship with Jesus *is* participation in the messianic banquet in anticipation of the completion of all things in the end time. What then are the theological themes found in this parable?

A rich cluster of theological motifs combine to give the parable unique power. Among these are:

1. Jesus is God's unique agent calling for participation in the messianic banquet of salvation.

2. The messianic banquet promised by Isaiah (Isa. 25:6-9) is inaugurated in the table fellowship of Jesus (realized eschatology). But the parable is left open-ended. All the guests are not assembled. The parable breaks off with the house not yet full. Thus there is an unfulfilled future anticipated by the parable (futuristic eschatology). The full vision of the messianic banquet is yet in the future, when the faithful will sit down in the kingdom with Abraham, Isaac, and Jacob (Luke 13:28-29). Thus the messianic banquet of the end times is both now and not yet.

3. The excuses people offer for refusal to respond to the invitation to join in the banquet are stupid and insulting. The original guests have their counterpart in every age.

4. The invitation to table fellowship at the banquet is extended to the unworthy who can in no way compensate the host for his grace. These outcasts may be from within or from without the community.

5. Grace is unbelievable. This is so true that some special pleading is required for many of the undeserving to be convinced that the invitation is genuine.

6. There is a centrifugal force of mission taught in the parable. The servant, with his invitation, is told to go out beyond the city. If God's salvation is to reach to the ends of the earth (Isa. 49:6) someone must take the message out and present it with all the winsomeness possible (Luke 14:23).

7. There is a self-imposed concept of judgment. Those who by their own choice reject the invitation thereby shut themselves off from fellowship with the host and his guests.

8. There is a warning addressed to the presumptuous in the believing community. God can get along without them. If they fail to respond to His invitation, He will proceed with outsiders.

9. Time runs out on the invitation. As Charles Smith has said, "Places are not kept open indefinitely at the Messianic table and those who assume . . . that there will always be room for them are likely to receive a rude shock" (C. Smith, 125).

10. The guests must be invited. No one "storms the party." Attendance is by invitation only. Yet the guests must respond and come in. There is no participation at a distance.

Containing as it does this rich series of tightly packed theological motifs, it is little wonder that this parable was given a prominent place along with the other parables spoken in defense of the gospel to the outcasts. Indeed, it speaks powerfully in any age.

The question of the believing communities' continuing table fellowship with Jesus is a question that is beyond the scope of a study of the parable itself. The parable, as we have observed, is not finished. Surely a part of the meaning of the communion service is the concept of continuing table fellowship with the now risen Lord in anticipation of the completion of the banquet of the end times. This parable profoundly relates to that understanding. Those who ate and drank with him during his earthly ministry were engaged in a proleptic celebration of the messianic banquet of the end times. This parable offers at least a part of the theological rationale for that celebration. Is not the communion service then an extension of this same celebration? Depending on our various traditions different answers can be given to this question. Yet surely all Christian theological traditions must deal with what is set forth so brilliantly in this banquet of the seven speeches.

One final consideration that is also beyond the scope of the study of the parable itself, but worthy of note in passing, is to observe the different ways Matthew and Luke deal with the problem of presumption. In Luke there is a series of parables that proclaims the concept of God's free offer of grace. These include (in order) the Great Banquet, the Lost Sheep, the Lost Coin, the Prodigal Son, and (as we understand it) the Unjust Steward (Bailey, *Poet,* 86–109). The reader of Luke's Gospel may well ask, If grace is free, is it not also cheap? The arrangement of material gives the reader the answer. In between two great banquet parables, each declaring pure grace (the Great Banquet and the Prodigal Son), is set a collection of sayings that speaks of the high cost of discipleship in clear and demanding terms (Luke 14:25–35). Matthew deals with the same problem in a different way. There, in a sequel to the Great Banquet, the guests (also freely invited) are held accountable to appear in proper garments. The banquet is free but acceptance carries with it responsibilities (Matt. 22:11-14).

Thus the Great Banquet sets forth weighty theological themes in a brief but unforgettable parable that continues to speak with power in every age.

Chapter 7

THE OBEDIENT SERVANT
(Luke 17:7-10)

This little parable's significance far outweighs the attention it usually receives. In the Lucan account the reader has already been told that the master who returns from the wedding banquet will serve his servants (12:35-38). In a few verses the reader will discover that Jesus is among his disciples; not as one who sits at a table, but "as one who serves" (22:27). For the insensitive these texts are invitations to presumption. If Jesus came and is coming to serve us, fine; here we are, expecting to reap the benefits of his service! While in no way denying the thrust of the above parables, here Jesus clearly asserts his authority over his disciples. He is the master! They are his servants, and let there be no misunderstanding! Because this parable uses some of the precise imagery of the parable of the Waiting Servants in 12:35-38, that parable will need to be examined briefly prior to our study of 17:7-10.

In the overall outline of the central section of Luke (Bailey, *Poet*, 79-85), 17:1-10 appears as a miscellaneous collection of sayings on offenses (vv. 1-2), forgiveness (vv. 3-4), faith (vv. 5-6), and duty (vv. 7-10). Thus we see no need to find a relationship between this parable and the dialogue with the apostles that precedes it, or the healing of the ten lepers that follows it. We would rather examine it in the light of the two other major discussions of the master-servant theme mentioned above. If, then, this parable is a part of a miscellaneous collection, to whom is it addressed?

The three previous paragraphs are addressed to the disciples (v. 1) and to the apostles (v. 5). In this parable the text of Luke assumes the same audience. The phrase, "which one of you," is used to introduce sayings to disciples, crowds, and opponents (Bailey, *Poet*, 139f.; against Jeremias, *Parables*, 103, 145, 193). It would appear that Luke is right and the disciples are the audience. The major argument against this view is the assumption that the disciples would not have had servants. Such is not the case. In the West, having a servant puts a person in (at least) the upper middle class, but not so in the East. The poorest of the poor let their children out as servants so that they can be fed, and the people of very little means have such servants in their homes. James, John, and their father, Zebedee, own a boat and have hired servants (Mark 1:20). Other disciples may have been people of similar means. Furthermore, only *one* servant is involved. The plowman/herdsman is also the cook. Thus the master is a man of modest income. Applebaum writes, "Talmudic traditions assume, as a matter of course, that the ordinary man has at least one slave" (*JPFC,* II, 627). Also, the parable does not assume that the master is a landowner. The servant may be plowing a rented field. There is no specific hint in the Gospels that the disciples were from among the poorest of the poor. Finally, the parable appeals to the audience on the basis of commonly known cultural assumptions. It does not necessarily peg the listener in a particular economic class. That is, the parable does not say, "Listen, you masters of servants." Rather it says, "Does not the servant-master relationship, as you know it, presuppose these things?" The same is true in the parable of the Lost Sheep, where Jesus addresses Pharisees with the identical introductory phrase used here ("Which one of you, having . . ."). Shepherds were among the proscribed trades for the Pharisees (Bailey, *Poet,* 147). Thus they were *certainly not* shepherds. In the same way Jesus is appealing here to the common Middle Eastern understanding of how servants and masters act and is not necessarily affirming that they owned slaves or engaged servants. Thus there seems to be no remaining reason for questioning Luke's judgment that the parable was originally addressed to the disciples/apostles.

The parable is a simple three-stanza ballad such as that which we have already observed in 11:9-13; 11:29-32; 15:3-7; and 16:9-13 (Bailey, *Poet,* 69f., 112, 135, 144). It is as follows:

(1)   "Can you imagine having a servant,   SERVANT
          plowing or keeping sheep,   FULFILLING ORDERS
             who on coming in from the field   ORDERS FULFILLED
                you say to him, 'Come at once and recline to REWARD?
                eat'?

(2)   Will he not rather say to him,
                 '*Prepare for me* something and I shall dine,
                      and gird yourself and *serve me,*   SERVE THE MASTER
                 till *I eat* and *drink*;   THEN YOURSELF
                 and afterward *you shall eat* and *drink*'?

(3)   Does the servant have special merit   SERVANT
          because he did what was commanded?   ORDERS FULFILLED
             So you, also, when you have done what was commanded
                                                              ORDERS FULFILLED
                say, 'Nothing is owing us servants, we have only done our
                duty.' "   REWARD?

As in the case of Luke 15:3-7, the third stanza is application, yet it deals with a series of themes introduced in the first stanza. These themes (noted on the right) are presented in stanza one and repeated in stanza three. In two cases we have diverged from the traditional translation of the passage. These will be examined in detail below. In the central section we have two couplets of parallelism. *Prepare for me* matches *serve me*, and *I eat and drink* parallels *you shall eat and drink.* Some of the words in the central stanza seems at first glance redundant. Thus the RSV has the first line read simply, "Prepare supper for me," condensing two verbs into one. With the extra verb each line in this central stanza has two major verbs. The three-stanza literary form reinforces Marshall's view that there is no need to identify the central stanza as redactional (Marshall, 646). In most of the parabolic stanzas under study, direct speech occurs at the beginning of the stanza. By contrast here the first and last stanzas end with direct speech. Thus the literary form is again complete, artistically satisfying, and provides an important key to interpretation.

Before proceeding to the interpretation of the parable we must examine the Waiting Servants in Luke 12:35–38, because some of the identical images occur there and function in reverse of what appears here. It is not our intention to make a full study of the parable of the Waiting Servants but to observe its literary form and the use of its images. The form is as follows:

A	1	Let your waist be girded,	SERVANTS PREPARE
	1'	and your lamp burning.	SERVANTS PREPARE
B	2	And be like men who are waiting	SERVANTS WAIT TO SERVE
	3	for their master to return from the wedding,	MASTER COMES
	3'	so that when he comes and knocks,	MASTER COMES
	2'	immediately they may open to him.	SERVANTS SERVE
C	4	Blessed are those servants	SERVANTS BLESSED
	5	whom coming the master finds awake.	MASTER COMES
	6	Truly I say to you, he will gird himself,	MASTER PREPARES
	7	and have them recline at table,	SERVANTS HONORED
	6'	and come and serve them.	MASTER SERVES
	5'	If (in the second or third watch) he comes and finds thus,	MASTER COMES
	4'	blessed are those servants.	SERVANTS BLESSED

In this case the literary form is built on a very sophisticated use of the phenomenon of the split parallelism. If all the repetitions are ignored the seven movements of the parable can easily be identified. They are as follows:

1. Servants prepare to serve the master.

2. Servants wait to serve the master.

3. The master's return is anticipated.

4. The servants are blessed in their vigilance.

5. The master comes.

6. The master prepares and serves the servants.

7. The servants recline to be served.

By following the numbers this flow of ideas can be easily traced. Each line/idea, except line 7, is repeated. A prosaic telling of these same seven ideas without the parallel repetitions would read as follows: "Prepare yourselves (1) and wait to serve (2) your returning master (3). You are blessed (4) if the master comes and finds you awake (5). For then he will gird himself to serve you (6) while *you* recline" (7). However, the extra words are not redundant but a part of the literary form. The split parallelism is an artistic device observable in the Old Testament. Freedman writes, "It is as though the poet deliberately split a bicolon or couplet, and inserted a variety of materials between the opening and closing halves of the unit to form a stanza" (Freedman, xxxvi). A clear case of this in the New Testament is in the Lucan Beatitudes (Luke 6:20–26; cf. Bailey, *Poet,* 64). There a very precise series of four couplets is formed with the key words "blessed" and "for." That is,

> *Blessed* are the poor,
> *for* yours is the kingdom of God.

The text has three couplets structured in this fashion. But the fourth of this series has some extra material inserted in between the first and second lines of the couplet. This is as follows:

> *Blessed* are you when men hate you,
> (and when they exclude you and revile you, and cast out your name as evil, on account of the Son of man. Rejoice in that day, and leap for joy, for your reward is great in heaven;)
> *for* so their fathers did to the prophets.

The couplet is intact. Yet extra material is added in the middle. At the same time this extra material in the center is ordered according to a precise pattern. There are three negatives matched by three positives and a reference to the Son of man in the center. This can be seen as follows:

> *Blessed* are you when men hate you,
>   and when they exclude you   −
>   and revile you,   −
>   and cast out your name as evil,   −
>   on account of the *Son of man.*
>   Rejoice in that day,   +
>   and leap for joy,   +
>   for your reward is great in heaven;   +
> *for* so their fathers did to the prophets.

Thus this text is clearly a New Testament example of the phenomenon Freedman has identified in the Old Testament. A two-line parallelism has been split and, in this case, seven lines added in the center. These seven lines have a literary form of their own with a climax in the middle. Thus the larger text has four couplets and the fourth is split to make up a stanza.

Here in Luke 12:35–38 we have the remarkable case of this phenomenon happening twice in a row. The first couplet is a simple synonymous parallelism.

Let your waist be girded,	SERVANTS PREPARE
and your lamp burning.	SERVANTS PREPARE

The first of these two images has to do with being prepared to undertake any strenuous task. The servant must put on a belt and tuck his long, loose-fitting outer garment into that belt to get the edge of the garment up out of the way. The second has to do with preparing to guide the master out of the dark. Only if one has lived in a world without electricity is it possible to appreciate how important it is to prepare and light the lamps before dark. When we compare stanza A and stanza B it is clear that the reference to the *servants* (with their preparation and wait) is repeated on the outside (2), and new material referring to the master is inserted into the center. This can be seen as follows:

Stanza A	*Stanza B*
1 Let your *waist be girded,*	2 And be like men who are *waiting*
	(a couplet on the master's return)
1' and your *lamp burning.*	2' immediately they may *open* to him.

The servant *girds* his waist in preparation (1) and *waits* for his orders from the master on his return (2). The lighting of the *lamps* (1') is for the purpose of opening the door for him with lamp in hand (2'). Thus two lines have been expanded into four by repeating the basic ideas (which have to do with the servants) and inserting between them two new lines (which have to do with the master). Then, remarkably, this process is repeated. Now the four lines are restated (in slightly different form) and again new material is inserted into the center. The matching nature of stanza B and the four outside lines of stanza C can be seen as follows:

Stanza B	*Stanza C*
2 Be like *men waiting*	4 Blessed are *those servants*
3 for the *master* to return,	5 *coming the master* finds awake.
3' so that when *he comes*	5' If *he comes* and finds thus
2' *they may open* to him.	4' blessed are *those servants.*

The outside lines tell of the servants who *wait* (2) to *open* (2') and who are thereby blessed (4,4'). All four inner lines talk of the *coming* of the *master*. The repetitions are needed to complete the parallelisms.

If the parable/poem had ended with these lines it would have made complete sense. The theology would have been in harmony with other things Jesus had taught and the missing three lines would not have been detected. Yet, the perceptive original listener/reader has already seen the first stanza split and new material added to its center to form the second stanza, and thus he may have expected the same stanza-splitting phenomena to take place in the third stanza. If so, he was not disappointed. The third stanza is also split and three new lines are added in the center. Thus the third stanza has seven lines and they are inverted. When parallel lines are inverted in biblical literature, the center is usually the climax (Bailey, *Poet*, 50f.). This is dramatically the case in this parable. The master takes the position of a *servant* and serves his own servant *as if he were the master*. This climax to the parable is such a shock that it is introduced by the phrase, "Amen, I say to you," which is a striking formula. It occurs only six times in Luke and in each case introduces something that comes as a shock, or is a hard saying, or a saying on which there is special emphasis. It also may indicate Luke's use of material he has not redacted (Marshall, 536). Here it introduces a shocking reversal of roles.

In the Middle East the traditional roles of master and servant are well-defined. For a master to serve his own servants is unheard of! This dramatic reversal is enacted by Jesus himself in the footwashing scene in John 13:3–5, and is described theologically and poetically in Philippians 2:6–7. In this parable the message is dramatic and powerful. The one who is prepared and willing to serve, and waits patiently for the final culmination of God's rule, will find himself *served* by the one for whom he is waiting. This scene is set in the *parousia*, but Luke 22:27 and John 13:3–5 make it clear that Jesus is *already* among them as a master who serves. Yet all of this rich imagery when taken alone can lead to a gross misrepresentation of a crucial aspect of Jesus' relationship to his disciples. He *is* among them as one who serves, indeed as *their* servant. At the same time he is still the *master,* and they need to remember who they are as servants. Thus this parable in Luke 17:7–10 is crucial in its presentation of Jesus as a master to whom his servants owe loyalty and obedience.

With this background in mind, we turn to the parable itself.

STANZA ONE

"Can you imagine having a servant,	SERVANT
plowing or keeping sheep,	FULFILLING ORDERS
who on coming in from the field	ORDERS FULFILLED
you say to him, 'Come at once and recline to eat'?"	REWARDS?

In a technological age with the forty-hour week, powerful labor unions, and time and a half for overtime, the world of this parable seems not only distant but unfair. After a long, hard day in the field, such a servant surely has earned the right to a little appreciation, some comforts, and a few rewards. But Jesus is building on well-known and widely accepted patterns of behavior in the Middle East. The master-servant relationship, in its ancient and modern expressions, implies acceptance of authority and obedience to that authority. Yet the outsider needs to be sensitive to the security that this classical relationship provides for the servant and the sense of worth and meaning that is deeply felt on the part of a servant who serves a great man. These qualities of meaning, worth, security, and relationship are often tragically missing from the life of the modern industrial worker with his forty-hour week. The servant offers loyalty, obedience, and a great deal of hard work, but with an authentic Middle Eastern nobleman the benefits mentioned above are enormous. Because of these things, this master-servant image is profoundly appropriate for illustrating the believer's relationship to God and to His unique agent/Son.

Jeremias has convincingly demonstrated that the introductory phrase (17:7) *tis ex humōn* ("which of you") is a phrase unique to Jesus that always expects an emphatically negative answer (Jeremias, *Parables*, 103; Bailey, *Poet*, 121f.). Certainly no one in any Middle Eastern audience could imagine any servant expecting special honors after fulfilling his duty in the field. The master is not *indebted* to him for having plowed the field or guarded the sheep. Then too, the afternoon meal (here specifically referred to in v. 8 by the verb *deipnēsō*, "I shall eat supper/dine"), is not at eight in the evening but rather in the late afternoon around three o'clock (Jeremias, *Eucharistic*, 44f.). Thus we are not dealing with harsh hours imposed by an unfeeling master but rather the normal expectations of a relatively short day's chores. The point is not, "Does the master allow the servant food and rest?" but rather, "Does he extend privilege to the servant who fulfills the daily assignment?" The clear answer is—no!

STANZA TWO

> "Will he not rather say to him,
> '*Prepare for me* something and I shall dine,
>   and gird yourself and *serve me*,
> till *I eat and drink*,
>   and afterward *you shall eat and drink*'?"

SERVE THE MASTER
THEN YOURSELF

The master is the master and is *not* the equal of his servant. Here the master does not eat with the servant. Again, there is a great deal of imagery on the other side of the coin in the New Testament taken from the language of common meals. Jesus eats with his disciples *and* even with sinners. The disciples are called friends, not servants (John 15:15), even though the servant is not greater than his master (John 15:20). Jesus stands at the door eager to enter and eat with anyone who will open (Rev. 3:20). Whatever these images mean, they do not mean an easy equality between the master (Jesus) and his servant disciples. The easy equality reflected in the popular chorus, "My God and I go through the fields together," is unknown in the New Testament. Again this little parable is a crucial corrective to a disastrous misunderstanding of the above texts. As in Luke 15:3–7 (cf. Bailey, *Poet*, 144f.), the third stanza is commentary and thematically matches the first stanza.

STANZA THREE

"Does the servant have special merit   SERVANTS
  because he did what was commanded?   ORDERS FULFILLED
    So you, also, when you have done what was commanded   ORDERS FULFILLED
      say, 'Nothing is owing us servants, we
        have only done our duty.' "   REWARDS?

The first stanza began with a question expecting an emphatically negative answer. This matching stanza begins in the same way. The four major themes set
out in the first stanza are carefully repeated here, as we have observed. In this case
the disciples/apostles are called on to identify with the servant of the parable and
to see their position illustrated by his. This position is properly understood only
when the text is examined carefully in the light of the language and the cultural
assumptions of the story. Two key words that we have translated "special merit"
and "nothing owing" need special scrutiny.

The traditional understanding of the first line of this stanza is reflected in
the RSV, which translates, "Does he thank the servant...?" The common
Greek verb "thank" (*eucharisteō*) occurs twice in Matthew, twice in Mark, and
four times in Luke. It is used in the account of the healing of the ten lepers in
Luke 17:16. Thus Luke knows the word and uses it more than the other
evangelists. Yet in this parable the actual words in the text are *mē echei charin tō
doulō*. Literally this reads, "Does he have any grace/favor for the servant?" The
word *charin* is the common New Testament word for grace. The theological
weight of this great word must not be overlooked, as we will note below. But here
we need ask only what is meant by the phrase, "have grace/favor for...." In the
Epistles there are clear cases where "to have grace for" means "to be grateful
to" (cf. I Tim. 1:12; II Tim. 1:3; Rom. 7:25; II Cor. 9:15; Bauer, 886). Yet in
Luke the word *grace* has to do primarily with credit (6:32–34) and favor (1:30).
Bauer lists a series of passages, most of them in Luke-Acts, where the word
grace appears in the phrase "to have grace," and says of them, "in these
passages the mng. comes close to reward" (Bauer, 885; cf. Luke 2:52; 6:32;
Acts 2:47; 7:10, 46). The relational situation implied by the use of this word (in a
Middle Eastern context) can be seen clearly in Luke 1:30. There Mary is told,
"You have found favor with God." Immediately after this comes the announcement, "You will conceive in your womb and bear a son...." This mirrors the
Old Testament refrain, "If I have found favor... then..." (cf. Gen. 18:3; Num.
11:15; I Sam. 20:29; Est. 5:8). If the servant or inferior has favor from his
superior, then the superior is indebted to the petitioner and is expected to grant
some special request or offer some special gift. It is true that these texts talk of
"*finding* favor" while Luke 17:8 speaks of "*having* favor." But in the first case
the petitioner has been granted favor as a gift; it is too great to be earned. Thus he
has only *found* favor as a gift. This parable is clearly talking of work accomplished and its results. After all of this work does the servant *have favor*? Is the

master indebted to him? Is there any *credit* due him (Luke 6:32–34)? Has he earned any merit? Is there anything owing him? The question is much deeper than a verbal expression of thanks. The master may well express appreciation to a servant at the end of a day's work with a friendly word of thanks. The issue is much more serious than this. Is the master *indebted* to his servant when orders are carried out? This is the question that expects a resoundingly negative answer in the parable.

The above understanding of the text is reflected in the great thirteenth-century Arabic version of Hibat Allah Ibn al-'Assāl, who translates, "Is there to this servant merit because he did what was commanded him?" Montefiore quotes one Merx (?) who writes,

> "Has he (the servant) any favor (i.e., in the sight of his master) because he did what he was told?" Does he acquire any special favor or merit? The sense is improved by this reading (Montefiore, *Gospels*, II, 1009).

Trench translates "doth he count himself especially beholden to that servant?" (Trench, 476). These two scholars differ only on the question of the subject of the verb *to have*. For Montefiore the servant is the subject, and for Trench the master is the subject. In the matching line in the first stanza we also find the verb *to have* and there the master is the subject and the servant the object. This seems to be the best understanding of the present line. This comes across somewhat awkwardly in English and reads literally, "Does he have special merit for the servant? . . ." Semitic languages have no verb *to have* and this further complicates any attempt to understand the language precisely, yet the sense is clear. The point is, does the master *owe* the servant anything because he has carried out his orders? Clearly not.

So, finally, the application is made to the audience. The passive "when you have done *what was commanded*" has been identified by Jeremias as "a periphrasis for the divine name" (Jeremias, *Parables*, 193). The final line, like its counterpart in the first stanza, ends with direct speech. Here again we are faced with a long-standing translation problem. The traditional understanding of this concluding statement is "we are miserable/useless servants, we have only done what was our duty." The key word is *achreios*, which has two shades of meaning. The first is *useless* (which would refer to their unprofitable functions as servants). The other is *miserable*, which is somewhat stronger and refers not to their work but to themselves. B. T. D. Smith summarizes the problem and notes a widely held solution:

> Clearly a slave who does all that is required of him is not useless to his master, and many would therefore omit the adjective as a gloss (B. T. D. Smith, 184).

Yet Smith accepts the adjective and translates it "good-for-nothing." Jeremias rejects *useless* in favor of *miserable* and decides that it is ". . . an expression of modesty" (Jeremias, *Parables*, 193). In summary, the meaning "useless/

worthless'' (in reference to their work) cannot be correct because the servant does his duty and is not worthless. The meaning ''miserable/good-for-nothing'' (in reference to themselves) seems harsh and unnecessarily self-critical for a hard-working servant. Thus a long list of scholars have decided that the word must be a gloss (Bauer, 128), though *only* the Sinai Old Syriac supports this decision textually. However, there is another way to understand the problematic word *achreios*. The Greek word is actually *chreios* with what the grammarians call an alpha privative prefix. We have this same construction in English with the words moral and amoral. The prefixing of the *a* negates the word. In this case, *chreios* by itself means ''need'' and thus the word *achreios* very literally means ''without need.'' It is easy to see how such a word could evolve in meaning. The person for whom you are ''without need'' is the one who is useless. Then the one who is useless usually has some undesirable character traits and so is miserable/good-for-nothing. But in this case, we need to return to the very literal translation of the word that gives us ''without need.'' This understanding of *achreios* was suggested by Bengel:

> akhreios is one *hou ouk esti okreia* or *khreos,* of whom there is no need, a person we can dispense with, dispensable, one to whom God the Master owes no thanks or favor (Bengel, II, 160).

The difficulty here is that Bengel leaves a basic ambiguity unresolved. When we opt for ''without need,'' does it mean the master is ''without need'' of the servant, or does it mean the servant is ''without need'' (of reward)? Bengel stated the first and hinted at the second and thus left the question unresolved. T. W. Manson defined unprofitable as ''not claiming merit'' (*Sayings*, 303). Yet he does not indicate how he reaches this conclusion linguistically. It is our view that he is right and that this understanding *is* linguistically defensible.

We begin with the Syriac and Arabic versions. A number of the major Arabic translations from the eleventh century onward agree with Hibat Allah Ibn al-'Assāl, who translates, ''We are servants to whom nothing is owing'' (*naḥnu khuddām la ḥāja lana*). Literally this reads, ''We are servants and we have no need.'' Clearly Hibat Allah has read *achreios* as meaning ''without need.'' The question then becomes, Does this translation make any sense in the context? The answer is yes, if the phrase is placed in a Middle Eastern cultural setting. This phrase is unambiguous idiomatic speech among Palestinian and Lebanese village people. One village workman renders some small service to a house owner and the following conversation takes place:

House owner:	*fī ḥāja?*	(Literally: ''Is there any need?''
		Meaning: ''Do I owe you anything?'')
Workman:	*ma fī ḥāja*	(Literally: ''There is no need.''
		Meaning: ''You owe me nothing.'')

This idiomatic speech form is widespread and, to our knowledge, universal in our Middle Eastern world. With vocabulary variants we have traced it from Syria to the Sudan. Obviously Hibat Allah is translating in a fashion that will make sense to his readers. His thirteenth-century translation gives the reader the above meaning. Furthermore, this translation of "without need" for *achreios* occurs in the Harclean Syriac, which reads *la ḥoshḥo* (Vat. Syr. 268, folio 110ʳ; cf. Bailey, *Hibat Allah,* 22–24). It is well-known that this seventh-century Syriac version is an extremely literal translation of the Greek. Thus the Harclean reading may be merely an attempt at literalism. Yet, at the same time, the translator must have expected his readers to understand *something* by the above phrase. He clearly rejected "unprofitable" for "without need." Is it not possible to affirm that he also recognized the latter as the intent of the text and for that reason chose it over the Peshitta with its traditional reading of "unprofitable"? Following Hibat Allah's lead we can suggest that the original editor/author/compiler of the Travel Narrative has used *achreios* as the equivalent of *ouden chreian.* That is, he has taken the negative and attached it to the word. Thus the original parable instructs the disciples to say, "We are servants to whom nothing is owing, we have only done our duty." This translation is etymologically possible. It makes profound sense in the context of the overall parable. Important early Arabic and Syriac translations give this reading, and we would submit that it is the best understanding of the text. With this meaning the problem of hard-working, "useless" servants is solved without any need to eliminate the word as a supposed gloss.

This is not the only case in the parables where a Greek word with an alpha privative is perhaps better understood as a root word with a negative. In Luke 11:8 the problematic *anaideia* as a Greek composite word means "shamelessness." But when one begins with the root of the word and adds a negative the meaning becomes "avoidance of shame," which we have argued is the original intent of *anaideia* in that parable (Bailey, *Poet,* 125–133).

The word "servant" is *doulos* and means "slave" also. Because the word "slave" in our society has totally negative connotations it is problematic to use it as a translation for *doulos* in this parable. Paul calls himself a "slave of Jesus Christ" (Rom. 1:1) and obviously means it in a positive sense. Here also a positive sense is meant. The disciple is not an employee who can work and expect payment. He is a slave for whom the master accepts total responsibility, and who enjoys total security, and who, at the same time, labors out of a sense of duty and loyalty, not in the hope of gaining rewards. Indeed, after he has fulfilled *all* commands he says, "Nothing is owing me, I have only done my duty."

The theological application of this carefully written parable is weighty indeed. Clearly we are again talking about salvation and good works. The Jewish commentary on the Psalms (*Midrash Tehillim*), in explaining Psalm 46:1, reads,

> Not for their works were the children Israelites redeemed from Egypt, but so that God might make himself an eternal name, and because of his favor . . . (Montefiore, *Rabbinic,* 361).

In commenting on this parable Montefiore mentions the rabbinic doctrine of "tit-for-tat":

In no other point is Jesus' antagonism to, and reaction against, certain ten-
dencies in that teaching more justified and more wholesome than here
(Montefiore, *Gospels*, II, 1009).

For Jesus salvation was a gift.

In addition to works and salvation there is the related topic of motivation
for service and its results. Do we serve in order to gain? Having served do we
have claims on God? This parable says no to both questions.

Some contemporary voices supported Jesus' view here set forth. In the
Sayings of the Fathers (*Pirke Aboth*) one Simeon the Just (*ca.* 300 B.C.) is
reported to have said, "be like slaves who serve the master not with a view to
receiving a present: and let the fear of Heaven be upon you" (Mishna *Pirke
Aboth*, 1:3, Charles, II, 691; cf. also 2:9). Hunter observes,

> The parable of the Farmer and his Man therefore warns us against importing
> into religion that book-keeping mentality which imagines we can run up
> credit with God by our works. Jesus says it can't be done. So does the Apostle
> Paul (Hunter, *Then*, 84).

The Egyptian commentator Saʿīd sees the parable as relating specifically
to the doctrine of justification and affirming that God's grace cannot be earned
(Saʿīd, 424). This becomes abundantly clear when the original language is
allowed to surface from under the traditional translation. The parable asks the
question, "Does he (God) have grace/merit for the servant because he did what
was commanded?" The answer is clearly, No! Jeremias is correct in identifying
the parable as "a demand for renunciation of all Pharisaic self-righteousness"
(Jeremias, *Parables*, 193).

A final question is, Who is the master? The first and foremost answer is
clearly God. Are there then any Christological implications for the parable?
Again these are perhaps more overheard than heard. Yet they are unavoidably
present. Jesus is addressed as "Master" all through the tradition. The disciple in
the Oriental world has always been and remains in traditional society a servant of
the master. The student/disciple literally waits hand and foot on the teacher. He
often sleeps in his quarters and provides the services of a house servant. Foerster
describes the first-century disciple:

> The pupil took his turn in preparing the common meal and catering for the
> general needs of the group. He performed personal services for his teacher,
> observed his conduct and was his respectful, loving, humble companion
> (*JPFC*, II, 964).

Jesus is God's unique agent/Son, and as such he is the master of the disciples and
they are his servants. Certainly these Christological implications develop in the
understanding of the post-Easter Church, but we would suggest that they are
already present in the parable in its original setting.

Finally, we need to ask what was the response that the parable intended to evoke from the disciples and what is the theological cluster used to elicit that response?

The listening disciples were perhaps pressed to perceive, "We are servants whose finest efforts earn us no merit with our master. As servant/slaves we do our duty and expect no pay." This hoped-for response is evoked by the use of a number of theological motifs. We would cautiously suggest the following:

1. The believer is a servant/slave. He is expected to obey and know his place as a servant.

2. Grace/salvation is a gift, not a reward for services rendered.

3. The servant of God labors to fulfill a duty. He does not develop a claim on God nor serve to receive rewards.

4. God is the master of the believer. Yet, at the same time, the believer's servanthood is appropriately fulfilled in obedience to God's unique agent/Son Jesus, who should be served with diligence and loyalty.

In passing, we note that the entire question of rewards is given a great deal of attention in the synoptic material. Bultmann succinctly summarizes the subject: "Jesus promises rewards to those who are obedient without thought of reward" (Bultmann, *Theology*, I, 14).

Thus the mighty theme of the nature of God's grace is set forth. Here it is stated negatively. The most hardworking servant/slave knows that nothing is owing him because of who he is. He does his duty and earns no merit. Obviously the master's gifts come unmerited and unearned, and so it is with God.

Chapter 8

THE JUDGE AND THE WIDOW
(Luke 18:1-8)

As in many of the parables, here also a deceptively simple story hides a complex series of theological themes and interpretive problems. Yet hopefully a close look at the literary background, the rhetorical form, and the culture will help unlock for us at least some of the theological secrets of this treasured story.

Here in the parable of the Judge and the Widow there is a clearly identifiable literary background. As we observed in the parable of the Barren Fig Tree, a careful comparison between the parable in the mouth of Jesus and its prototype is crucial. By doing so we are able to see what he has borrowed, what he has transformed, and, of equal importance, what he has left out. In this case, our prototype is in Ben Sirach. The text in question is as follows:

> He will not ignore the supplication of the fatherless,
>   nor the widow when she pours out her story.
>
> Do not the tears of the widow run down her cheek
>   as she cries out against him who has caused them to fall?
>
> He whose service is pleasing to the Lord will be accepted,
>   and his prayer will reach to the clouds.
>
> The prayer of the humble pierces the clouds,
>   and he will not be consoled until it reaches the Lord.
>
> He will not desist until the Most High visits him
>   and does justice for the righteous and executes judgment.
>
> The Lord will not delay,
>   neither will he be patient with them,
>
> till he crushes the loins of the unmerciful,
>   and repays vengeance on the gentiles (Ben Sirach 35:15-19).

Points of similarity and dissimilarity are many and significant. These need to be examined in three categories: points of complete similarity, points of similarity (but with a difference), and points of complete dissimilarity.

POINTS OF COMPLETE SIMILARITY

1. In each, the text begins with the topic of prayer in general. Then, after an illustration, each moves on to discuss the specific topic of justice for the righteous in the face of oppression.

2. Both use the rabbinic principle of "from the light to the heavy" (from a "light" illustration from daily life to a "heavy" application).

POINTS OF SIMILARITY (BUT WITH A DIFFERENCE)

1. The basic figure of a widow crying out for help is similar in both stories. (Yet the repeated nature of the widow's actions in Jesus' parable is more prominent. Unlike Jesus, Ben Sirach shifts to the persistent humble *man* who will not be consoled until he has an answer. That is, Jesus makes more of persistence *and* Ben Sirach shifts to a male figure.)

2. The patience of God is mentioned in both texts. (Yet Ben Sirach says God *is not* patient with the *ungodly*. As we will see, Jesus affirms that God *is* patient with the *godly*.)

3. Both texts discuss the vindication of the righteous. (Yet in Sirach God acts in two ways. He executes justice for the righteous and vengeance on the unrighteous. In Jesus' parable the second is omitted.)

4. Each has a concrete illustration, a widow. (Yet Jesus' use of the illustration is expanded into a full parable.)

POINTS OF COMPLETE DISSIMILARITY

1. In Sirach the way to get your prayers heard is to render service that is "pleasing to the Lord." Such a one is accepted and his prayers reach the clouds. None of this God-hears-you-if-you-serve-Him theology is reflected in Jesus' parable.

2. The figure of the unjust judge is a dramatic new thrust in Jesus' parable. It is bold and risky. A negative character symbolically represents God. This then gives a sharper cutting edge to the "from the light to the heavy" principle of interpretation.

Thus it is obvious that some material from Sirach has been used, some transformed, and some omitted. The similarities are so numerous that we assume with Montefiore that there is conscious borrowing. These points of similarity and dissimilarity will be examined in detail as we proceed.

The topic of the parable of the Judge and the Widow and that of the parable which follows it obviously relate to prayer. The close parallels with Luke 11:5-8 have often been noted. Elsewhere I have argued that the central section of Luke has an outline that brings Luke 11:1-13 into a parallel position with 18:1-14 (Bailey, *Poet,* 79-82). In the first case there are three units of tradition on the subject of prayer; in the second there are two. At the same time the passages relates to the question of the coming of the Son of man and thus to the previous passage in 17:22-37. This latter relationship is reinforced by the Lucan introduction in 18:1 and by the conclusion in 8b. Thus two themes are woven into the passage: the topic of prayer and that of the paradoxical suddenness/delay of the parousia. Indeed, as we will observe, each of these two passages (18:1-8, 9-14) has a unique thrust in relation to prayer.

The question of authenticity for the present passage is too crucial to be ignored. The passage breaks down into three sections. First is the evangelist's introduction (v. 1), second, the parable proper (vv. 2-5), and finally, the Dominical application of the parable (vv. 6-8). The introduction is clearly the work of Luke or his source and is not a part of the parable. Significantly, the following parable (18:9-14) also begins with the evangelist's introduction which, as we will see, is also his commentary on what the parable is all about. It is our view that these introductions must be taken seriously as important indications of the original meaning of the parable. Bultmann has placed this parable in a list of parables for which the original meaning is irrecoverably lost (Bultmann, *History,* 199). Yet if we take the literary background in Sirach and the evangelist's introduction seriously, we have evidence for the original intent of the parable.

In regard to the parable and, in particular, the Dominical application at the end, opinion is sharply divided. Linnemann argues that both are secondary (Linnemann, 187f.). Jeremias presents weighty linguistic arguments for the authenticity of both (Jeremias, *Parables,* 154-56; cf. Marshall, 669-671). Kümmel finds specific features that mark the Dominical application as original and argues that it is "in no way a re-interpretation, since the parable, as a metaphor, can bear a particular as well as a general application" (Kümmel, 59). Kümmel's main point is that the text talks of God's salvation coming quickly and that this particular emphasis was strong in Jesus' own teaching (*ibid.,* 54).

In the prototype of the parable (found in Sirach), we noted an application of the figure of the weeping widow to prayer in general, which then turned at the end of the passage to a specific discussion of God's intervention for the community of the faithful. The same move occurs here. Marshall observes an historically closer parallel:

In fact, we have a structure similar to that in the parable of the prodigal son, where a story, whose central character appears to be the father and whose central concern is to depict the character of God, turns out to have a "sting in the tail" as it presents the picture of the elder brother and asks the audience whether they behave like him. So here, after depicting the character of God, the parable turns in application to the disciples and asks whether they will show a faith as persistent as the nagging of the widow (Marshall, 670f.).

Thus from linguistic, theological, and literary points of view there are important reasons for affirming both the parable and the Dominical application as authentic to Jesus.

THE INTRODUCTION

And he was saying a parable to them to the effect that they ought always to pray and not lose heart/be afraid.

The audience is assumed by the text to be the disciples (17:22). The following parable (18:9–14) is addressed to those with a self-righteous spirit like some Pharisees. In the parallel teaching material on prayer (Luke 11:1–13) we can observe the identical shift. There the initial material is spoken to the disciples (11:1–8) and the parable/poem on the Father's Gifts (vv. 9–13) is most likely spoken to the Pharisees (Bailey, *Poet,* 139–142).

The introduction reinforces the general theme of persistence in prayer. At the same time, the specific application at the conclusion of the parable is hinted at in this introduction. Not only in regard to God's decisive intervention in history are the faithful to be persistent in prayer, but they are to seek Him whenever He seems far away and the confidence of the believer wavers. The solution to fear is prayer. In Shakespeare's famous play Macbeth is fearful lest their plans fail. His wife tries to steel his nerves with the command, "But screw your courage to the sticking place, and we'll not fail!" (act 1, scene 7). Macbeth does so and yet his grand plans disintegrate into tragedy for himself and all around him. Here a simple piety expressed in trusting prayer is commanded as a solution to the fear that robs the believer of his tranquility and the will to endure. Jesus and his little band were faced with intensified rejection and hostility on all sides. Surely this generalized introduction/interpretation of the parable can be seen as authentic to the specific situation Jesus faced, as well as an appropriate introduction to the parable at a later stage in the life of the early Church.

THE PARABLE

The first stanza tells of the judge and the second of the widow. The third returns to the judge (with the same motifs), and the fourth then returns to the widow. The three themes of JUDGE–GOD–MAN of stanza one are repeated in the identical order in the third stanza. Stanzas two and four on the widow have the same themes, but in the last stanza the order is reversed. It is pointless to commit one more rash act *metri causa* and suggest that the last stanza may have

Luke 18:1-5

1	A certain judge there was in a certain city.	JUDGE
	God he did not fear	GOD
	and man he did not respect.	MAN
	2 And a widow there was in that city,	WIDOW
	and she was coming to him	COMING
	saying, "Vindicate me from my adversary."	VINDICATE
3	He did not want to for a (certain) time.	JUDGE
	Then he said to himself, "Although I do not fear God	GOD
	and do not respect man,	MAN
	4 yet because she causes me trouble, this widow,	WIDOW
	I will vindicate her,	VINDICATE
	lest in continual coming she wear me out."	COMING

had the theme of vindication at the end (like stanza three). Such may be the case, or the language originally may not have been that precisely aligned (as in many cases of parallelism in the Psalms). Yet the stanzas are intact, without any extra interpretive details. Each theme has a balancing line and the overall effect is symmetrical and artistically satisfying.

STANZA ONE—THE PAGAN JUDGE

A certain judge there was in a certain city.	JUDGE
God he did not fear	GOD
and man he did not respect.	MAN

In II Chronicles 19:4-6 Jehoshaphat chooses judges for the land and tells them,

> ... consider what you do, for you judge not for man but for the Lord; ... now then, let the fear of the Lord be upon you, take heed what you do, for there is no perversion of justice with the Lord our God, or partiality, or taking bribes.

Such admonitions are always needed in every society, and the Old Testament keeps trying to establish justice in the gate. Amos in particular was upset over the corruption of the judges (Amos 2:6-7; 5:10-13). In New Testament times the same problem surfaced. Edersheim (*Life*, II, 287) describes judges in the city of Jerusalem who were traditionally so corrupt that they were called *Dayyaney Gezeloth* (Robber-Judges) rather than *Dayyaney Gezeroth* (Judges of Prohibitions), which was their real title. The Talmud speaks of village judges who are willing to pervert justice for a dish of meat (B.T. *Baba Kamma* 114a). In perversion of Jehoshaphat's directive the judge in our parable cares neither for man nor for God. Plummer points out that the word often translated "respect" (*entripō*) can also mean "being abashed, having a feeling of awe" (Plummer,

412). The active of the verb is to "make ashamed" and the passive is either "be put to shame" or "have respect for" (Bauer, 269). But starting with the Old Syriac, down through all the other Syriac and all the Arabic versions for another thousand years, the only translation we have had here in the Middle East is, "He is not ashamed before people." A very important aspect of the description of the judge is thereby overlooked when we read with our Western translation tradition, "have respect for." The point is that Middle Eastern traditional culture is a shame–pride culture to a significant degree. That is, a particular pattern of social behavior is encouraged by appeals to shame. The parent does not tell the child, "That is wrong, Johnny" (with an appeal to an abstract standard of right and wrong) but "That is shameful, Johnny" (an appeal to that which stimulates feelings of shame or feelings of pride). In such a society the vocabulary that surrounds the concept of shame is very important (Bailey, *Poet*, 132). One of the sharpest criticisms possible of an adult in the Middle Eastern village today is *mā jikhtashī* ("he does not feel shame"). The point is that such a person does a shameful thing; you cry "Shame" to him but he does not feel ashamed. His inner sense of what constitutes a good act and what is a shameful act is missing. He cannot be shamed.

In this regard we are dealing with another case where very ancient attitudes are reflected. Jeremiah had the same problem. We are told, "the wise men shall be put to shame" (Jer. 8:9), but in regard to the prophets and priests he writes,

> Were they ashamed when they committed abomination?
>   No, they were not at all ashamed;
> they did not know how to blush (8:12).

The Hebrew text uses two strong words for shame (*bwsh, klm*) and speaks precisely to the problem faced with the judge. *Nothing* shames him. There is no spark of honor left in his soul to which anyone can appeal.

The problem with this judge is not a failure to "respect" other people in the sense of respecting someone of learning or high position. Rather it is a case of his inability to sense the evil of his actions in the presence of one who should make him ashamed. In this case he is hurting a destitute widow. He should feel shame. But the whole world can cry "Shame!" and it will make no impression on him. He does not *feel shame* before men. We have precisely the same concept and the same word in the parable of the Rebellious Tenants in Luke 20:13. The tenants refuse to give some of the fruits of the vineyard to the owner. They treat the servants of the owner shamefully. Finally the master says, "I will send my beloved son; it may be they will feel shame before (*entrapēsontai*) him (so translated in all Syriac and Arabic versions). The hope is not that they might treat him kindly, but rather that in his presence they might feel ashamed of what they have done and give up their rebellious acts. But there also the tenants involved *could not be shamed.* In both texts the Greek word carries this meaning. Middle Eastern culture requires it and Middle Eastern fathers give us this meaning in their translations. Thus we have in Luke 18 a clear picture of a *very* difficult man. He has no fear of God; the cry of "for God's sake" will do no good. He also has no inner sense of what is right and what is shameful to which one can appeal. Thus the cry, "For the sake of this destitute widow!" will likewise be useless. Obviously the only way to influence such a man is through bribery. To such a man comes the widow.

STANZA TWO—THE HELPLESS WIDOW

And a widow there was in that city,	WIDOW
and she was coming to him	COMING
saying, "Vindicate me from my adversary."	VINDICATE

The widow in the Old Testament is a typical symbol of the innocent, powerless oppressed (cf. Ex. 22:22–23; Deut. 10:18, 24:17, 27:19; Job 22:9, 24:3, 21; Ps. 68:5; Isa. 10:2; also Jth. 9:4). Isaiah 1:17 calls on the rulers and the people to "plead for the widow." Then, in verse 23, we are told, "everyone loves a bribe . . . and the widow's cause does not come to them." The Jewish legal tradition required that on the basis of Isaiah 1:17 "the suit of an orphan must always be heard first; next, that of a widow . . ." (Dembitz, 204). Thus this woman had legal rights that were being violated. Bruce writes of her, "too weak to compel, too poor to buy justice" (Bruce, *Parabolic*, 159). Plummer observes, "she had neither a protector to coerce, nor money to bribe" (Plummer, 412; cf. Marshall, 669). Ibn al-Ṭayyib comments on the plight of the widow in Middle Eastern society:

> In every time and place the greedy have found the widow vulnerable to oppression and injustice for she has no one to protect her. Thus God commands the judges to give her special consideration, Jer. 22:3 (Ibn al-Ṭayyib, Manqariyūs edition, II, 312).

Jeremias suggests that "a debt, a pledge, or a portion of an inheritance is being withheld from her" (Jeremias, *Parables*, 153); and, as Bruce observes, "A widow was one who was pretty sure to have plenty of adversaries if she had anything to devour" (Bruce, *Parabolic*, 159). The issue is clearly money because, according to the Talmud, a qualified scholar could decide money cases sitting alone (B.T. *Sanhedrin* 4b, Sonc., 15).

Her cry is a call for justice and protection, not vengeance. Smith translates it, "Do me justice with regard to my opponent" (C. W. F. Smith, 186).

By way of summary, the parable thus far makes three assumptions.

1. The widow is in the right (and is being denied justice).
2. For some reason, the judge does not want to serve her (she has paid no bribes?).

3. The judge prefers to favor her adversary. (Either the adversary is influential or he *has* paid bribes.)

Smith comments,

> She may be presumed to have been incapable of rewarding him, and we may assume further that it would probably be to his advantage to let her oppressor have his way (C. W. F. Smith, 186f.).

In the last century a Western traveler witnessed a scene in Iraq that gives us the wider picture behind the parable. He writes,

> It was in the ancient city of Nisibis, in Mesopotamia. Immediately on entering the gate of the city on one side stood the prison, with its barred windows, through which the prisoners thrust their arms and begged for alms. Opposite was a large open hall, the court of Justice of the place. On a slightly raised dais at the further end sat the *Kadi*, or judge, half buried in cushions. Round him squatted various secretaries and other notables. The populace crowded into the rest of the hall, a dozen voices clamouring at once, each claiming that his cause should be the first heard. The more prudent litigants joined not in the fray, but held whispered communications with the secretaries, passing bribes, euphemistically called fees, into the hands of one or another. When the greed of the underlings was satisfied, one of them would whisper to the *Kadi*, who would promptly call such and such a case. It seemed to be ordinarily taken for granted that judgment would go for the litigant who had bribed highest. But meantime a poor woman on the skirts of the crowd perpetually interrupted the proceedings with loud cries for justice. She was sternly bidden to be silent, and reproachfully told that she came there every day. "And so I will," she cried out, "till the *Kadi* hears me." At length, at the end of a suit, the judge impatiently demanded, "What does that woman want?" Her story was soon told. Her only son had been taken for a soldier, and she was alone, and could not till her piece of ground; yet the tax-gatherer had forced her to pay the impost, from which as a lone widow she could be exempt. The judge asked a few questions, and said, "Let her be exempt." Thus her perseverance was rewarded. Had she had money to fee a clerk, she might have been excused long before (Tristram, 228f.).

A long list of commentators from Plummer to Jeremias has noted this account as helpful in filling out the cultural details that are the background of the parable. Yet there is a crucial element both in the parable and in Tristram's account that has gone unnoticed. Ordinarily women in the Middle East do not go to court. The Middle East was and is a man's world and women are not expected to participate with men in the pushing, shouting world described above. There is, furthermore, Jewish evidence for this from talmudic times. Tractate *Shebuoth* reads,

> Do, then, men come to court, and do not women ever come to court? . . . —You might say, it is not usual for a woman, because "all glorious is the King's daughter within," (note: Ps. XLV, 14; the King's daughter [i.e. the

Jewish woman] is modest, and stays within her home as much as possible)
(B.T. *Shebuoth* 30a, Sonc., 167).

In the light of this reticence to have women appear in court one could understand
her presence there as meaning that she is entirely alone with no men in an
extended family to speak for her. This may be the assumption of the story. In
such a case her total helplessness would be emphasized.

Yet there is another even more important element. During the Lebanese
civil war of 1975–76 a Palestinian peasant woman of my acquaintance was
caught in a tragedy. Her cousin disappeared. He was assumed to be kidnapped by
one of the many armed groups fighting in the city of Beirut. The entire extended
family searched in vain for him or his body. He was the only son of his widowed
mother and was not a member of any paramilitary group. In desperation the
family sent a delegation of three peasant *women* to the political/military leader of
the leftist forces in the area where he had disappeared. The man they went to see
was an internationally known, powerful military and political figure. These three
women shouted their way into an audience with him and, once there, flung a
torrent of hard words in his face. The entire scene was vividly described to me
by my peasant friend the following day. I specifically asked, "What would have
happened if the men of your family had said such things to this man?" With
raised eyebrows and a shake of the head she answered, "O, they would have
been killed at once." Tristram heard ". . . a dozen voices clamouring at once,
each claiming that his cause should be the first heard." Thus *many* people were
shouting. How did the *widow* get attention? Obviously her shouting was different
from the others. In traditional society in the Middle East women are generally
powerless in our man's world. But at the same time, they are respected and
honored. Men can be mistreated in public, but not women. Women can scream at
a public figure and nothing will happen to them. In the case of my Palestinian
friend, the family had *deliberately* sent the women because they could express
openly their sense of hurt and betrayal in language guaranteed to evoke a response. The men could not say the same things and stay alive. This same
background is reflected in the rest of the parable.

STANZA THREE—THE RELUCTANT JUDGE

He did not want to for a (certain) time.	JUDGE
Then he said to himself, "Although I do not fear God	MAN
and do not respect man,"	GOD

STANZA FOUR—THE VINDICATED WIDOW

"yet because she causes me trouble, this widow,	WIDOW
I will vindicate her,	VINDICATE
lest in continual coming she wear me out."	COMING

The word "certain" we have cautiously accepted in the text. It occurs in Codex Bezae and some of the Syriac, Latin, and Coptic versions. It reinforces the parallelism between stanzas one and three, but may not be original. In any case, the judge confesses the accuracy of the judgment passed on his character. He knows that he does not fear God and that no one can call him into account and make him feel ashamed. If anyone flings even such accusations at him it will have no effect.

In the phrase "he said to himself," we have what Black has called "a well-known Semitism . . . 'to speak the mind', 'to think' " (Black, 302). This kind of soliloquizing is common in the parables (cf. the Rich Fool; the Prodigal Son; the Unjust Steward; the Master of the Vineyard), and with the Semitic idiom noted above marks the parable's genuineness.

The word here translated "wear me out" is a prizefighting term for a blow under the eye (cf. I Cor. 9:27) and has led many commentators to suggest that the judge is fearful lest the woman get violent (Linnemann, 185). But the language does not require this interpretation and the cultural milieu of the Middle East excludes it. The widow can shout all kinds of insults at him, but if she tries to get violent she will be forcibly removed and not allowed to return. Enough is enough! Derrett argues that the word means "to blacken the face" (Derrett, *Judge*, 189–191). He correctly observes that the phrase is common throughout the East. However, it means "to destroy the reputation of" and describes a man with a sense of personal honor, which he is anxious to preserve. Our judge has no such personal honor. Derrett observes this objection and tries to defend his interpretation by suggesting that the phrase "have no respect for man" is really a compliment offered to an impartial judge. Against Derrett we would argue that "God he did not fear and man he did not respect" is clearly meant to be a double-edged negative statement, not part compliment and part insult. Thus the judge is indeed shameless and as a result you cannot "blacken his face." Again we prefer the long, rich Arabic translation tradition that gives variations of "lest she give me a headache!" Ibn al-Ṭayyib is particularly helpful. He notes that the language can refer to a blow on the head and comments, "This exaggeration on the part of the judge is to indicate the extent to which her persistence has irritated him" (Ibn al-Ṭayyib, Manqariyūs edition, II, 312).

The Greek *eis telos* we have translated "continual." Ibn al-'Assāl gives this an added emphasis with the wording, "lest she forever continue coming and wearing me out." The Greek phrase is strong and implies a will to go on forever. The judge is convinced that the woman will never give up. T. W. Manson calls it a "war of attrition" between the two of them (*Sayings,* 306).

As we have observed, the parable is a clear case of the rabbinic principle of "from the light to the heavy" (*qal waḥomer*). The woman is in an apparently hopeless situation. She is a woman in a man's world, a widow without money or powerful friends. The judge cannot be appealed to out of duty to God, and no human being can make him ashamed of any evil act he may perpetrate on the innocent. *Yet* this woman not only gets a hearing but has the case settled in her favor. Taken with its introduction the main thrust is clearly persistence in prayer. If this woman's needs are met, *how much more* the needs of the pious who pray not to a harsh judge but to a loving Father. However discouraged and hopeless their situation may seem to be, it is not as bad as that of this widow. They can rest assured that their petitions are heard and acted upon. When fear grips the heart the believer is challenged to pray, and to pray continually in the face of all discouragements with full confidence that God will act in his best interests.

Verses 6–8 have long been called a *crux interpretum*. It is not our intent to review all the traditional solutions and debate each in turn (Marshall, 674–77); rather we shall set forth our own understanding with the hope that it may help contribute to a solution of the problems involved. A literal translation of the text with its parallelisms displayed is as follows:

1 *Shall* not *God make vindication for his elect*   (future)

2   the ones crying to him day and night?   (present)

3   Also he is slow to anger over them.   (present)

4 I say to you that *he shall make vindication for them* speedily. (future)

5 Yet when the Son of man comes will he find faith on the earth?

The third line is traditionally read as a question and the key word *makrothumeō* translated as "patience" or "delay" (cf. RSV "will he delay long over them?"). The fifth line is problematic and is thought by many to be a concluding reflection of the evangelist or the Church, or a separate saying of Jesus attached here by the evangelist or his source. Granting any of these as possibilities, this final phrase clearly indicates an uneasiness about the quality of faith in the believing community. *Someone* (either Jesus, or the Church, or Luke's source, or Luke) is nervous because of the less than perfect specimens of faith around him who do not exhibit the will to endure that the woman in the parable exhibited (on *pistis* with the article cf. Marshall, 676). The author of this line is apparently afraid that the believers will fail to pray and will then indeed lose heart and, in the process, lose faith. Why then is this nervousness expressed here? We would suggest that the answer to this question is in the four lines immediately preceding. Line three contains the focus of the discussion.

In considering line three, we are faced with two problems. What is the meaning of the word that the RSV translates "delay"? And is it a statement or a question? First then, the translation of this key word. The word itself (*makrothumeō*) is one of the great New Testament words for patience. But the above translation of "delay" does not do justice to it. The New Testament has three words for patience and they are all applied to God. The first is *anochē* and appears in Romans 2:4 and again in 3:26. God has a divine *forbearance* in passing over former sins. The second type of patience is *hupomonē*, which is the patience of the sufferer and is most clearly illustrated by Christ on the cross. Then in Romans 2:4 *anochē* is linked with our word (*makrothumia*) and is used in the context of judgment and mercy. Literally *makrothumia* applies to the one who can and does "put his anger far away." It is the patience of the victor who refuses to take vengeance. T. W. Manson translates it as "removes his wrath to a distance" (*Sayings*, 307). A classical example of this virtue can be seen in David as he stands over the sleeping body of Saul with spear in hand. Saul has come to kill David. David has penetrated Saul's camp and can easily kill him. David's bodyguard wants to take vengeance and David shows great *makrothumia*; he puts his anger far away and refuses the request (I Sam. 26:6-25). Obviously this is a quality God must exercise if He is to deal with sinners. In Exodus 34:14 God tells Moses that He is both "slow to anger" and at the same time "gracious." Horst, in his article on *makrothumia*, describes this quality of God as it appears in His dealings with His people. Horst writes that He is the God "who will restrain this wrath and cause His grace and loving-kindness to rule. The wrath and the grace of God are the two poles which constitute the span of His longsuffering" (Horst, *TDNT*, IV, 376). This same willingness of God to restrain His wrath and thus be merciful appears in the Book of Wisdom (*ca.* 50 B.C.). This text describes God as "slow to anger" and at the same time "merciful" (15:1). The author in this connection writes, "We are yours even though we have sinned, since we acknowledge your power." Thus God puts aside His wrath and shows mercy to the believer even though the believer has sinned. Again Horst is helpful where he describes this understanding and writes, "alongside this wrath there is a divine restraint which postpones its operation until something takes place in man which justifies the postponement" (Horst, *TDNT*, IV, 376). A marvelous illustration of this (observed by T. W. Manson) is provided by the rabbis. They tell of a king who wondered where to station his troops. He decided to quarter them at some distance from the capital so that on the occasion of civil disobedience it would take some time to bring them. In that interim the rebels would have an opportunity to come to their senses and "So, it is argued, God keeps His wrath at a distance in order to give Israel time to repent" (T. W. Manson, *Sayings*, 308; cf. P.T. *Taanith*, 11.65b). At the same time, according to Ben Sirach (35:19-20), God has no *makrothumia* toward the gentiles. As we noted above he writes,

> And the Lord will not delay,
>   neither will he be slow to anger (*makrothumia*) with them,
> till he crushes the loins of the unmerciful,
>   and repays vengeance on the nations.

Here again *makrothumia*, which is a part of the language of salvation, is used to describe God's actions toward His people, *not* toward the nations. Toward the gentiles/nations He has *no makrothumia*.

In the New Testament we see this same background reflected in the parable of the Unforgiving Servant (Matt. 18:23-35). The servant owes his master ten thousand talents and he is not able to pay (v. 25). The master (obviously in anger) orders the entire family sold into slavery. The servant falls on his knees imploring him, "Lord, have patience with me (*makrothumēson ep' emoi*), and I will pay you everything." That is, he calls for the master to set aside his anger, to have patience. This the lord does.

Turning to the rest of the New Testament, the same meaning of "setting aside wrath" is evidenced in each case where the word is applied to God. In Romans 2:4 it is an attribute of God and is attached to repentance. In Romans 9:22 it is connected to wrath. In I Timothy 1:16 Jesus puts aside his anger for Paul. In I Peter 3:20 God exercised His *makrothumia* with the disobedient, and in II Peter 3:9 God exercised *makrothumia* "not wishing that any should perish, but that all should reach repentance." Finally in 3:15, which is parallel to verse 9, the reader is told to "count the *makrothumia* of our Lord as salvation" (obviously this setting aside of wrath is a necessary part of salvation). This unchanging understanding of *makrothumia* must now be applied to the present text.

In his article on *makrothumia* Horst discusses our parable. He links the question of longsuffering in line three with the vindication theme in line four. He affirms that *ekdikasis* ("vindication") in our passage means

> not only final judgment for adversaries but also serious self-examination for the elect. When the Son of Man comes, will He find faith on the earth? (v. 8b). Only in faith can they go into the *ekdikasis* (vindication) of the last judgment and pray for its coming. Thus God's *makrothumein* (slowness to anger) is for them a necessary interval of grace which should kindle the faith and prayer that moves mountains (17:6 par.). In the *makrothumein* of God there now lies the possibility of the existence of believers before God . . . in confidence that they may beseech His righteousness and grace (Horst, *TDNT*, IV, 381).

Furthermore, Horst argues that the phrase under question is a statement, not a question, that it applies to the elect, and that it cannot mean "delay" (*ibid.*; cf. also Bruce, *Parables*, 164). We would submit that Horst's understanding is correct and that it is essential to a proper interpretation of the parable. The phrase in question should be read as a statement, and *makrothumia* does not mean "delay" but has to do with God's willingness to put His anger far away because of the sins of the elect. God will *indeed* vindicate His elect, who cry to Him day and night. But these same elect are also sinners, not sinless saints. If He is not willing to put aside His anger, they cannot approach Him in prayer and dare not call out for vindication lest, with Amos, the Day of the Lord be a day of darkness and not light (Amos 5:18-20). The act of seeking vindication *does not* make them righteous. As in the case of the political enthusiasts encountered in Luke 13:1-5, a righteous cause does not produce righteous people. So here, a sincere cry for God's intervention to vindicate the elect does not in itself make them holy in His presence. Only as God is willing to "put His anger aside" is it possible for them to invoke Him day and night and to "pray and not be afraid." Only with a liberal exercise of His *makrothumia* toward *them* can God vindicate them at all.

The inverted parallelism of the four lines helps to reinforce the above understanding of the text. The first two lines pose the question and the second two provide the answer. The tenses of the verbs reinforce the parallelism with an ABBA sequence. The first line asks, "*Shall* God (future) vindicate his elect?" This is answered in the matching fourth line, "He *shall* vindicate them (future) speedily!" In the second line we find out that they cry (present) to Him day and night. This cry is answered in the third line where God is (present) slow to anger with them.

The theological divergence from Ben Sirach is crucial. As we observed, Ben Sirach also uses the parable of the widow. His parable also shifts from general prayer to a discussion of the vindication of God's people. He also mentions God's slowness to anger. But in Sirach this recollection calls forth an almost vindictive attack on the gentiles. God will *not* be slow to anger with the gentiles but will crush their genitals. In sharp contrast the Lucan text offers *no* words of judgment against the adversaries of the faithful. Rather, the account concludes with a challenging question, a wistful hope that the Son of man will find faith on the earth, and a clear statement that only in the willingness of God to set aside His wrath can they even cry to Him at all. So this text is not a simple question of God delaying salvation, but of God's willingness to put off judgment.

Finally, the question of the nature of God's vindication requires brief reflection. For Ben Sirach the form of this vindication is spelled out. The wicked will be crushed, eliminated, broken, and repaid for their deeds. His people will rejoice in His mercy (35:23). In our parabolic application there are no details. The vengeance on the gentiles is (as we noted) significantly absent. But, in regard to the faithful, how does God vindicate them? Is it only a promise for the end times (near though these times may be), or does the text hint at a dynamic for the present? The tenses of the verbs referring to vindication are future. But must it necessarily mean the distant future? This passage is in Luke 18. The beginning of the passion story is only a few verses away. Jesus' enemies are gathering strength for the final act of their opposition. Will God vindicate *him*? The reader is given a clear answer, but what an answer! Yes, God will vindicate His Son who also prays to Him day and night, but that vindication *will be seen in resurrection and will come by way of a cross*. For centuries the house of Islam has stumbled at the offense of the cross. For them Jesus is a great prophet. In the Psalms God says, "Touch not my anointed ones, do my prophets no harm" (Ps. 105:15). If these things are true, asks Islam, where is God's vindication for His prophet in the passion narratives? How could the story of the cross be true? In an attempt to assure vindication by God for Jesus, the story of the cross is reshaped in Islamic tradition to allow for a divine rescue operation before Good Friday and the crucifixion of a substitute. But is not the Islamic question the right question? Where is God's vindication? And surely the right answer is that God's vindication of *this* prophet far exceeded his followers' wildest dreams. He was vindicated at an empty tomb, and the path to that empty tomb led across Golgotha. If such was the vindication of Jesus, what of his disciples?

The concluding verses of the passage (18:6–8) have been read for centuries in the context of the expectation of the *parousia*. It may well be that this is the context in which Luke himself understood them and perhaps appropriately so. But is it not possible to see an initial application of these texts in the ministry of Jesus himself? Is God going to vindicate him and the little band of fearful followers that have cast their lot with him? T. W. Manson points out that election was to service and not to privilege.

> They are not the pampered darlings of Providence, but the *corps d'élite* in the army of the living God. Because they are what they are, they are foredoomed to suffering at the hands of the wicked; and in many cases the seal of election is martyrdom (*Sayings, 307*).

As fear intensifies during the final approach to Jerusalem, it is addressed in this parable. The clear promise is made that God will indeed vindicate them and will do so quickly!

Finally, to what precise understanding were the disciples pressed to come, and what cluster of theological motifs compose the fabric of the meaning of the parable? For the disciples the hoped-for response was surely something like this:

> In the gathering gloom of intensified opposition we need not fear. God has put His anger far away and He hears us. We must trust and be steadfast in prayer. We do not appeal to a disgruntled judge but to a loving Father who will vindicate His elect and will do so quickly.

The cluster of theological motifs include the following:

1. Prayer conquers fear.
2. Persistence in prayer is appropriate to piety.
3. In prayer the believer addresses a loving Father (not a capricious judge).
4. God must, and indeed does, put His anger aside to hear the prayers of the faithful, for their cry for vindication does not make them holy.
5. God is at work in history and *will* accomplish His purposes and vindicate His elect.
6. A woman is used as an example for the faithful to emulate. Ben Sirach starts with a woman and then shifts to a male figure. Jesus starts with a woman and then makes application to the elect in general. The sexist bias of Ben Sirach is missing. Thus the status of women in the believing community is enhanced by the way the parable is told.
7. The cry for vindication requires self-examination lest the faithful themselves fail to keep faith.

Again a series of weighty theological themes speaks to us out of a deceptively simple story.

Chapter 9

THE PHARISEE AND THE TAX COLLECTOR
(Luke 18:9–14)

The Text:

	And he said to certain people who considered themselves righteous and despised others, this parable.	(INTRODUCTION)
1	"Two men went up into the temple to pray, one a Pharisee, and the other a tax collector.	TWO GO UP PHARISEE, TAX COLLECTOR
2	The Pharisee stood by himself thus praying, 'God, I thank thee because I am not like other men,	HIS MANNER HIS PRAYER
3	extortioners, unjust, adulterers, even like this tax collector.	TAX COLLECTOR (THE IMAGE)
4	I fast twice a week. I give tithes of all that I possess.'	HIS SELF-RIGHTEOUSNESS
5	But the tax collector, standing afar off, would not even lift up his eyes to heaven,	TAX COLLECTOR (THE REALITY)
6	but he beat upon his chest saying, 'God! Make an atonement for me, a sinner.'	HIS MANNER HIS PRAYER
7	I tell you, he went down to his house made righteous, rather than that one."	TWO GO DOWN TAX COLLECTOR, PHARISEE
	For every one who exalts himself will be humbled, and he who humbles himself will be exalted.	(CONCLUSION)

This famous parable has long been considered a simple story about pride, humility, and the proper attitude for prayer. These themes are certainly present. Yet, as in the case of many of the parables we have examined, a closer look uncovers a weighty theological presentation that is traditionally overlooked. Here also a key

142

word can be translated in a fashion significantly different from the translation tradition common among us. Again a closer look at culture and style unlocks otherwise obscured theological content. The parabolic ballad form noted in many of the previous parables is also evidenced here. In this case the stanzas are inverted in their relationship to one another. This parabolic ballad form will be examined first, then the cultural and religious background of the parable. Our interpretation will attempt to keep these factors in focus. First, then, is an examination of the literary form set forth above.

A series of parallel themes marks out this parable as another of the seven-stanza parabolic ballads (cf. Luke 10:30–35; 14:16–23; 16:1–8). After the introduction (which is supplied by Luke or his source), the parable opens with two men going up to the temple (1). The parable concludes with the same two men going down, but now their order is reversed. The tax collector is now mentioned first (7). Stanzas 2 and 6 clearly form a pair also. The exterior manner of each man is listed first (in each case), then his direct address to God. The second line in each stanza is an explanation of each worshiper's self-understanding. Stanzas 3 and 5 concentrate on the tax collector. He is specifically named in each. Yet there is a sharp contrast between the two pictures. Stanza 3 is the tax collector as seen through the eyes of the Pharisee, while stanza 5 is the reality of the man as portrayed by the storyteller. The center in stanza 4 is a presentation of the Pharisee's case for his self-righteousness. This theme of righteousness is then repeated at the end of the seven stanzas (a feature common to this literary form). Another literary device common to this form of inverted parallelism is the point of turning which occurs just past the center of the structure (cf. Bailey, *Poet,* 48, 51, 53, 62). This feature appears here in stanza 5 where the story turns around with the startling phrase, "But the tax collector. . . ." Only one parallelism is not in precise balance. We are told how each of the participants was standing. But the first appears in stanza 2 and the second in 5. It is possible to see the movement of the parable in a simplified manner that would bring these two ideas in balance. This would be as follows:

Two went up

The Pharisee stood
and prayed

The tax collector stood
and prayed

Two went down

The difficulty with this structure is that the prayer of the Pharisee is five lines while the tax collector's prayer is only one. Also, the ground for the Pharisee's self-righteousness (stanza 4) loses its prominence in the center. Other close parallelisms in the ballad are blurred when this element of how they stand is brought into juxtaposition. Thus we prefer to see the first structure suggested above as that intended by the author. This parable, like that of the Good Samaritan, is seen as deliberately structured with seven stanzas that invert with a climax in the center. The introduction has been added by the editor, and the structure would reinforce the opinion that the conclusion may also be exterior to the parable, which ends with stanza 7. Each double line will need to be examined in turn.

INTRODUCTION

> And he said to certain people who considered themselves righteous and despised others, this parable.

This introduction is clearly added by the evangelist or his source. As such it is an interpretation of the parable. The interpreter tells the reader that the subject is *righteousness* and, in particular, self-righteousness. T. W. Manson comments that the parable is addressed to those who

> had the kind of faith in themselves and their own powers that weaker vessels are content to have in God, and that the ground of this confidence was their own achievements in piety and morality (*Sayings,* 309).

Centuries earlier Ibn al-Ṭayyib came to the same conclusion. In his comment on this verse he remarks, "Christ saw that some of those who gathered around him relied on their own righteousness for their salvation rather than on the mercy of God" (Ibn al-Ṭayyib, Manqariyūs edition, II, 313). As we have observed, the question of humility in prayer is indeed dealt with. Yet the theme of righteousness and how it is achieved is pointed up by verse 9 as a central thrust of the parable.

We have argued elsewhere that the material in the Lucan central section was compiled by a pre-Lucan editor (Bailey, *Poet,* 79–85). That editor/theologian placed this parable into his outline along with other material on the subject of prayer. Thus *he* identified it as a parable about prayer, and indeed it is. It is not too likely that this editor/theologian, having placed the parable in a collection of material on prayer, then wrote an introduction that highlighted a different aspect of the theology of the parable. Therefore this interpretative introduction is either traceable to a very early Christian commentator who wrote prior to the compilation of the Travel Narrative or to Luke himself. Yet whether this introduction is traceable to a very early evangelist, the editor of the Travel Narrative, or to Luke, it must be taken seriously. As we will observe, the parable is virtually studded with vocabulary pointing to the topic of righteousness and how it is achieved. Thus this introduction is clearly appropriate to the internal message of the parable. This brings us to the parable itself.

1 "Two men went up into the temple to pray,	TWO GO UP
one a Pharisee, and the other a tax collector."	PHARISEE, TAX
	COLLECTOR

The Pharisee is mentioned first, then the tax collector. They both *go up*. But when it comes time to *go down,* the tax collector will be in the lead.

We have traditionally assumed that the setting of the parable is that of private devotions. This assumption has deeply colored the way we in the Western tradition have translated and interpreted the text. Middle Easterners read the same text and assume a parable about public worship. Ibn al-Ṭayyib's remark is typical where he comments on the publican standing "afar off" and says, "that is, apart from the Pharisee and *from the rest of the worshipers in the temple*" (Ibn al-Ṭayyib, Manqariyūs edition, II, 315; emphasis mine). Here Ibn al-Ṭayyib affirms the presence of a worshiping congregation almost in passing. This assumption has a basis in the text, as we will see.

A part of our problem in the West is that the English verb "pray" is almost exclusively applied to private devotions, and the verb "worship" is used for corporate worship. However, in biblical literature, the verb "pray" can mean either. In Luke 1:10 Zechariah is participating in the daily atonement sacrifice in the temple and takes his turn at burning the incense in the Holy Place. In the meantime, "The whole multitude of the people were praying outside. . . ." Jesus quotes from Isaiah 56:7 where the temple is called "a house of prayer" (Luke 19:46). The famous listing of early Christian concerns in Acts 2:42 includes the apostles' teaching and fellowship, the breaking of bread, and *the prayers*. In this list the word "prayers" is a synonym for community worship. Acts 16:13, 16 speak of a place of public worship as "a place of prayer." These and many other texts make clear that the context of a given passage must determine whether the verb "pray" means corporate worship or private devotions. When Jesus goes up on a mountain alone to pray, obviously the context is private devotions. But in this parable there is a series of clear indicators that we are here dealing with corporate worship, not private devotions. First, specifically, *two* people go up to a place of public worship at the same time. Second, they go down at the same time (presumably after the service is over). Third, the temple (a place of public worship) is specifically mentioned. The contemporary Middle Easterner has the same double meaning attached to the verb "pray." But when he, as a Christian, says, "I am going to *church* to pray," or, as a Muslim, remarks, "I am on my way to the *mosque* to pray," everyone knows that they mean corporate worship, not private devotions. Even so with the parable, the mention of the temple adds considerable weight to the assumption that corporate worship is intended. Fourth, as we will note below, the text tells us that the Pharisee "stood by himself." The obvious assumption is that he stood apart from the other worshipers. Fifth, we also are told that the tax collector "stood afar off." Afar off from whom? It can mean afar off from the Pharisee, but can also mean afar off from the rest of the worshipers. This is especially the case if it can be substantiated that there *are* worshipers present, apart from whom the Pharisee has also chosen to stand. Finally, the tax collector specifically mentions the *atonement* in his prayer. The temple ritual provided for a morning and evening atoning sacrifice to be offered each day and a congregation was normally present. Indeed, it is always assumed in the discussions of the service (cf. Mishna *Tamid*, Danby, 582–89; Sir. 50:1–21). In summary, the verb "pray" gives us two interpretive options. It can mean private devotions or corporate worship. The weight of evidence in the parable suggests the latter. It is with this assumption that we will proceed through the parable. Yet one can ask, does not each man in the parable offer a private prayer?

Quite likely the traditional assumption that the parable is talking only about private devotions is related to the fact that each of the principal figures in the parable offers a private prayer. Does this not lead the reader to conclude that no service of public worship is involved? Not so. Safrai describes the worship of the temple in the first century.

> Many Jews would go up daily to the Temple in order to be present at the worship, to receive the priestly benediction bestowed upon the people at the end, (and) *to pray during the burning of the incense* (Safrai, *JPFC*, II, 877; emphasis mine).

He also states that they are there to "worship and pray during the liturgy" (*ibid.*, 876). Ben Sirach has an elaborate description of the atonement ritual in the temple (Sir. 50:1-21). He mentions hymns of praise sung by the cantors

> as the people pleaded with the Lord Most High,
>   and prayed in the presence of the Merciful,
> until the service of the Lord was completed
>   and the ceremony at an end (Sir. 50:19).

Clearly, the people are praying *during* the service. The time of the offering of the incense was the often mentioned time of personal prayer (as in Luke 1:10 noted above). Safrai writes, "During the incense-offering, the people gathered for prayer in the court" (Safrai, *JPFC*, II, 888). This was so commonly accepted as the right time for private prayers that people not in the temple were known to offer their own special petitions at that time, particularly during the afternoon sacrifice (cf. Jth. 9:1). Thus there is conclusive evidence that private prayers are offered as a part of the corporate worship during the atonement sacrifice ritual held twice daily.

If then the two men are on their way to participate in corporate worship, can we be sure that the service was the morning or evening atonement sacrifice? Indeed yes, since this was the only *daily* service of public worship in the temple. Thus anyone on any unspecified day on his way to corporate prayers in the temple would naturally be assumed to be on his way to the atonement sacrifice. This service was the sacrifice of a lamb (for the sins of the people) at dawn. A second similar sacrifice was held at three in the afternoon. The elaborate rituals connected with these sacrifices have been fully described (Dalman, *Sacred*, 302f.; Edersheim, *Temple*, 152-173; Safrai, *JPFC*, II, 887-890). The time of incense was especially appropriate as a time of personal prayer because by this time in the service the sacrifice of the lamb had covered the sins of Israel and thus the way to God was open. The faithful could *now* approach Him (Edersheim, *Temple*, 157). The incense arose before God's face and the faithful offered their separate petitions to Him. This background appropriately combines for us the idea of private prayers (which the two actors in this drama do indeed offer) in the context of corporate worship (in that the atonement sacrifice is mentioned in the parable) in a place of public worship like the temple (which is specified as the scene of the action).

If, however, one concludes that the evidence for corporate worship is yet unconvincing as a specific setting for the parable, we are still obliged to assume this same background in general. At dawn each day the atonement sacrifice took place. The smoke from the sacrifice arose over the altar and the temple area. Any believer offering private prayers in the temple any time between the two services stood in the presence of this altar with its burning sacrifice. He knew that it was possible for him to address God with his private needs *only* because the atonement sacrifice had taken place. Any private prayers were, as it were, sandwiched in between the two daily atonement sacrifices. Thus any kind of prayer in the temple area (private devotions or prayer in connection with corporate worship) necessarily presupposes the context of the twice daily atonement sacrifice that is specifically mentioned in the parable itself.

First-century attitudes toward Pharisees and tax collectors are sufficiently well-known as to need no explanation. The one is the precise observer of the law, and the other is a breaker of the law and a traitor to the nation. With the actors on stage, the play proceeds.

> 2   "The Pharisee stood by himself thus praying,   HIS MANNER
> 'God, I thank thee because I am not like other men,'"   HIS PRAYER

The first line of this couplet has within it both a textual and a translational problem. We have opted for the text selected by Kurt Aland *et al.* in the United Bible Societies Text (Jeremias accepts the same reading and identifies it as a Semitic style of speech; *Parables*, 140). The deeper problem (which has most likely created the textual variants) is the question, did he *stand by himself* or *pray to himself*? The phrase *pros heauton* can be read "by himself" and attached to the previous word "stood," which gives us the above translation. Or it can be read "to himself" and attached to the word "praying" which follows. In this latter case it then reads, "The Pharisee stood praying thus to himself." It has been argued for some time that the prepositional phrase *pros heauton* must refer to his manner of praying because to modify the verb *standing* it should read *kath heauton* in accord with the classical Greek usage (Plummer, 416).

However, a number of things can be said against Plummer. First, in the Lucan parables a soliloquy is introduced with the phrase *en heautō*, not *pros heauton* (cf. 7:39; 12:17; 16:3; 18:4). Second, we are told how the tax collector stood in relation to others and it is only natural to have a similar description of the Pharisee. Third, the traditional understanding of the text may be an additional example of the spilling phenomenon. This phenomenon occurs where texts have been read together for so long that, like two rivers flowing together, one text "spills" into the next. That is, meaning is carried over inadvertently from one text to another. An important example of this phenomenon can be seen in Luke

11:5–13, where the idea of persistence has spilled from verses 9–13 back into the parable in verses 5–8 (cf. Bailey, *Poet,* 128f.). So here, in the previous parable the judge talks *to himself (en heautō)*; thus perhaps inadvertently the Pharisee has gradually been seen as also offering a soliloquy. Fourth, Codex Bezae (D), along with a few other minor manuscripts, has *kath heauton,* which indicates that its editors clearly understood the Pharisee to be standing alone, not praying alone. Fifth, the very important Old Syriac from the second century translates this text in an unambiguous fashion and has the Pharisee *standing by himself.* Delitzsch, in his famous Hebrew version of the New Testament, also translates the phrase "standing by himself," as do a number of our Arabic versions. Sixth, when we read the text as a soliloquy this detail adds nothing to the parable. But when the Pharisee is seen as standing apart from the other worshipers, the detail is in precise harmony with everything else that is said and done in the parable and adds considerably to the entire dramatic effect (with Manson, *Sayings,* 310). Seventh, classical Greek usage can hardly be determinative in the Lucan Travel Narrative with its many parables and Semitisms and obvious translation Greek. Thus, with these considerations in mind, we prefer to see the Pharisee standing apart from the remainder of the worshipers about him.

The Pharisee's reasons for standing apart can be easily understood. He considers himself righteous and indeed "despises others," as we see from his description of them. Those who kept the law in a strict fashion were known as "associates" (*haberim*). Those who did not were called "people of the land" (*am-haaretz*). These latter Danby defines as

> those Jews who were ignorant of the Law and who failed to observe the rules of cleanness and uncleanness and were not scrupulous in setting apart Tithes from the produce (namely, Heave-Offering, First Tithe, Second Tithe, and Poorman's Tithe) (Danby, 793).

In our parable, paying the tithe is specifically mentioned. In the eyes of a strict Pharisee the most obvious candidate for the classification of *am-haaretz* would be a tax collector. Furthermore, there was a particular type of uncleanness that was contracted by sitting, riding, or *even leaning against* something unclean (*ibid.,* 795). This uncleanness was called *midras*-uncleanness. The Mishna specifically states, "For Pharisees the clothes of an *am-haaretz* count as suffering *midras*-uncleanness" (Mishna *Hagigah* 2:7, Danby, 214). With this background in mind it is little wonder that the Pharisee wanted to stand aside from the rest of the worshipers. If he accidentally brushes against the tax collector (or any other *am-haaretz* who might be among the worshipers), he would sustain *midras*-uncleanness. His state of cleanliness is too important. It must not be compromised for any reason. Physical isolation, from his point of view, would be a statement and an important one at that. Thus the Pharisee carefully stands aloof from the others gathered around the altar.

Furthermore, the problem of the proud man standing aloof in worship was a contemporary problem. One of the intertestamental books called The

Assumption of Moses gives us an illuminating illustration. This book, written most likely during the lifetime of Jesus (Charles, II, 411), has some very sharp things to say about the leadership of the nation during the time of the unknown author. These "impious rulers" are described as follows:

> And though their hands and their minds touch unclean things, yet their mouth shall speak great things, and they shall say furthermore: "Do not touch me lest thou shouldst pollute me in the place (where I stand)..." (7:9–10, Charles, II, 420).

This remarkable text has striking parallels with our parable. In each case the leaders are under attack. In each they "speak great things." The Pharisee in the parable goes down to his house not justified in God's sight, and here the impious rulers are described as defiled with unclean things. Improper attitudes are criticized in each account. We know from John 11:48 that "the place" can mean the temple area, and it is possible that the above text carries this same meaning and is therefore also set in the temple. Thus Jesus' criticism is in harmony with others of his time. Finally, and most important for our discussion, each talks of someone who wants to stand in physical isolation from the others.

Jesus' criticism of the Pharisee is also in harmony with advice offered earlier by the great Hillel, who said, "Keep not aloof from the congregation and trust not in thyself until the day of thy death, and judge not thy fellow until thou art thyself come to his place" (Mishna *Pirke Aboth* 2:5, Danby, 448). Hillel's remark is further evidence that some religious leaders had a tendency to "keep aloof from the congregation."

In summary, the Pharisee in the parable goes up to attend the morning or afternoon atonement sacrifice. In a gesture of religious superiority he stands apart from the other worshipers.

When the problematic phrase *pros heauton* is attached to his mode of standing, it is then possible to understand his prayer as offered out loud. The Sinaiticus original, along with some important early Latin and Coptic versions, leaves out the "to/by himself" entirely and thereby deliberately affirms that he is praying out loud. Marshall observes that "Jewish practice was to pray aloud" (Marshall, 679). This possibility adds further color. The Pharisee is thus preaching to the "less fortunate unwashed" around him. They have little chance to get a good look at a truly "righteous" man like himself, and he is "graciously" offering them a few words of judgment along with some instruction in righteousness. (Most of us, at some point in our worship experience, have been obliged to listen to some misguided soul insult his neighbors in a public prayer.) The officiating priest (as we have observed) is most likely in the Holy Place offering up the incense. At this particular point in the service the delegation of Israel was responsible for making the unclean stand at the eastern gate (Mishna *Tamid* 5:6, Danby, 587). The Pharisee may be wondering why this publican was not ushered out. In any case, during this pause in the liturgy, the Pharisee probably takes advantage of the opportunity to instruct the "unrighteous" around him.

The opening volley of the Pharisee's attack on his fellow worshipers reveals more of himself than he perhaps intended. Prayer in Jewish piety involved primarily the offering of thanks/praise to God for all of His gifts, and petitions for the worshiper's needs. This Pharisee does neither. He does not thank God for His gifts but rather boasts of his own self-achieved righteousness. He has no requests. Thus his words do not fall under the category of prayer at all but degenerate to mere self-advertisement. Jeremias translates a striking illustration of a similar prayer from the period (Jeremias, *Parables*, 142; B.T. *Berakhoth* 28b, Sonc., 172; cf. Edersheim, *Life*, II, 291). Thus Jesus is not portraying a caricature but a reality most likely known to his audience. We have taken the option of translating the *hoti* as "because" rather than "that," since the former strengthens the self-congratulatory thrust of his opening sentence. As he proceeds the prayer goes "from bad to worse."

> 3   " 'extortioners, unjust, adulterers,   TAX COLLECTOR
>   even like this tax collector.' "   (THE IMAGE)

These first two words can also be translated *rogues* and *swindlers* (Jeremias, *Parables*, 140). Obviously the words are selected because they specifically apply to the tax collector, who is already spotted standing at some distance. The tax farmers of the Roman empire were traditionally known as extortioners and swindlers. The third word, "adulterers," is thrown in by the Pharisee for good measure (like the older son in Luke 15:30). It tells us nothing about the tax collector but does inform us regarding the mindset of the speaker. Ibn al-Ṣalībī makes the thoughtful comment,

> We know that the one who is not a thief and adulterer is not necessarily a
> good man. Furthermore experience demonstrates that the search for the faults
> and failures of others does the greatest harm of all to the critic himself and
> thus such action must be avoided at all costs (Ibn al-Ṣalībī, II, 181).

Thus we see a man tearing up the fabric of his own spirituality.

The point at issue in this stanza is the translation of the beginning of the second line (*ē kai hōs*). We need to examine the first word *ē* and the third, *hōs*. The question is, Are we presented with two lists or one? Is the Pharisee saying, I am not like type A (extortioners, unjust, adulterers), nor am I like type B (tax collectors)? Or do we have one list, of which the tax collector is a part and an illustration? We will attempt to demonstrate the second.

A clear translation of the traditional view of this stanza is found in the Good News Bible of the United Bible Societies, which reads, "I thank you, God, that I am not greedy, dishonest, or an adulterer, like everybody else. I thank you that I am not like that tax collector over there." The particle *ē* is the key word in making our choice between the two alternatives suggested above. This particle is relatively rare in Matthew and Mark but common in Luke. In Luke it occurs only eight times in the opening chapters and six times in the passion narrative, but in the central section (9:51–19:49) it is found twenty-three times. Thus it is especially important to observe its use here in the central section. As a word this particle is often translated "or." Yet, as an English word, the particle "or" exclusively joins contrasting elements in a sentence. Someone is asked, "Do you want this or that?" The weight of usage and thus meaning is that of joining contrasting items. However, the Greek particle *ē* can join either contrasting or similar elements in a sentence. Bauer observes that this particle can separate "opposites, which are mutually exclusive," or it can separate "related and similar terms, where one can take the place of the other or one supplements the other" (Bauer, 342). He then lists Matthew 5:17 as a clear case of the latter. For this verse the RSV reads, "Think not that I have come to abolish the law and (*ē*) the prophets." Here the continuity and similarity of the two terms ("law" and "prophets") are so close that *ē* is translated "and." In the Travel Narrative in Luke, nineteen of the twenty-three occurrences of *ē* separate *similar* terms. In only five cases does it separate *contrasting* elements. In four texts the *ē* could just as easily be translated "and," as in Matthew 5:17 (cf. Luke 11:12; 13:4; 14:31; 15:8). An interesting case of the use of *ē* as a particle connecting similar terms is in Luke 17:23. In this verse we have three textual alternatives. These are:

> 'Lo, there,' or 'Lo, here,'
> 'Lo, there,' and 'Lo, here,'
> 'Lo, there,'   'Lo, here,'

That is, the particle *ē* so often connects similar terms that in the textual tradition it is at times replaced by *kai* ("and") or omitted and in translation replaced with a comma. In summary, we can see that *ē* in the Travel Narrative connects similar (not contrasting) terms in three out of four cases. In some texts it can be translated with an English "and" and perhaps even replaced with a comma. The English word "or," which inevitably implies contrasting terms, is thus inadequate. In our text here in 18:11, with adjectives especially selected to apply to tax collectors, we clearly have a case of similar and not contrasting terms. Thus our translation should communicate this linkage of similar terms. The precise combination of *ē kai* that we have in this text also occurs in 11:11, 12 (?). There also it connects similar and not contrasting terms. To this must be added an examination of *hōs*.

The Greek word *hōs* ("like") is a comparative particle common throughout the New Testament. However, one of its "noteworthy uses" (Bauer, 906) is to introduce an example. The longer text of Luke 9:54 reads, "Lord, do you want us to bid fire come down from heaven and consume them as (*hōs*) Elijah did?" The general statement occurs first, then the specific illustration introduced by *hōs*. The same usage occurs in I Peter 3:6, where a general statement about submissive wives is made and then Sarah (introduced with the word *hōs*) is mentioned as a specific illustration. The well-known phrase "as (*hōs*) it is written" is another common example of this use of *hōs* (cf. Luke 3:4). We would submit that our text here is a further case of this special use of *hōs*.

In summary, the Pharisee gives a list of characteristics selected to apply to the tax collector standing nearby. He concludes his list with an illustration, the tax collector himself. The $\bar{e}$ connects the similar/identical terms. We opt for joining the adjectives with the illustration and translating "even like this tax collector." Thus the prayer comes through as a ruthless attack on a stereotype, a public accusation of a fellow worshiper at the great altar, that is based on preconceived notions formulated by the Pharisee's own self-righteousness, which he then proudly displays.

> 4   " 'I fast twice a week.   HIS SELF-
>   I give tithes of all that I possess.' "   RIGHTEOUSNESS

The basis of the Pharisee's assumption of righteousness is here verbalized. Moses stipulated a fast for the day of atonement (Lev. 25:29; Num. 39:7). This man goes far beyond that admonition and fasts twice *each* week, a practice that "was confined to certain circles among the Pharisees and their disciples" (Safrai, *JPFC*, II, 816). Regarding the tithe, the Old Testament regulation was clear and limited. Tithes were levied on grain, wine, and oil (Lev. 27:30; Num. 18:27; Deut. 12:17; 14:13). But as Safrai observes, "in tannaitic times the law was extended to take in anything used as food" (Safrai, *JPFC*, II, 825; cf. Mishna *Maaseroth* 1:1, Danby, 66). But even this ruling had exceptions because rue, purslane, celery, and other agricultural products were exempt (Mishna *Shebiith* 9:1, Danby, 49). The practice of tithing nonagricultural products was just beginning to appear, and "the custom was never really widespread, and was confined to those who were particularly strict" (Safrai, *JPFC*, II, 825). Even tax collectors paid *some* tithe (*ibid.*, 819). But this Pharisee—well, he tithed *everything*. Ibn al-Ṣalībī observes, "He is comparing himself with the great examples of righteousness like Moses and the Prophets" (Ibn al-Ṣalībī, II, 181). His acts are works of supererogation (Jeremias, *Parables*, 140). Amos had some sharp words for this type of religion (cf. Amos 4:4). Indeed, we have a picture of a man who prides himself on his more than perfect observance of his religion.

This stanza is the climactic center. We can see the move to this climax in the flow of the action in the previous lines. Standing aloof lest he be defiled by the "unrighteous" around him, he congratulates himself (2) and offers scathing criticism of a tax collector nearby (3). He then brags of having not only kept the law but exceeded its demands (4). The dramatic point of turning is then introduced as the major themes begin to repeat, but with a difference.

> 5   "But the tax collector, standing afar off,   TAX COLLECTOR
>   would not even lift up his eyes to heaven,"   (THE REALITY)

The point of turning in the literary form is intense and dramatic. The image of the tax collector in the mind of the Pharisee (3) is in sharp contrast to the reality of the broken, humble man standing some distance away from the assembled worshipers (5). This same contrast between image (seen through self-righteous eyes) and reality was observed above in our study of Simon and the woman in Luke 7:36–50. There also a self-righteous man looked on a dramatic expression of genuine piety and saw only a defiling sinner to be scrupulously avoided.

This repentant tax collector does not stand aloof but "afar off," for he feels he is not worthy to stand with God's people before the altar. As he comes to voice his petition, he (like the woman in 7:38) breaks into an unexpected dramatic action.

6	"but beat upon his chest saying,	HIS MANNER
	'God! Make an atonement for me, a sinner.' "	HIS PRAYER

The accepted posture for prayer was to cross the hands over the chest and keep the eyes cast down (Edersheim, *Temple,* 156). But this man's crossed arms do not remain immobile. Rather he beats on his chest. This dramatic gesture is still used in villages all across the Middle East from Iraq to Egypt. The hands are closed into fists that are then struck on the chest in rapid succession. The gesture is used in times of extreme anguish or intense anger. It never occurs in the Old Testament, and appears only twice in the Gospels, both times in Luke. The remarkable feature of this particular gesture is the fact that it is characteristic of women, *not men*. After twenty years of observation I have found only one occasion in which Middle Eastern *men* are accustomed to beat on their chests. This is at the *'Ashūra* ritual of Shiite Islam. This ritual is an enactment of the murder of Hussein, the son of Ali (the son-in-law of the prophet of Islam). The murder scene is dramatically presented and the devotees lacerate their shaved heads with knives and razors in a demonstration of intense anguish as they recollect this community-forming event. At this ritual the *men* beat on their chests. Women customarily beat on their chests at funerals, but men do not. For men it is a gesture of *extreme* sorrow and anguish and it is almost never used. It is little wonder that in all of biblical literature we find this particular gesture mentioned only here and at the cross (Luke 23:48). There we are told that "*all* the multitude" went home beating on their chests. The crowd naturally included men and women. Indeed, it takes something of the magnitude of Golgotha to evoke this gesture from Middle Eastern men.

Furthermore, we are told that he beats on his *chest*. Why the chest? The reason for this is given in an early Jewish commentary on Ecclesiastes 7:2:

> R. Mana said: *And the Living will lay it to his heart:* these are the righteous who set their death over against their heart; and why do they beat upon their heart? as though to say, "All is there," (note: . . . the righteous beat their heart as the source of evil longing.) (*Midrash Rabbah,* Eccl. VII,2,5, Sonc., 177).

The same underlying rationale is affirmed by Ibn al-Ṣalībī in his eleventh-century commentary where he writes regarding the tax collector,

> his heart in his chest was the source of all his evil thoughts so he was beating it as evidence of his pain as some people do in their remorse, for they beat upon their chests (Ibn al-Ṣalībī, II, 182).

Thus this classical Middle Eastern gesture is a profound recognition of the truth of the fact that "out of the heart come evil thoughts, murder . . . theft, false witness, slander'' (Matt. 15:19). This kind of background gives us a picture of the depth of the tax collector's remorse. What then is his specific prayer?

For centuries the Church, East and West, has translated *hilastheti moi* in this text as ''have mercy on me.'' However, later in the same chapter the blind man cries out, *eleeson me* (18:38), which clearly means ''have mercy on me.'' But this common Greek phrase is not used in 18:13. Our word *hilaskomai* occurs as a verb only here and in Hebrews 2:17. As a noun it appears four times (Rom. 3:25; Heb. 9:5; I John 2:2; 4:10), and it clearly refers to the atonement sacrifice. Expiation and propitiation as English words must be combined with cleansing and reconciliation to give the meaning of the Hebrew *kaffar*, which lies behind the Greek *hilaskomai*. The tax collector is not offering a generalized prayer for God's mercy. He specifically yearns for the benefits of an atonement. Both the classical Armenian and the Harclean Syriac versions of the early centuries of the life of the Church translate our text literally as ''make an atonement for me.'' Dalman's brief account helps set the total scene. He describes the temple area:

> One coming here in order to pray at the time of the evening sacrifice i.e. at the ninth hour (three o'clock in the afternoon) . . . would see first of all the slaughtering and cutting up of the sacrificial lamb, and would then notice that a priest went to the Holy Place to burn incense (Lk. i.9). Both these were acts at which the Israelite was not merely an onlooker, for they were performed in the name of the people, of whom the priest was a representative, in order to affirm daily Israel's relationship to God, according to His command; and when, after the censing from the steps to the ante-hall was accomplished, the priests pronounced the blessing with outstretched hands . . . and put God's Name upon the children of Israel . . . it was for the reception of the blessing that the people ''bowed themselves'' (Ecclus. 1.21) to the ground on hearing the ineffable Name. . . . This was followed, in the consciousness that God would graciously accept the gift, by the bringing of the sacrifice to the altar (Dalman, *Sacred*, 303).

Dalman goes on to explain the other elements of the liturgy, the clash of cymbal, the blasts on the trumpets, the reading of the Psalms, the singing of the choir of the Levites, and the final prostration of the people. On reading Dalman and Edersheim (*Temple*, 156f.) one can almost smell the pungent incense, hear the loud clash of cymbals, and see the great cloud of dense smoke rising from the burnt offering. The tax collector is there. He stands afar off, anxious not to be seen, sensing his unworthiness to stand with the participants. In brokenness he longs to be a part of it all. He yearns that he might stand with ''the righteous.'' In deep remorse he strikes his chest and cries out in repentance and hope, ''O God! Let it be for me! Make an atonement for me, a sinner!'' There in the temple this humble man, aware of his own sin and unworthiness, with no merit of his own to commend him, longs that the great dramatic atonement sacrifice might apply to him. The last stanza tells us that indeed it does.

> 7   ''I tell you, he went down to his house   GO DOWN
>   made righteous, rather than that one.''   TAX COLLECTOR, PHARISEE

In stanza 1 two went up to the temple at the same hour with the Pharisee in the lead. Now the same two go down (again at the same time). The service is over. The tax collector is now mentioned first. *He* is the one justified in God's presence. For centuries the Church debated whether the sacraments have an automatic effect on the believer irrespective of his spiritual state. Here in this simple parable we already have an answer, and the answer is no! The Pharisee was wasting his time. The self-righteous returns home unjustified. Indeed as Ibn al-Ṣalībī notes, "The false pride of the Pharisee has intensified his guilty condition and increased his sin" (Ibn al-Ṣalībī, II, 182). The sacrifice of the lamb for the sins of the people is made—but the broken of heart, who come in unworthiness trusting in God's atonement, they alone are made right with God. With this the parable ends. A general statement is then attached as a summarizing conclusion.

CONCLUSION

For every one who exalts himself will be humbled,
and he who humbles himself will be exalted.

This statement, in various forms, occurs in a number of places in the New Testament (cf. Matt. 18:4; 23:12; Luke 14:11; I Pet. 5:6). It is an antithetical parallelism and is quite likely a proverb of Jesus that Luke or his source may have attached to the end of the parable, which comes to its own conclusion. At the same time, a significant number of the major parables have wisdom sayings attached to their conclusions (cf. Luke 8:8; 12:21, 48; 16:8b; 18:8b; 19:26). There is no reason to deny that Jesus could have attached wisdom sayings to his own parables. This may be the case here. In any event, the saying is profoundly appropriate to the parable and focuses on its major topic of righteousness. As we observed above, either Luke or his source attached an introduction to the parable that highlighted the theme of righteousness and how it is achieved. That introduction is here balanced by this concluding wisdom saying, which discusses the same theme.

This final verse affirms that only the humble will be exalted. The great word "exaltation" has an important place in New Testament theology in relation to the person of Christ. Here, however, we see it used in its Old Testament sense. In regard to this Old Testament usage, Bertram writes, "As God's name alone is exalted ... so He alone can elevate and exalt men" (Bertram, *TDNT*, VIII, 606). Thus "exalt" approaches the meaning "deliver, redeem" (*ibid.*, 607). Bertram explains, "Exaltation means drawing close to God; the righteous man who is meek and humble may hope for this and claim it" (*ibid.*). In regard to the use of this word in the synoptic Gospels Bertram observes, "Along the lines of the Old Testament revelation of God all exaltation on man's part is repudiated.... Exaltation is the act of God alone" (*ibid.*, 608). Thus it is clear that verse 14 in our text is not talking about social rank or man's humility or elevation among his fellow men. Again Bertram observes that exaltation "always has an eschatological reference for the Christian hearer and reader" (*ibid.*). Clearly the verse has to do with man being elevated in relation to God. As in the Old Testament it is almost synonymous with "to deliver" and "to redeem." The introduction to the parable speaks of those who elevate themselves (that is, consider themselves righteous) and humiliate others (that is, despise others). At the end, the self-exalted is humbled and the humble one is exalted.

Finally, then, what is the original listener pressed to understand or do, and what motifs comprise the theological cluster of the parable?

The original self-righteous audience is pressed to reconsider how righteousness is achieved. Jesus proclaims that righteousness is a gift of God made possible by means of the atonement sacrifice, which is received by those who, in humility, approach as sinners trusting in God's grace and not their own righteousness. As Jeremias has succinctly observed, "Our passage shows . . . that the Pauline doctrine of justification has its roots in the teaching of Jesus" (Jeremias, *Parables*, 114).

The theological motifs present in the parable include the following:

1. Righteousness is a gift of God granted by means of the atonement sacrifice to sinners who come to Him in confession of their sin and in a full awareness of their own inability to achieve righteousness.

2. The atonement sacrifice is worthless to anyone who assumes self-righteousness.

3. There is a pattern for prayer set forth. Self-congratulation, boasting of pious achievements, and criticism of others are not appropriate subjects for prayer. A humble confession of sin and need, offered in hope that through the atonement sacrifice this sin might be covered and those needs met, is an appropriate subject for prayer. Along with the subjects for prayer appropriate attitudes for prayer are also presented. Pride has no place. Humility is required.

4. The keeping of the law, and even the achieving of a standard beyond the requirements of the law, does not secure righteousness.

5. Self-righteousness distorts the vision. A profoundly moving demonstration of remorse was enacted by a sincerely repentant man before the eyes of the self-righteous Pharisee. He saw only a sinner to be avoided.

The parable has no evident Christology. The atonement service highlighted is that of the Old Testament. The person of Jesus and his role in salvation history is nowhere mentioned or suggested. Yet a rich theological understanding of righteousness through atonement is set forth in clear and unforgettable terms. This understanding (we would suggest) then becomes the foundation of the early Church's theology. In short, the starting point for the New Testament understanding of righteousness through atonement is traceable to no less than Jesus of Nazareth.

Chapter 10

THE CAMEL AND THE NEEDLE
"What must I do to inherit eternal life?"
(Luke 18:18-30)

The major themes of this remarkable dialogue are inverted. If we reduce the passage to these themes, this inversion can be seen as follows:

1   Inherit eternal life

    2   Five old requirements set forth with special emphasis on:
        —loyalty to family
        —attitude towards property

        3   The demands of the new obedience:
            —sell everything you have
            —come and follow me

            4   The new obedience seen as:
                —too hard

                5   The PARABLE OF THE CAMEL AND THE NEEDLE
                    (Enter the kingdom)

            4'   The new obedience seen as:
                —too hard
                —possible only with God

        3'   The demands of the new obedience are fulfilled:
            —we have left everything
            —we have followed you

    2'   Five new requirements set forth with special emphasis on:
        —attitude toward property
        —loyalty to family

1'   Receive eternal life

The entire text with its structure is as follows:

1   A certain ruler asked him,   ETERNAL LIFE
     "Good Teacher, what having done I shall inherit *eternal life*?"

    2   And Jesus said to him,
          "Why do you call me good?   THE OLD REQUIREMENTS
             No one is good but one, even God.   —fulfilled
          You know the commandments.
             Do not commit adultery.   7 (loyalty to family)
             Do not kill.   6
             Do not steal.   8 (property)
             Do not bear false witness.   9
             Honor your father and mother."   5 (loyalty to family)
     And he said, "All these I have observed from my youth."

    3   And hearing, Jesus said to him,
             "One thing you still lack.   THE NEW OBEDIENCE
          Sell everything you have   —explained (the ruler)
             and distribute to the poor.
             And you will have treasure in heaven.
          And come and follow me."

      4   And hearing this
               he became deeply grieved,   NEW OBEDIENCE
               for he was very rich.   —too hard

        5   And seeing him Jesus said,
                    "How *hard* it is
                       for those who have possessions   ENTER THE
                          to *enter the kingdom of God.*   KINGDOM

        5'   It is *easier* for a camel to go through a needle's eye
                       than for a *rich man*
                          to *enter the kingdom of God.*"

      4'   And those who heard said,
               "And who is able to be saved?"   NEW OBEDIENCE
               But he said, "What is impossible with men   —too hard
               is possible with God."   —possible with God

    3'   And Peter said,
             "Lo, we have *left what is ours*   THE NEW OBEDIENCE
             and *followed you.*"   —fulfilled (disciples)

  2'   And he said to them,
          "Truly, I say to you,
          there is no one who has left   THE NEW REQUIREMENTS
             house   (property)   —fulfilled (all believers)
             or wife   (loyalty to family)
             or brothers   "
             or parents   "
             or children   "
          for the sake of the kingdom,

1'   who will not receive much more in this time,
     and in the age to come—*eternal life.*"   ETERNAL LIFE

In Luke 10:25-37 we studied the same question set forth here. In the overall outline of the Lucan Travel Narrative that passage parallels this text (cf. Bailey, *Poet,* 80-82). In each passage there is first a discussion about the law. In each there follows a dialogue with a parable in its center. Yet, at the same time, the two passages are structured differently. The first passage (10:25-37) has two rounds of debate with two questions and two answers in each round. This passage, however, has five inverted topics with a parable in the center. We turn then to the details of this structure.

The passage begins with the topic of eternal life and comes full circle back to the same topic at the end. But yet there is a difference. In the opening stanza the rich young ruler wants to *do* something to gain eternal life as an inheritance. At the end of the discussion eternal life is received as a gift, not awarded as an earned right. In the second stanza five commands are selected from the Decalogue. These five are then placed out of their original order (note the numbers to the right of the laws above). We are almost obliged to assume that the rearrangement is intentional and serves some purpose. Those responsible for the text in its present form obviously knew the original order and would not leave Jesus to repeat such a rearrangement to no purpose. Granted, the commandment on adultery is often placed before the commandment on murder (Deut. 5:17; Rom. 13:9; James 2:11; Nash Papyrus). Yet Hosea has it at the end of his list and Jeremiah has it in the middle (Hos. 4:2; Jer. 7:8-9). To our knowledge the placing of the commandment on honor to parents at the end of a selection of the Decalogue is without precedent. Marshall affirms that no reason for the present arrangement has been found (Marshall, 685). We would cautiously suggest such a reason. It is our view that the selection and arrangement is deliberate.

What purpose then does the rearrangement serve? We suggest that the present text is edited to give special emphasis to the subjects of loyalty to family and attitudes toward property. The question of adultery (i.e., loyalty to family) heads the list. The command to honor one's parents concludes it. "Do not steal" is placed in the middle. It is possible that a full inversion is intended. This would give us:

> Do not commit adultery   (loyalty to family)
> Do not kill   (physical destruction of another)
> Do not steal   (respect for property)
> Do not bear false witness   (verbal destruction of another)
> Honor your father and mother   (loyalty to family)

The list in Luke 14:26 is somewhat similarly arranged (see following page). There is an introduction and a conclusion with seven specifics in the center. Clearly the high points of the list are the beginning (the father) and the end (the self). These two are the highest demands for loyalty that any person in the Middle East could or can imagine. These two loyalties are given special prominence by their position at the beginning and the end of the list of seven. In a similar

Luke 14:26

If anyone comes to me and does not hate

    his own father
      and mother
      and wife
      and children
      and brothers
      and sisters,
    yes, even his own life,

    he cannot be my disciple.

fashion, here in Luke 18:20 the rearrangement of laws gives special emphasis to the topic of loyalty to family by placing it at the beginning and at the end of the list. The question of respect for property is given prominence by placement in the center. Then, in stanza 2', there is a second list of demands. There we again see five specifics and, significantly, the two topics of loyalty to property and family make up the entire list. Thus the selection and rearrangement of material from the Decalogue can be seen as a deliberate effort to make stanzas 2 and 2' balance thematically.

In stanza 3 two demands are made of the ruler. In the matching stanza (3') the disciples specifically state that they have met these demands. In stanza 4 the ruler finds the new demands too difficult. In the matching stanza 4', the bystanders agree. Stanza 4' is also the point of turning for the entire passage. In many of these literary structures we have observed a crucial change of direction just past the center. Here also an important new element is introduced as the inversion begins. This theme is the affirmation that only with God is salvation possible.

A further shift at center can be seen in the move from singular to plural. The first half is addressed to a particular case, the ruler, and all the verbs are in the singular. In the center the parable makes a generalizing application, and from then on the text deals with plurals and collectives. This particular observation is crucial for an understanding of the passage. The discussion with the rich ruler sets the stage for a discussion of the significance of the same question for *all disciples*.

The center of the structure has a short parable that informs the entire drama. Then finally, as is often the case, a major theme that occurs at the beginning and at the end of the structure is repeated in the center. This feature is also present here. The theme of eternal life, which appears at the beginning and at the end of the passage, relates thematically to the theme of "enter the kingdom of God," which is twice repeated in the parable in the center. Thus the overall passage has all of the major features of inverted parallelism. The themes are presented and then repeated in an inverted fashion. The center repeats the theme with which the structure opens and closes. There is a point of turning just past the center. With such a carefully constructed structure it is obvious that the passage must be examined as a whole and the parable studied in the light of the entire theological mosaic in which it is placed.

This literary structure is strikingly similar to the form we studied in Luke 7:35–50. There also we observed a brief parable that forms the climax of a much longer discussion. In both texts the inversion principle is used throughout. In both, dialogue forms a crucial part of the passage with its inversions. Thus we have two clear examples of a brief parable functioning as the center of a much larger discussion of which it is a part and in the light of which it must be understood. With this structure in mind, the separate stanzas must be examined.

STANZA 1

A certain ruler asked him,
"Good Teacher, what having done I shall inherit *eternal life*?"

There is a significant cluster of parallel terms used throughout the passage. These are:

inherit/receive eternal life = follow me = enter the kingdom = be saved.

The parallel nature of this set of terms will become evident as we proceed.

Our literal translation is awkward English but perhaps highlights the thrust of what the ruler is saying. He clearly wants to achieve eternal life by his own efforts. His focus is on the future. He assumes that a certain standard of performance now will secure eternal life for him in the future. The topic of eternal life has significance for him only for that future. This emphasis is shifted by Jesus in his reply at the end of the passage, as we have noted. The question of rewards in the kingdom is also raised (although indirectly). It is also dealt with at the end of the discussion but in an entirely new context. The act of God that is "impossible with men" must take place first, and only then can rewards be brought into focus. The question as stated here is identical to the lawyer's question in Luke 10:25 with the one addition of the word "good." Jesus' response begins with a focus on this unusual address.

STANZA 2

And Jesus said to him,
"Why do you call me good?
  No one is good but one, even God.
You know the commandments.

Do not commit adultery.	7	(loyalty to family)
Do not kill.	6	
Do not steal.	8	(property)
Do not bear false witness.	9	
Honor your father and mother."	5	(loyalty to family)

And he said,
  "All these I have observed from my youth."

Jesus' initial response has been problematic for centuries. The phrase, "No one is good but one, even God," has often been quoted to deny any form of high Christology in the self-understanding of Jesus. A return to the sterile polemics of the past would be meaningless, yet in fairness to the passage the intent of this phrase must be examined.

One possible approach to the text is to understand Jesus to be asking, "Why do you call me good? Do you mean what you are saying? 'Good' is only appropriate for God. Are you serious in applying this title to me?" However, the ruler does not answer. Would we not expect an answer if this kind of high Christology was the intent of the text? Yet it could be argued that the question is left unanswered deliberately so that the reader must answer the question for himself. Many parables end unfinished, and the reader is left with the tension of responding to the dialogue. A clear example of this is in Luke 9:57–62, where the reader has no hint regarding the final response of any of the three potential disciples. We do not know how the older brother responds to the plea to come in to the banquet hall (Luke 15:32), nor do we know what happens at the end of the great banquet (14:24). The final fate of the unjust steward is likewise unknown (16:8). In this same vein, here in 18:19 we may have a case of a bold question that means, "Are you serious in attributing to me a title that is appropriate only for God? Are you ready to accept the implications of such an affirmation?" Leaving this possible option as an alternative we would examine another possibility.

The title "Good Teacher" is found only once in the rabbinic tradition where a rabbi is asked to report a dream and says,

> To me in my dream the following was said: Good greetings to the good teacher from the good Lord who from His bounty dispenseth good to His people (B.T. *Taanith* 24b, Sonc., 126).

In this text we are dealing with a dream, not a normal salutation. Furthermore there is clearly a dramatic repetition of the word "good." In any case the greeting is extremely rare. Thus Jesus is best understood as responding to a tendency on the part of the ruler to "overdo it." The ruler is trying too hard. He tries to impress with a compliment and perhaps hopes to be greeted with some lofty title in return. In the Oriental world, one compliment requires a second. The ruler starts with "Good Teacher" and may expect "Noble Ruler" in response from Jesus. This seems to be the tension of the text because Jesus answers with *no* title at all, and this response can indicate irritation in the Gospels (cf. Luke 15:29; John 4:17). This abrupt, almost harsh response of Jesus is a technique we observe on his lips on a number of occasions. The purpose is apparently to test the seriousness of the inquirer's intentions (cf. Matt. 15:25; John 3:3). The same type of an introduction and response can be seen in Luke 12:13–14 where the inquirer begins with a title and is spoken to in a somewhat harsh manner. This forthright challenge to the seriousness of the questioner's intentions thus seems to be the best understanding of Jesus' answer.

But going beyond the mood of Jesus' response, we still must ask if the text is affirming the insignificance of his person, particularly in relation to God. When the full passage is examined, this is clearly not the case. In stanza 1 the ruler wants to know what he must *do* to inherit eternal life. Jesus tells him (3) to sell everything and "come and follow *me.*" If the passage intended to affirm the insignificance of Jesus in contradistinction to God, it would have Jesus tell the ruler to "follow the way of God (even as I follow the same way)," or some such affirmation. Rather the ruler is told that to *follow Jesus* is the climax of what is required of him. Thus Jesus appears again as God's unique agent through whom obedience to God is appropriately expressed.

We have noted the special emphasis on family and property in the selection and arrangement of the laws listed. The ruler's reply that he has observed all of these since his youth can be paralleled and is yet somewhat presumptuous. In the Talmud, Abraham, Moses, and Aaron are reported to have kept the whole law (Plummer, 423). The rich ruler seems to calmly put himself in rather exalted company. Thus Jesus' response comes almost as a judgmental challenge flung in the face of a comparatively self-righteous ruler.

STANZA 3

And hearing, Jesus said to him,
  "One thing you still lack.
Sell everything you have
  and distribute to the poor.
  And you will have treasure in heaven.
And come and follow me."

The theme of "one thing lacking" also follows the question of eternal life in Luke 10:42 in the story of Mary and Martha. The one thing that Mary has and Martha lacks is an appropriate expression of loyalty to the person of Jesus. This lawyer lacks the same thing. As happens again and again in Luke, a theme is dealt with twice, and in one case it is illustrated by a woman and in the other, by a man (cf. 4:25-27; 15:3-10; etc.).

There is the possibility that the two lines, "and distribute to the poor" and "you will have treasure in heaven," may be an editorial expansion of the original text. The matching lines in stanza 3' omit any reference to treasure in heaven. This particular concern has clearly been edited into the text in Luke 6:23 (as we observed in chapter six). The literary structure of 14:12-14 suggests that 14:14b, on the same topic, is also a brief comment added by way of explanation (the treasure in heaven is the eternal life he seeks). The case for two literary layers (an original composition, then an addition to that composition) can be made with ease in the case of Luke 6:23. It can be affirmed with less confidence in 14:14b and 18:22. Such pious expansions (when they can be demonstrated) are evidence of an old piece of literature, revered in the life of the early Church, being reused with some expansion. They oblige us to place a pre-Lucan date to the composition of the material itself.

The demands themselves (sell everything and follow me) touch at the heart of the same two primary values suggested by the rearrangement of the commandments, namely property and family. The family estate is of supreme value in Middle Eastern society because it is a symbol of the cohesiveness of the extended family. One must observe at close range the lengths to which a Middle Eastern family will go to keep a part of the extended family in the ancestral home (even in today's mobile society) to sense the thrust of what is demanded of the ruler. He is asked to place loyalty to the person of Jesus higher than loyalty to his family and his family estate, for in a very deep sense the latter two are one. Abraham was faced with a similar type of demand on two occasions. He left his estate in Ur in a response of obedience. Then on Mount Moriah God required of him a willingness to put his obedience to God on a higher level than his loyalty to his own family. Abraham passed that great test of obedience/faith. The ruler failed even on the first type of test. Had he measured up to the demand he might have received his estate back as a gift of God to be used in His service. Regarding these things we can only speculate. What is clear is that the focus of the language on the question of possessions clearly implies a discussion of family (as stanzas 3' and 2' make eloquently clear). Thus, in this stanza, a self-assured man is faced with the radical demands of obedience. His response is recorded in stanza 4.

STANZA 4

And hearing this
he became deeply grieved,
for he was very rich.

The new obedience does not contradict the old law but rather goes beyond it. The new standard set for the ruler is beyond his ability to fulfill. Yet surely the ruler's deep grief is not just a result of his love for his wealth. More than this, he comes to the painful awareness that he cannot *earn* his way into God's graces. People of wealth are often proud of their own achievements. They accept no favors, ask for no special consideration, and with exceptional effort achieve wealth. But status in God's presence cannot be earned. It can only be received with gratitude. When a self-made person senses a need for acceptance in God's presence, his entire understanding of merit and worth must be painfully reevaluated. With God there is no pulling up of one's self by the bootstraps. The self-confidence of the self-made person crashes and dissolves like a mighty wave on a sandy shore when eternal life is at issue. The ruler *hears* (4) as do the bystanders (4'), who put a tongue to their (and perhaps his) thoughts. No doubt he grieves because of his love of wealth. But, as we have indicated, a significant portion of that wealth is his family estate, which is a visible symbol of the extended family itself, of which he, as a ruler, is a leader. Jesus is demanding that loyalty to him must be higher than loyalty to even such a treasured symbol. The ruler grieves in silence. His brash self-confidence is destroyed. Observing this, Jesus responds with a six-line parable set in step parallelism.

STANZA 5

And seeing him Jesus said,
"How *hard* it is
   for those who have *possessions*
      to *enter the kingdom of God.*
It is *easier* for a camel to go through a needle's eye
   than for a *rich man*
      to *enter the kingdom of God.*"

Standing alone, the second three lines have a four-line structure as follows:

It is easier for a camel
   to go through a needle's eye
than for a rich man
   to enter the kingdom of God.

But, as we observed in Luke 7:44–48, line length is not crucial for a semantic parallelism that has no need to fit poetical molds. Here a brief proverb of four lines may be reworked, with the addition of three extra lines, to make the six-line stanza. The three ideas that bring the six lines together are "how hard," "wealth," and "entering the kingdom." The two sets of three lines are parallel, yet there is progression. Entering the kingdom through reliance on possessions and wealth is hard (1); indeed, it is impossible (2). Anyone with possessions has a natural tendency to want to earn his way into God's good graces. It is hard, indeed impossible, both to set aside this drive to "make it on one's own" and to accept grace.

In the history of interpretation there are two attempts to soften the blow of the text. One attempt is linguistic and very ancient. It involves a change of a Greek vowel. Rather than *kamēlon,* if we read *kamilon* (as some ancient manuscripts give us) we are not talking about a large, four-footed animal but rather a rope. Thus, if you imagine a thin rope (string?) and a large enough needle, it becomes difficult, but not impossible, for the rope to be pulled through the needle. It would appear that some copyists in the early centuries tried to soften the text and make salvation somehow possible for a rich man if he tried hard enough. Yet the textual evidence for "rope" is slight and unconvincing. This option was already discarded by Ibn al-Ṭayyib in the eleventh century:

Some say that the word "camel" in the text means a thick rope. Others think that it is the large beam that provides support for the foundation of the roof, and others say that it simply means the well-known animal; and this is the correct opinion (Ibn al-Ṭayyib, Manqariyūs edition, I, 323).

A second alternative comes from the Middle Eastern village scene. Here peasant homes sometimes have a large set of double doors that open from the street into the courtyard of the family home. In the village these doors must be large enough to allow the passage of a fully loaded camel. Thus the doors must be at least ten feet high and together some twelve feet wide. Such doors are constructed of massive timbers. So much manpower is required to move them that they are opened only when loaded camels are transporting something through them. The ordinary movement of people in and out of such doors is facilitated by a small door cut in the large door. This small door is easily opened. In the past some commentaries explained that this is the "needle's eye" of the text. F. W. Farrar quotes private correspondence recollecting travels in the Middle East in 1835 in which the correspondent did find such a door called the needle's eye (Farrar, 375f.). Yet a few years later Scherer, a longtime resident in the Middle East, wrote bluntly, "There is not the slightest shred of evidence for this identification. This door has not in any language been called the needle's eye, and is not so called today" (Scherer, 37). Our experience substantiates Scherer. In any case, Farrar himself opts against his correspondent's suggestion in favor of evidence from the Talmud.

In the Talmud Rabbi Nahmani suggests that a man's dreams are a reflection of his thoughts. We are then told,

> This is proven by the fact that a man is never shown in a dream a date palm of gold, or an elephant going through the eye of a needle (B.T. *Berakhoth* 55b, Sonc., 342).

That is, a man is never shown something that is clearly impossible. The elephant was the largest animal in Mesopotamia and the camel the largest in Palestine. In each case we are illustrating something that is quite impossible, as the text itself affirms (v. 27). We would see both of the above attempts to explain away the thrust of the text as misunderstandings of it. The parable deliberately presents a concrete picture of something *quite impossible*. As Ellis succinctly states, "The camel-needle proverb (25) is to be taken very literally. Anyone's salvation is a miracle" (Ellis, 219). A rich man (through his own efforts) *cannot* enter the kingdom. The decision to dethrone his wealth he cannot make unaided. The profounder levels of the theological content of the parable miss the bystanders. What they do understand is that rich men cannot themselves enter the kingdom. These sentiments are expressed in the following stanza.

STANZA 4'

And those who heard said,
"And who is able to be saved?"
But he said, "What is impossible with men
  is possible with God."

The bystanders' question emerges out of a special mentality. This mentality says,

> Rich men are able to build synagogues, endow orphanages, offer alms to the poor, refurbish temples, and fund many other worthwhile efforts. If anyone is saved, surely it is they. Jesus says that such people cannot enter the kingdom by such noble efforts. We commoners do not have the wealth to carry out such noble deeds. Who then can be saved?

The ruler found the demands of Jesus too hard (4). The bystanders echo this feeling and shape it as a question (4').

We have noted the fact that just past the center of an inverted literary structure there is usually a point of turning. Something crucial is usually introduced just past the center that informs the entire passage. True to form, a key statement of this kind appears at precisely this point in this structure. Salvation is affirmed as an action of God. No one unaided *enters* the kingdom. No one achieves great things and *inherits* eternal life. An inheritance is a gift, not an earned right. No one has rights in the kingdom, not even rich men with all their potential for good works. Indeed, if Jesus had given the rich man a list of expensive good works to be funded or carried out, the ruler would likely have begun on them with great enthusiasm. Rather, he is told that his best efforts are worthless in the achievement of his goal of *entering* the kingdom. Salvation is impossible with men and possible only with God. As Marshall succinctly states, "God can work the miracle of conversion in the hearts even of the rich" (Marshall, 686). The flow of the inverted dialogue naturally returns to the demands the ruler found too hard (3). The question becomes, Has anyone met them? Stanza 3' gives the answer.

STANZA 3'

And Peter said,
"Lo, we have *left what is ours*
and *followed you.*"

The parallelism between the requirements laid before the ruler and the speech of Peter is noticed already by Ibn al-Ṣalībī (I, 387). This can be seen as follows:

The Ruler (3)	*The Disciples* (3')
Jesus said to him,	Peter said,
"Sell everything you have . . .	"We have left what is ours
Come and follow me."	and have followed you."

We have argued that the demands laid on the ruler are not only dealing with wealth, but also with the dethronement of the demands of the extended family. This same background is significant here also. It becomes all the more evident in the stanza that follows. Peter says, "We have left *ta idia* and have followed you." We grant that this is a neuter plural that ordinarily refers to things. In John

1:11 we have, "He came into his own home (*ta idia*) and his own people (*hoi idioi*) did not receive him." Thus a distinction is made between the home (*ta idia*) and the people (*hoi idioi*). The first is neuter and the second masculine. Yet here in Luke it is clear from Jesus' response that Peter is talking about far more than buildings and furniture. This broader understanding of *ta idia* in Peter's speech is caught in many of the early Arabic versions, which read, "We have left what is ours." The phrase can imply both people and property. Thus Peter and the disciples, for whom he is a spokesman, are living examples of the miracle of which Jesus speaks. They also had families and possessions. They too were Middle Easterners, and the cultural pressures to make these things absolutes were felt by them as well. But with them the miracle happened. What was impossible with men was demonstrated as possible by God in their own concrete discipleship. Indeed, men and women of faith in every age discover that the impossible demands of obedience are made possible through the miracle of God's grace. Peter affirms the reality of this miracle having happened in their lives. Ibn al-Ṣalībī comments, "Indeed their following of Jesus was the only reason they were able to leave everything" (Ibn al-Ṣalībī, I, 387f.). Jesus' response to Peter forms stanza 2' and stanza 1'.

STANZA 2'

And he said to them,	
"Truly, I say to you,	
there is no one who has left	
house	(loyalty to property)
or wife	(loyalty to family)
or brothers	"
or parents	"
or children	"
for the sake of the kingdom,	

STANZA 1'

who will not receive much more in this time,
and in the age to come—*eternal life*."

In the case of the ruler we observed that his relationship to his wealth was such that he could not submit to a higher loyalty. So here, Ibn al-Ṣalībī observes,

> He does not mean by these words that we should dissolve marriages or break the ties to families but rather he teaches us to give honor and priority to our fear of God over marriage, brothers, race, and relatives (Ibn al-Ṣalībī, I, 389).

It is no mistake that "house" occurs first on this list of specifics. Members of the family then make up the other four items in the list of five. We have already observed that in stanza 2 five commandments are selected and rearranged in order to give special prominence to the question of property and family. Here these two themes are the only items on the list. A comparison between the old and the new requirements of obedience is revealing.

In the old obedience the faithful were told not to steal another's property. In the new obedience, one's own property may have to be left behind. In the old obedience one was told to leave the neighbor's wife alone. In the new obedience the disciple *may* be required to leave his *own* wife alone. In the old obedience the faithful were to honor father and mother, which of course, popularly understood, meant (and still means) to stay home and take care of them until they die and are respectfully buried. In the new obedience the disciple may have to *leave* them in response to a higher loyalty. It is nearly impossible to communicate what all of this means in our Middle Eastern context. The two unassailable loyalties that any Middle Easterner is almost required to consider more important than life itself are *family* and the *village home*. When Jesus puts both of these in *one* list, and then demands a loyalty that supersedes them both, he is requiring that which is truly impossible to the Middle Easterner, given the pressures of his culture. The ten commandments he can manage, but this is too much. Only with God are such things possible. Surely the shock of the passage cuts deeply into the presuppositions of any culture. Our point is that this shock is felt all the more intensely in a traditional culture where these particular values are supreme. Jesus is fully aware of the radical rupture of the fabric of cultural loyalties that his words create. Thus he introduces these incredible statements with "Amen, I say to you." In Luke this phrase occurs only six times and in each case it introduces a saying of awesome proportions that shocks the listener. Its use here is no exception.

The final stanza returns again to the question of rewards. Here we see this important topic presented in two aspects. The ruler already had his reward in mind. He wants eternal life. He asks about what he must do to inherit this reward. The standard is presented and he fails to meet it, for indeed it is impossible to achieve. Salvation is demonstrated to be a work of God, not an achievement of people. The disciples were given the grace to respond to the new pattern of obedience. They did so in the past (we have left what is ours). They broke the pattern of their cultural demands and placed obedience to Jesus higher than loyalty to family and property. Jesus responds and confirms that the kingdom has boundless rewards for those who respond in obedience with no thought of rewards. Marshall affirms that Peter's speech is not a "claim for a selfish reward." Rather it is "an opportunity to give a promise that self-denial for the sake of the kingdom will be vindicated" (Marshall, 688). In addition, these rewards are for this time *and* the age to come. Furthermore, they will *receive* eternal life, they cannot *earn* it. There also is an emphasis in the text on the theme of assurance. *No one* who has responded to the call to obedience will be left out. Thus this final stanza, with its return to the opening theme of eternal life, is rich in theological affirmations.

In conclusion, then, what is the response expected from the ruler and what cluster of theological motifs comprise the theological content of the passage? The ruler is pressed to understand that eternal life is not inherited through good works but *received* by those who allow God to work the impossible within them. The ruler's ability to do good works (through his wealth) proves only a stumbling block to his humble acceptance of a miracle of grace that could enable him to respond with the radical obedience demanded of him.

The theological motifs that appear in the passage are as follows:

1. Salvation is beyond human reach; it is possible only with God.

2. There is a new obedience that does not cancel the old, but rather builds on it and surpasses it.

3. Salvation, entering the kingdom, receiving eternal life, are all integrally related to following Jesus. Thus the passage affirms a high Christology. Jesus is God's unique agent through whom obedience to God is to be expressed.

4. The life of faith is defined in terms of loyalty to the person of Jesus. This loyalty must surpass loyalty to family and property.

5. Those who seek to earn rewards, like the ruler, find insurmountable obstacles in their path.

6. Disciples like Peter, who accept the miracle of God's work of salvation and respond in radical obedience, are assured the rewards of the kingdom. These are offered freely to all disciples and are for this life as well as the life to come.

7. Possessions and what they represent can be a major obstacle to an obedient response to the call, "Follow me."

Our study closes as it began. Not only is the literary form of this passage parallel to the scene in the house of Simon, but each passage proclaims salvation as a free gift of grace. In each we see some who accept and some who reject. It is our earnest hope that this modest effort may have made a little clearer the winsomeness of the person of Jesus, the clarity of his mind, and the attractiveness of his costly discipleship.

CONCLUSION

At the end of our brief study it is perhaps appropriate to tie together a few threads. We are anxious to summarize general observations and major themes. Can any general observations be made and are there any theological themes that appear especially prominent?

Our first general observation is that the parables do fall into a series of short dramatic scenes, and that these scenes relate to one another in a variety of recognizable patterns. Four are in a straightforward sequence. The ABAB pattern was noted twice. In six cases there was some form of inverted parallelism. A recognition of these scenes and patterns became an important aid to interpretation.

A second observation is the fact that the person of Jesus in the flesh takes on more clarity. At a banquet he is sharply critical of his host, and yet he is careful not to suggest that the host should have washed his feet. He subtly attacks racial prejudices by making a hero out of the hated Samaritan. He elevates the place of women by pairing them with men as examples of faith. He emerges as courteous and compassionate, and yet willing to use words like naked steel. Keen perception and penetrating intelligence are woven together, and these two elements are so fused that to touch one is to touch the other. The Middle Eastern details of the encounter in the house of Simon are culturally so precise as to have the ring of authenticity. Remarkable personal courage surfaces on numerous occasions. Indeed, we are able to sense the emergence of a more distinct personality that maintains its integrity through the theologies of the evangelists.

Our third observation is the emerging picture of Jesus as a theologian. The range of his mind is in itself remarkable. We have long been conditioned to think only of Paul, John, Luke, Mark, and the other New Testament authors as theologians. Jesus has been seen as the one through whom God acts to bring in the kingdom, but about whom little is known due to the heavy editing of the early

171

Church theologians. The preacher turns to him for ethical examples, not theological content. If the findings of this study can be sustained, this view will need some revision. We are convinced that it is indeed possible to speak of Jesus the theologian, and that, in the parables we have studied, four themes are especially prominent. These are as follows:

1. The love of God is offered freely and cannot be earned. Righteousness through human effort cannot be achieved. The Pharisee, proud of his works of supererogation, is unjustified. The servant labors but earns no merit. The ruler has kept the law but has not earned eternal life. The guests at the great banquet are totally unworthy to be present. The lawyer's attempt to justify himself fails.

2. The theme of the costly demonstration of unexpected love surfaces again and again. The Samaritan risks his very life to complete his acts of mercy. The woman before Simon knows Jesus will be despised for what he accepts from her and for what he says in her defense. The unexpected love offered to the outsiders at the banquet will infuriate the original guests and everyone knows it. This theme is more fully presented in the parable of the Prodigal Son but is yet deeply embedded in a significant number of parables here studied. It relates to the passion.

3. The acceptance of the freely offered love of God triggers a response in the form of costly acts of love. The woman in the house of Simon shows great love. The disciples have left houses and families. The servant labors, knowing that nothing is owing him. The eager volunteers are challenged with the cost of discipleship.

4. The person of Jesus functions as God's unique agent whose call of "Follow me" is seen again and again as equivalent to "Follow the way of God." He mediates forgiveness and personally accepts the gratefully offered response of love. He is the host of the great banquet, and unwavering service to him is equated with participation in the kingdom of God.

Thus, an examination of the Middle Eastern culture and literary forms of these sayings of Jesus can bring us, if ever so slightly, to a clearer perception of the person of Jesus and a more precise understanding of him as a theologian.

SELECTED BIBLIOGRAPHY

Aland, K., "Evangelium Thomae Copticum," *Synopsis Quattuor Evangeliorum*. Stuttgart: Württembergische Bibelanstalt, 1964.

Aland, K., M. Black *et al.*, editors. *The Greek New Testament*. Second Edition. New York: The United Bible Societies, 1968.

Arberry, A. J. *The Koran Interpreted*. London: George Allen Ltd., 1955.

Arndt, W. F. *The Gospel According to St. Luke*. St. Louis: Concordia, 1956.

Bailey, Kenneth E. *The Cross and The Prodigal*. St. Louis: Concordia, 1973. (Cited as: *Cross*)

————, "Hibat Allah Ibn al-'Assal and His Arabic Thirteenth Century Critical Edition of the Gospels (with special attention to Luke 16:16 and 17:10)," *Theological Review* (Near East School of Theology, Beirut, Lebanon), 1 (April 1978), 11–26. (Cited as: *Hibat Allah*)

————. *Poet and Peasant: A Literary-Cultural Approach to the Parables in Luke*. Grand Rapids: Eerdmans, 1976. (Cited as: *Poet*)

————, "The Manger and the Inn: The Cultural Background of Luke 2:7," *Theological Review* (Near East School of Theology, Beirut, Lebanon), 2 (November 1979), 33–44. (Cited as: *Manger*)

————, "Women in Ben Sirach and in the New Testament," *For Me To Live. Essays in Honor of James L. Kelso*. Cleveland: Dillon/Leiderback, 1972, 56–73. (Cited as: *Women*)

————, "Recovering the Poetic Structure of I Cor. i 17–ii 2: A study in Text and Commentary," *Novum Testamentum*, 17 (1976), 265–296.

Barth, K. *The Doctrine of the Word of God*. Vol. I, Part II in *Church Dogmatics*. Edinburgh: T. and T. Clark, 1956.

Bauer, W. *A Greek-English Lexicon of the New Testament*. Translated and adapted by W. F. Arndt and F. W. Gingrich. Chicago: University Press, 1957. (Cited as: Bauer)

Bengel, J. A. *Gnomon of the New Testament*. 2 vols. New York: Sheldon, 1963 (1742).

Bertram, G., "Symmetrical Design in the Book of Ruth," *Journal of Biblical Literature*, 84 (1965), 165–68.

Bishop, E. F. F. *Jesus of Palestine*. London: Lutterworth Press, 1955.

Black, M. *An Aramaic Approach to the Gospels and Acts*. Third Edition. Oxford: Clarendon Press, 1967.

Blass, F. W. and A. Debrunner. Translated and revised from the 9th and 10th German ed. by R. W. Funk. *A Greek Grammar of the New Testament and Other Early Christian Literature*. Chicago: University of Chicago Press, 1961.

Blauw, Johannes. *The Missionary Nature of the Church*. London: McGraw-Hill, 1962.

Bornkamm, G. *Jesus of Nazareth*. New York: Harper, 1960.

Bruce, A. B. *The Parabolic Teaching of Christ*. New York: A. C. Armstrong and Sons, 1896. (Cited as: *Parabolic*)

――――. *The Synoptic Gospels*. Vol. I of *The Expositor's Greek Testament*. New York: Doran, n.d. (Cited as: *Synoptic*)

Brueggemann, W., "The Bible and The Consciousness of the West," *Interpretation*, 29 (1975), 431–35.

Buckingham, J. S. *Travels in Palestine*. London: Longman, Hurst, Rees, Orme, and Brown, 1821.

Bullinger, E. W. *The Companion Bible*. Oxford: University Press, 1948 (1913).

Bultmann, R. *The History of the Synoptic Tradition*. Oxford: Basil Blackwell, 1963. (Cited as: *History*)

――――. *Jesus and the Word*. New York: Charles Scribner's Sons, 1958 (1934). (Cited as: *Jesus*)

――――. *Theology of the New Testament*. 2 vols. New York: Harper, 1951. (Cited as: *Theology*)

Burton, Richard F. *Personal Narrative of a Pilgrimage to al-Madinah and Meccah*. London: G. Bell and Sons, 1924 (1855).

Cadoux, A. T. *The Parables of Jesus*. London: James Clarke, n.d.

Carlston, C. E. *The Parables of the Triple Tradition*. Philadelphia: Fortress Press, 1975.

Charles, R. H., editor. *The Apocrypha and Pseudepigrapha of the Old Testament*. 2 vols. Oxford: The Clarendon Press, 1963 (1913).

Cohen, A., translator. *Midrash Rabbah Lamentations*. London: The Soncino Press, 1939. (Cited with reference and Sonc.)

Creed, J. M. *The Gospel According to St. Luke*. London: St. Martin, 1930.

Crossan, J. *In Parables*. New York: Harper, 1973.

Dalman, G. *Sacred Sites and Ways*. London: SPCK, 1935. (Cited as: *Sacred*)

————. *The Words of Jesus.* Edinburgh: T. and T. Clark, 1902. (Cited as: *Words*)

Danby, H., editor and translator. *The Mishnah.* Oxford: The Clarendon Press, 1933.

Daube, David, "Inheritance in Two Lukan Pericopes," *Zeitschrift der Savigny-Stiftung für Rechtsgeschichte, Romanistische Abteilung,* 72 (1955), 326–334. (Cited as: *Inheritance*)

Dembitz, L. N., "Procedure in Civil Causes," *The Jewish Encyclopedia,* X. New York: Funk and Wagner, 1905, 102–106.

Derrett, J. D. M. *Law in the New Testament.* London: Darton, Longman and Todd, 1970.

————, "Law in the New Testament: The Parable of the Unjust Judge," *New Testament Studies,* 18 (1971–72), 178–191. (Cited as: *Judge*)

Dodd, C. H. *More New Testament Studies.* Grand Rapids: Eerdmans, 1968. (Cited as: *More*)

————. *The Parables of the Kingdom.* Revised edition. New York: Charles Scribner's Sons, 1961. (Cited as: *Parables*)

Edersheim, A. *The Life and Times of Jesus the Messiah.* 2 vols. New York: Longmans, Green and Co., 1896. (Cited as: *Life,* I or II)

————. *Sketches of Jewish Social Life in the Days of Christ.* Grand Rapids: Eerdmans, 1974 (1876). (Cited as: *Social*)

————. *The Temple: Its Ministry and Services as they were at the Time of Jesus Christ.* London: The Religious Tract Society, n.d. (Cited as: *Temple*)

Ehlen, A. J., "The Poetic Structure of a Hodayat from Qumran." Unpublished Ph.D. Thesis, Harvard Divinity School, Harvard University, Cambridge, Mass., 1970.

Ellis, E. Earle, editor. *The Gospel of Luke* in *The Century Bible.* London: Nelson and Sons, 1966.

Epstein, I., editor. *The Babylonian Talmud.* 35 vols. London: Soncino, 1935–1960. (Cited with tractate and verse and Sonc. with page number)

Farrar, F. W., "Brief Notes on Passages of the Gospels. II. The Camel and the Needle's Eye," *The Expositor (First Series),* Vol. 3 (1876), 369–380.

Freedman, D. N., "Prolegomenon," in *The Forms of Hebrew Poetry* by G. B. Gray. New York: Ktav Publishing House, 1972. Pp. vii–lvi.

Freedman, H., and M. Simon, editors. *Lamentations* in *Midrash Rabbah.* London: Soncino Press, 1939.

Glueck, N. *The River Jordan.* Philadelphia: The Westminster Press, 1946.

Gray, G. B. *The Book of Isaiah (ICC),* Vol. I. New York: Scribner's Sons, 1912.

Hunter, A. M. *Interpreting the Parables.* London: SCM Press, 1960. (Cited as: *Interpreting*)

————. *The Parables Then and Now.* Philadelphia: Westminster Press, 1971. (Cited as: *Then*)

Ibn al-Ṣalībī, Diyūnīsiyūs Jaʻqūb. *Kitāb al-Durr al-Farīd fī Tafsīr al-ʻAhd al-Jadīd.* 2 vols. (The Book of Unique Pearls of Interpretation of the New Testament.) Written in

Syriac *ca.* 1050. Translated into Arabic by Abd al-Masīḥ al-Dawlayānī in 1728. Published in Arabic in Cairo: n.p., 1914.

Ibn al-Ṭayyib. *Tafsīr al-Mishriqī* (The Commentary of al-Mishriqī). 2 vols. Edited by Jūsif Manqariyūs. Cairo: al-Tawfīq, 1908.

————. Commentary on the Four Gospels, Paris Arabic Manuscript 86. National Library of Paris.

Jeremias, J. *The Eucharistic Words of Jesus.* New York: Charles Scribner's Sons, 1966. (Cited as: *Eucharistic*)

————. *New Testament Theology.* New York: Scribner, 1971. (Cited as: *Theology*)

————. *The Parables of Jesus.* London: SCM Press, 1963. (Cited as: *Parables*)

————. *The Promise of the Nations.* London: SCM Press, 1958. (Cited as: *Promise*)

Jones, G. V. *The Art and Truth of the Parables.* London: SPCK, 1964.

Josephus. *Jewish Antiquities* (Loeb Classical Library). Cambridge: William Heinemann, 1961 (1926).

Jowett, William. *Christian Researches in Syria and the Holy Land.* Second Edition. London: L. B. Steeley, 1826.

Jülicher, A. *Die Gleichnisreden.* 2 vols. Tübingen: J. C. B. Mohr, 1910.

Kitāb al-Injīl al-Sharīf al-Tāhir (The Holy, Noble, Pure Gospel). Al-Shawayr (Lebanon): Monastery of St. John, 1818 (1776).

Kittel, G., and G. Friedrich, editors. *Theological Dictionary of the New Testament.* 9 vols. Translated and edited by G. W. Bromiley. Grand Rapids: Eerdmans, 1964–1974. (Cited as: *TDNT*) Articles cited:
    Bertram, G., "Hupsos," Vol. VIII, 602–620.
    ————, "Phrēn," Vol. IX, 220–235.
    Bultmann, R., "Euphrainō," Vol. II, 772–75.
    Foerster, W., "Klēros," Vol. III, 758–769.
    Horst, J., "Makrothumia," Vol. IV, 374–387.
    Windisch, H., "Aspazomai," Vol. I, 496–502.

Kümmel, W. G. *Promise and Fulfillment.* No. 23 in *Studies in Biblical Theology.* Naperville: Alec R. Allenson, 1957.

Lamartine, Alphonse. *A Pilgrimage to the Holy Land; comprising Recollections, Sketches, and Reflections, Made During a Tour in the East in 1823–1833.* Philadelphia: Carey, Lea, and Blanchard, 1838.

Lees, G. Robinson, "Village Life in the Holy Land," *Pictorial Palestine Ancient and Modern.* Compiled and edited by C. Lang Neil. London: Miles and Miles, n.d. Pp. 163–247.

Levison, L. *The Parables: Their Background and Local Setting.* Edinburgh: T. and T. Clark, 1926.

Lightfoot, John. *Horae Hebraicae et Talmudicae: Hebrew and Talmudical Exercitations upon the Gospels and the Acts.* 4 vols. Oxford: University Press, 1859.

Linnemann, E. *Parables of Jesus.* London: SPCK, 1966.

Louw, J. P., "Discourse Analysis and the Greek New Testament," *Technical Papers for the Bible Translator*, 24 (1973), 101–118.

Lund, N. W. *Chiasmus in the New Testament*. Chapel Hill: U. of North Carolina Press, 1942.

Manson, T. W. *The Sayings of Jesus*. London: SCM, 1937. (Cited as: *Sayings*)

_____. *The Servant Messiah*. Cambridge: University Press, 1966 (1953). (Cited as: *Messiah*)

_____. *The Teaching of Jesus*. Cambridge: University Press, 1935. (Cited as: *Teaching*)

Marshall, I. Howard, *The Gospel of Luke*. Exeter: Paternoster Press, 1978.

Martin, R. P., "Salvation and Discipleship in Luke's Gospel," *Interpretation*, 30 (1976), 366–380.

Meyer, H. A. W. *Critical and Exegetical Handbook to the Gospels of Mark and Luke*. New York: Funk and Wagnalls, 1884.

Miller, D. G. *Saint Luke*. London: SCM Press, 1959.

Montefiore, C. G. *Rabbinic Literature and Gospel Teaching*. London: Macmillan, 1930. (Cited as: *Rabbinic*)

_____. *The Synoptic Gospels*. 2 vols. London: Macmillan and Co., 1909. (Cited as: *Gospels*)

Moule, C. F. D., "Mark 4:1–20 Yet Once More," in *Neotestamentica et Semitica: Studies in Honour of Matthew Black*. Ed. by E. E. Ellis and M. Wilcox. Edinburgh: T. & T. Clark, 1969, pp. 95–113.

Muir, William. *The Caliphate: Its Rise, Decline, and Fall*. Second Edition. London: The Religious Tract Society, 1892.

Neusner, J., "Pharisaic Law in New Testament Times," *Union Seminary Quarterly Review*, 26 (1971), 331–340.

Newbigin, Lesslie. *The Open Secret*. Grand Rapids: Eerdmans, 1978.

Oesterley, W. O. E. *The Gospel Parables in the Light of their Jewish Background*. London: SPCK, 1936.

Plummer, A. *The Gospel According to S. Luke*. Edinburgh: T. and T. Clark, 1975 (1896).

Rice, E. W. *Orientalisms in Bible Lands*. Philadelphia: The American Sunday-School Union, 1912.

Rihbany, A. M. *The Syrian Christ*. Boston: Houghton Mifflin, 1916.

Robertson, A. T. *A Grammar of the Greek NT in the Light of Historical Research*. Nashville: Broadman, 1934.

Saʿīd, Ibrāhīm. *Sharḥ Bishārit Lūqā* (Commentary on the Gospel of Luke). Cairo: The Middle East Council of Churches, 1970 (1935).

Safrai, S., and M. Stern, editors. *The Jewish People in the First Century: Historical Geography, Political History, Social, Cultural and Religious Life and Institutions*.

Section One of Two Volumes in *Compendia Rerum Iudaicarum ad Novum Testamentum*. Philadelphia: Fortress Press, 1976. (Cited as: *JPFC*) Articles cited:

Flusser, D., "Paganism in Palestine," Vol. II, 1065–1100.

Foerster, G., "Art and Architecture in Palestine," Vol. II, 971–1006.

Rabin, Ch., "Hebrew and Aramaic in the First Century," Vol. II, 1007–1039.

Safrai, S., "Education and the Study of the Torah," Vol. II, 945–970.

——, "Home and Family," Vol. II, 728–792.

——, "Religion in Every Day Life," Vol. II, 793–833.

——, "The Temple," Vol. II, 865–907.

Stern, M., "Aspects of Jewish Society. The Priesthood and Other Classes," Vol. II, 561–630.

——, "The Reign of Herod and the Herodian Dynasty," Vol. I, 216–307.

Scharlemann, M. H. *Proclaiming the Parables*. St. Louis: Concordia, 1963.

Schegloff, E. A., "Notes on Conversational Practice: Formulating Place" in *Studies in Social Interaction*. David Sudnow, ed. New York: The Free Press, 1972. Pp. 78–89.

Scherer, G. N. *The Eastern Colour of the Bible*. London: The National Sunday-School Union, n.d.

Sim, K. *Desert Traveller: The Life of Jean Louis Burckhardt*. London: Victor Gollancz Ltd., 1969.

Smith, B. T. D., *The Parables of the Synoptic Gospels*. Cambridge: University Press, 1937.

Smith, C. W. F. *The Jesus of the Parables*. Revised edition. Philadelphia: United Church Press, 1975.

Strack, H. L. and Paul Billerbeck. *Kommentar zum Neuen Testament erläutert aus Talmud und Midrasch*. 6 vols. München: C. H. Beck'sche, 1924–61.

Summers, R. *Commentary on Luke*. Waco: Word Books, 1973.

Thomson, W. M. *The Land and the Book*. 2 vols. New York: Harper and Brothers, 1871.

Trench, R. C. *Notes on the Parables of Our Lord*. New York: D. Appleton and Company, 1881.

Tristram, H. B. *Eastern Customs in Bible Lands*. London: Hodder and Stoughton, 1894.

Vermes, G. *The Dead Sea Scrolls in English*. Baltimore: Penguin Books, 1962.

Via, D. O. *The Parables*. Philadelphia: Fortress Press, 1967.

ORIENTAL VERSIONS USED IN THIS STUDY

Century	Version
2 (?)	The Old Syriac
4 (?)	The Peshitta
7	The Harclean Syriac (Vat. Syr. 268)
9	Vatican Arabic 13
9 (?)	Vatican Borgianus Arabic 71

10 (?)   Vatican Borgianus Arabic 95

11   The Arabic Diatessaron

11   The Four Gospels of 'Abd Allah Ibn al-Ṭayyib (Vat. Syr. 269)

13   Vatican Coptic 9

13   The Four Gospels of Hibat Allah Ibn al-'Assāl (British Mus. Or. Mss. 3382)

17   The London Polyglot Version

17   The Propagandist Version

18   The Shawayr Version

19   The Shidiyāq Version

19   The Van Dyke-Bustānī Version

19   The Jesuit Version

(For a full description of these versions cf. Bailey, *Poet*, 208–212; the Shawayr Version is a Lectionary first published in Lebanon at the Monastery of St. John in Shawayr in 1776. The text was brought from Aleppo in the seventeenth century. Our copy was printed in 1818.)

INDEX OF AUTHORS

INDEX OF REFERENCES

OLD TESTAMENT

NEW TESTAMENT